REPORTING FOR CHINA

Reporting for China

HOW CHINESE CORRESPONDENTS
WORK WITH THE WORLD

Pál Nyíri

UNIVERSITY OF WASHINGTON PRESS

Seattle and London

Reporting for China was made possible in part by a grant from the
Chiang Ching-kuo Foundation for International Scholarly Exchange.

University of Washington Press
www.washington.edu/uwpress

Library of Congress Cataloging-in-Publication Data

Names: Nyíri, Pál, author.
Title: Reporting for china : how Chinese correspondents work with the world /
    Pál Nyíri.
Description: Seattle : University of Washington Press, [2017] | Includes
    bibliographical references and index.
Identifiers: LCCN 2016026505| ISBN 9780295741307 (hardcover : alk. paper) |
    ISBN 9780295741314 (pbk. : alk. paper)
Subjects: LCSH: Journalism—China. | Foreign correspondents—China. | Foreign
    News—China. | Press and politics—China.
Classification: LCC PN5364 .N95 2017 | DDC 079.51—dc23
LC record available at https://lccn.loc.gov/2016026505

DÁVIDNAK
MEGLEPETÉS!

Contents

Acknowledgments . . . . *ix*

Introduction: China and the World. 3
1. The Worldwide Expansion of China's Media 19
2. How Stories are Made 43
3. How Correspondents Work. 83
4. Finding the "China Peg" 133
   Epilogue: Cosmopolitan Professionals in the Service
   of the Nation 154

Notes *173*
Glossary of Chinese Terms *179*
References *184*
Index *194*

Acknowledgments

RESEARCH for this book was supported in large part by an Independent Social Research Fellowship. I thank the Independent Social Research Foundation for their flexible, unbureaucratic, and genuinely helpful way of advancing research.

I am grateful to the journalists, editors, and others who have put me in touch with their colleagues, particularly Zhang Hong, Yang Shanshan, Zhou Gufeng, Wu Chen, Vincent Ni, Guan Juanjuan, Zhang Xiaoyu, Yuan Zhenyu, Sam Xu, Jia Yanning, He Shenquan, Wang Fang, Zeng Guohua, Evan Osnos, Qi Fei, and Garrie van Pinxteren. I am indebted to Mikkel Bunkenborg, Iginio Gagliardone, and Garrie van Pinxteren for helpful discussions, and to Wang Zhongyuan and Zhang Jialu for pointing me to online discussions of Chinese media. Li Lin helped collate and analyse online texts.

Finally, thank you to Lorri Hagman, who advanced her trust in this book and then saw it to completion with her usual thoroughness, and to the two anonymous reviewers who were helpful, sympathetic, and very well informed.

Some material in Chapter 4 was previously published in Pál Nyíri, "Reporting for China: Cosmopolitan Attitudes and the 'Chinese Perspective' among Chinese Correspondents Abroad," *New Global Studies* 8(3): 223–44 (2014).

REPORTING FOR CHINA

China and the World

A T the beginning of the new millennium, relatively few Chinese traveled internationally, and blogging had not yet become popular. For most Chinese, international news came from official media, most of which relied, in turn, either on translated foreign sources or on the reports of the main news agency, Xinhua.

In 2015, 120 million Chinese travelled abroad to study, conduct business, buy brand-name handbags or real estate, spend time on the beach or see famous temples, work on construction sites, consult corporate clients, volunteer as English teachers in urban slums, and for a myriad other reasons. As tourists, they are the world's biggest spenders. As students, they have long been the largest group among those studying outside their home countries; as expatriate managers and engineers accompanying the globalization of Chinese companies, they are poised to become one of the largest groups working outside their home countries. China has even become the largest source country of international student volunteers placed by the world's largest student association, AIESEC.

As the ways Chinese people engage with the world and with non-Chinese expand, so does their need to understand and to be understood. Previously formed stereotypes and suspicions may be confirmed or contradicted by personal experiences. The Chinese state, which has long considered itself responsible for the management of all relations with foreign countries at any level, can no longer always keep control of them. When, in 2005, Chinese tourists staged a sit-in at the Malaysian gambling resort of

Genting because they were offended at receiving meal tickets with the image of a pig (apparently meant to indicate that they could be served pork, but taken as a slur), or when, in 2013, Chinese bus drivers in Singapore struck to demand better working conditions, neither local nor Chinese authorities were sure how to manage the conflict. The Chinese government is keen to promote the expanding presence of Chinese around the world as a testament to China's benevolent "rise," but is hesitant and ill-equipped to defend the interests of its citizens and corporations when they encounter conflicts, sometimes appearing heavy-handed and other times negligent, alternately stoking and fending off waves of angry nationalism. This expanding and sometimes conflicted global engagement is perhaps nowhere more poignantly illustrated than in the response by the Chinese people, government, and media to the disappearance of a Malaysia Airlines plane in 2014 with 154 Chinese passengers aboard, a story that will surface several times in this book.

In the West, most of the recent interest in China's emergence as a global economic, political, and increasingly military power has centered on the Party-state's desire and ability to impose its rules on others, and on how other countries might benefit or suffer from such imposition.[1] But China's entanglement with the world is not just a government affair. As Chinese people and businesses get more deeply involved with the world, their interests, in both senses of the word, sometimes coincide but at other times conflict with or are simply unrelated to the Chinese government's.[2] The protagonist of these engagements is an affluent, urban, and largely young population that frequently combines nationalism with individualism, curiosity about the world and a sense of being misunderstood by it, and hope for growing prosperity with anxieties about the environment, health, and the futures of their children. Even for many of those who are not already engaged with the world outside China in some personal capacity and do not have relatives or friends living abroad—most do—foreign countries are the subject of at least occasional discussion as destinations of one sort or another.

Few generations anywhere have been thrust into the world so rapidly yet—despite a consistent interest in foreign countries—know so little about it. This is where the prodigious amount of writing and images about the world, produced by professional journalists, semiprofessional online writers, and casual commentators with mobile phones, come into the picture.

FOLLOWING CHINESE CORRESPONDENTS

For over two decades, I have been studying the facets of the entrepreneurial migration from China that began with Chinese traders in the late 1980s and subsequently expanded geographically across much of the globe, and, in terms of business, from trade in cheap consumer goods to real estate, manufacturing, and the brokerage of complicated investment deals channeling capital from China. Throughout this research, I have been interested in the way Chinese migrants see the world in which they live and travel and their, as well as China's, place in it.

In the last few years, the motives for and ways of leaving China have become more diverse. But in terms of social composition, urban professionals make up an increasing share of those who leave. They are a diverse group, but, like expats from other countries, they are distinguished by a rapid mobility and a secure social position within the home society. They are strongly tied to organizations in China and often have relatively privileged living conditions abroad—particularly in relation to other Chinese—but their relations with the surrounding society have to be negotiated. Although they are exposed to more of the world than most other migrants, it is up to them to engage with it and let these engagements shape their worldviews.

Foreign correspondents are the exception. In many ways, they are socially close to other young, educated, temporary expats and relatively distant from entrepreneurial migrants, let alone contract laborers, who tend to face different problems, use different strategies, and are unlikely to be in the circle of their acquaintances back in China. But correspondents are professional mediators whose job it is to convey something of the place they are stationed in to their audiences in China, or vice versa as the case may be. The dictum that "journalism is the first rough draft of history," usually attributed to Phil Graham, the former publisher of the *Washington Post*, is widely known and quoted among Chinese journalists, including foreign correspondents. But whose history are they endeavoring to write? This question has been in the back of my mind since I started following the lives and work of these correspondents in 2012.

Right up till the 2008 Beijing Olympics, the view that Chinese society was cut off from the world—in part by the Great Firewall—and that greater contact would change the nationalistic attitudes towards foreign countries that had become increasingly visible in the 2000s retained some currency in the West. This view has proven naïve, as millions of Chinese study, work, and travel abroad without that experience necessarily weakening their nationalistic sentiments; indeed, sometimes it strengthens them. In other words, a cosmopolitan habitus may not lead to questioning a world view dominated by nations engaged in a zero-sum game against each other, a world view that dominates Chinese media, international relations scholarship, and political commentary today.[3] Yet we should not discount the potential of foreign correspondents, who offer and interpret vicarious contact with foreign places and people, to challenge such views. Foreign news, after all, attracts more interest in China than in many other media markets: *Reference News* (Cankao Xiaoxi), a digest of translated articles from foreign media published by Xinhua News Agency, evolved from an internal reference publication into China's largest-circulation daily.[4] *Global Times*, which started out as *People's Daily*'s foreign-affairs supplement, now far exceeds its mother paper in both circulation and profit.[5] And while foreign coverage in American media has been shrinking, in Chinese media it has been expanding.

But while a strong interest in foreign countries—and in what they think about China—has been undiminished since the 1980s and is broadly shared across China's social classes, the recent rise of an urban leisured class and the coming of age of their children may now mean that being a "well-informed citizen" is becoming an attribute of a certain social or educational status, and, if so, the question then becomes whether this includes a new type of demand for information on foreign countries.[6] This type of demand is potentially generative of a cosmopolitan sensibility with "a sense of responsibility beyond the nation-state," but "there is another sense of cosmopolitanism: a more cultural and experiential conception, referring to an awareness and appreciation of diversity in modes of thought, ways of life, and human products."[7] If this is so, then what is at stake is whether a more sophisticated reporting on the world can strengthen cosmopolitan sensibilities—or, on the contrary, reinforce nationalistic sentiments. Simply put, will more exposure to the world through professional mediators make people more open to or more fearful of the West and Japan, who are cast as China's enemies in dominant historical narratives? Will it arouse more interest in places outside the West? Can it, perhaps, generate "compassionate cosmopolitanism" in a society where cross-border philanthropy has not taken off and where there is popular opposition to development aid?[8]

Anthropologist Ulf Hannerz's book *Foreign News*, as well as a collection of interviews with Chinese journalists by Judy Polumbaum, went some way in convincing me that even—by anthropologists' standards—relatively fleeting encounters with foreign correspondents could yield significant insights into their world.[9] After all, they have been trained to talk: rather than being put off by my note-taking, some of them were surprised that I was not recording our conversations.

I have since talked with over seventy current and former foreign correspondents, stringers, and foreign desk editors in two North American, eight European, a Middle Eastern, and three African cities as well as Beijing, Shanghai, and Canton. These dialogues were sometimes set up as formal interviews, but most were informal conversations. I have kept in touch with a few of them over e-mail and telephone, and met several of them repeatedly, some in multiple countries as they changed assignments. My interlocutors included reporters for news agencies, television, radio, print and online media, spanning a wide range of positions from the Communist Party's mouthpiece *People's Daily* to the then still liberal *Southern Weekend.* I have sought to understand what factors shape the work and reporting of these journalists; to what extent their personal interests are influenced by encounters with foreign countries; and how they balance these interests with their organizations' business demands and the government's requirements and censorship. In particular, I was interested in the potential of more sophisticated reporting on the world to challenge or else strengthen the nationalistic views that dominate Chinese media today.

While correspondents for the official media proved hard to locate without introductions—their e-mails are usually not publicized, and they have tended not to respond to "cold" contacts via their social media accounts, which they check far more often than e-mail—most were willing to meet and talk once introduced by a mutual acquaintance. It is likely, of course, that those journalists I was being introduced to were deemed by their colleagues to be more inclined to talk to me. This may well mean that there is an overrepresentation of more open-minded journalists in this book, and that I have not managed to reach those who hold more conservative or nationalistic views. Nonetheless, by the end of this research, the number of correspondents I had talked to within some of the major media organizations—notably Xinhua, China Radio International (CRI), *21st Century Business Herald*, and Caixin—began to translate into a sense of the network itself, as by this time my new interviewees and I were likely to have several acquaintances in common.

An equally if not more serious limitation is that I had to rely on the correspondents' own description of how they worked. As every anthropologist knows, what one says about what one does is never quite like what one actually does. This is particularly so with journalists, who are, on the one hand, often eager and able to talk about their work in vivid terms, but, on the other hand, are also firmly in control of the messages and cues they are getting across and often have an idea—whether correct or not—of the cues and messages their interlocutor is looking for. In the mid-1990s, journalists and editors who talked to media scholars were very careful not to say anything out of the Party-defined mainstream: "Clearly, these journalists were carefully managing the space that they had cultivated for themselves. They knew that this space was fragile, and could be reduced or eliminated by the party. Being pinned down as an 'oppositional paper' or even an explicit alternative to party organs would only mean that nothing could be done."[10]

Twenty years later, the situation is more diverse. Market papers do want to be seen as alternatives to Party organs, but feel that their advantages are diminishing. Many liberal journalists, whose situations are increasingly precarious, have no qualms about their criticism of the system, whether in conversation or even in writing published in English or on Chinese-language websites run by foreign media such as the *New York Times*. But official media journalists have even more to lose, in terms of existential security and status, than they did twenty years ago. In the early years of media marketization, many journalists attempted to solve the tension between following the Party line and market demand in their work by couching innovative overtures to the market in terms of "news values" while depicting market-based operations and carrying out the Party's ideological work as mutually reinforcing.[11] I have still frequently encountered such discursive strategies among my interviewees, but a mixture of a cultural relativist stance—"all state media in the world advance national interests"—with a display of personal conviction is now a more common one among official media journalists, and one that is in line with the reinvented tone of Party media and their popular offshoots such as *Global Times*. Nonetheless, it remains difficult to separate genuinely held convictions from narrative performances in such situations. A number of interlocutors expressed concern with the possibility not so much that their identities might be revealed in an academic book, but that they might somehow be picked up either by media such as the *New York Times* that are the target of the current Chinese leadership's sanctions or, on the contrary, the

People's Daily or similar central organs that might attract attention from senior officials. Some did not want their opinions cited in a book that was critical of China, even if they could not be identified, because they did not want to lend any support to such criticism by a foreign researcher.

In any case, many aspects of the news production process—the process in which the idea of a news story is born, executed and transformed into a final product by journalists, editors, and managers—are so deeply internalized that they become second nature, and journalists are unable to reflect on them fully even if they are inclined to do so. Nothing can replace actually observing the process of news making.[12] But, having no hope of being allowed into a major newsroom as a fly on the wall, I had to content myself with observing the occasional editorial meeting and asking editors to describe a day at work. As for smaller organizations, their overseas bureaus are too small to have newsrooms in the proper sense of the word; in some cases, correspondents work from their homes.

The book draws on encounters in Europe and Africa in about equal measure, supplemented by conversations in China (with editors and former correspondents, often in one person) and the United States. While the choice of bureaus to visit was to some extent serendipitous, driven by personal introductions, observing work routines at news hubs and less important locations on the two continents provided a scope that was necessary to understand the diversity of Chinese media operations and journalists' lives abroad. Both Europe and Africa are regions thought to leave state media correspondents relatively wider room for reporting, as China's relations with them are less politically sensitive than those with East Asian countries or the United States.[13] On the other hand, precisely because Africa and Europe are relatively unimportant for Chinese foreign policy, they attract less attention, so it is possible that, as one CCTV correspondent in the Middle East suggested, weaker journalists would be sent to these regions.

But Europe and Africa are also very different places to report from. In London, an official media correspondent is likely to meet colleagues from the commercial media every now and then, and they may be tempted to follow each other's work on WeChat, a mobile application similar to WhatsApp used by most Chinese. At the same time, even if she moves frequently about town and sometimes has to look for accommodation or deal with the health care system, she is likely to spend most of her free time with other official media correspondents, while her working days are structured by communication with headquarters in Beijing. In Nairobi, the same correspondent is likely to live a more secluded life, in the Xinhua compound or within a gated community. As there are no commercial media correspondents present and movement around town is largely limited to chauffeured drives to familiar locations, there is little exposure to other life-worlds. Moreover, as Africa has been the site of a concentrated government effort to build up a Chinese media presence, journalists operate in a somewhat different atmosphere, one in which senior editors and managers—those referred to as the *lingdao*, the "leaders," with a term borrowed from Communist Party parlance—emphasize both the opportunity to compete in a market with a relatively weak Western media presence and the need to project a "Chinese voice" perhaps more than elsewhere. (In Europe, newsroom conversations are more likely to revolve around what interests Chinese audiences and how to fill reporting quotas.) But life at a small African bureau like Maputo or Yaoundé, located in a villa and manned by a single Chinese correspondent or a man-and-wife couple, with at most two other Chinese correspondents in town, is very different again from life in Nairobi, under the close watch of the *lingdao*.

Understanding how journalists work requires reading, watching, or listening to what they produce. Throughout, I focused on output produced for Chinese audiences, but most of my interlocutors were simultaneously working on foreign-language stories that, in some cases, constituted the bulk of their tasks. This book thus also offers glimpses of correspondents for state media as they carry out their task to assist the spread of China's soft power—a task towards which their attitudes range from enthusiasm to skepticism and even ridicule.

The public output of Chinese journalists today includes their print articles or broadcast "packages," those texts or video/audio files that are only published online, as well as blog and microblog posts. In addition, there are texts and images circulated on WeChat: although these are increasingly important, they constitute semi-public output because accessing them requires being accepted by the author as a "friend," even though in some cases this is more akin to a subscription than the creation of a personal relationship. (The ambiguity of whether WeChat constitutes public or private communication has led both to hopes that it would be less actively censored and to uncertain government moves to regulate its content.) Even leaving WeChat aside means dealing with a very large body of text (and image). On some days, a prolific news agency correspondent may file several stories, while an active microblogger may post a dozen or more times. Blog and especially microblog (Weibo) posts are part of how a journalist communicates with his or her audience, and are an important source of information about that journalist's personality and work. But their function is different from that of articles and varies greatly from person to person: some journalists use them actively to reflect on their work or on journalism in general; others to comment on issues that grab their attention at a given moment or just to vent their mood. The microblog posts of other users that they choose to repost—whether links to other journalists' work or private commentary—can also tell a lot about journalists. I have not subjected these texts to formal analysis but tried to follow them, with the help of Li Lin, a graduate student of media anthropology at Sun Yat-sen University in Canton, and distil an overall picture of their authors.

I chose to focus on journalists who have been sent abroad by media organizations based in mainland China to report for mainland Chinese audiences. This leaves out many others who write about foreign countries: freelancers who contribute to Chinese media from abroad; foreign desk journalists and opinion writers based in China; online commentators unaffiliated with media organizations; and reporters for Hong Kong-based Phoenix TV, which is popular on the mainland. My interlocutors, as I have already noted, are not even necessarily the most influential sources of foreign news in China: an online commentator with millions of followers or an opinion writer for a paper like *Global Times* or *Southern Weekend* is likely to weigh in more heavily on readers' opinions. Many papers without foreign correspondents dispatch reporters abroad occasionally to cover important stories, to take advantage of invitations, or even simply to gain a sense of a country (*Global Times*, for one, follows this practice). Nor is the choice to limit the analysis to what is written for mainland audiences as simple as it seems: after all, much Chinese content produced in Singapore, Taiwan, Hong Kong, or elsewhere in the world is accessible, and accessed, by many in the mainland. Indeed, popular articles that circulate on the Internet are often difficult to trace to their original source. Nonetheless, my choice is probably justifiable insofar as the questions I set out to ask concern a group of professionals who spend long periods of time in foreign societies, but whose work and remuneration depends on organizations inside mainland China—which operate differently from those in Hong Kong and elsewhere, both in terms of business models and editorial policies—and whose writing is intended to shape mainland Chinese understandings of the world. Nonetheless, I have tried to supplement the picture by talking to some editors, freelancers, and "firefighters"—foreign desk journalists who are regularly sent abroad for short assignments—at influential papers such as *Global Times*, *Southern Weekend*, and *Oriental Morning Post*, as well as at some of the magazines with relatively extensive foreign coverage, such as *Oriental Outlook*, *Globe*, and *Southern People Weekly*.

The research took place in a period of particularly rapid change for media worldwide and especially in China. It coincided with the retrenchment of traditional media and the growth of various forms of online and mobile reporting and with a period of political repression in China. Over its course, some of my interlocutors changed countries three or even four times—a testament to the extraordinary mobility of Chinese correspondents, particularly in the commercial media. I talked to some of them five or six times at different locations in three countries, keeping track of their movements via WeChat and availing myself of all opportunities to meet them wherever they and I happened to be. I have come to regard some of them as friends, introduced them to each other, and invited them to social or academic gatherings. With a small group of liberal journalists, I repeatedly discussed the possibility of a new independent Chinese medium devoted to quality foreign reporting. *Global Times*, known for its nationalist stance, invited me to contribute opinion pieces. After some hesitation, I did so on two occasions and saw my pieces published without alterations (but promptly denounced by commentators on the paper's website). My exchanges with *Global Times* editors remained civil.

Finally, a note on protecting the identities of my interlocutors: In anthropology, it is customary to use pseudonyms and change all other information—including place and company names—to make informants impossible to identify, and indeed many of my interlocutors agreed to talk to me on condition of anonymity. But consistently giving media organizations and the locations of foreign bureaus pseudonyms would have made writing this book pointless. In general, I have avoided naming my interlocutors and made their precise postings untraceable by using descriptions such as "a senior reporter for a central media organizations stationed in a Western European capital." This has meant that, in most cases, I could not link texts written by correspondents to their profiles, and I have had to omit most details of my observations of their work, an unfortunate but inescapable limitation. In some cases, notably with senior editors who spoke on the record and when quoting published texts, I retained real names.

COSMOPOLITAN ANTHROPOLOGY AND
THE ANTHROPOLOGY OF COSMOPOLITANISM

I wrote much of this book in Hungary at a time when the state of its media, relations with other countries, and coverage of international affairs increasingly resembled China. After years of frequent conflict with the European Union and the United States over issues ranging from judicial independence to media freedom, religious neutrality, and minority rights, the government of Prime Minister Viktor Orbán came to a full-blown clash with Western governments and the United Nations when those condemned its use of force against the extraordinary wave of refugees that marched through Europe in the summer of 2015. Orbán declared that the crisis showed the bankruptcy of the EU's "liberal blah blah" and provided an opportunity to stop Muslim immigration and return to Europe's Christian values and what he called "everyday nationalism." By this time, the government had built up a network of friendly print media through relations with crony capitalists and launched a new government-financed paper that was to focus on "positive reporting." Public radio and television were reorganised to eliminate opposition oversight, with reporting regulated by weekly verbal instructions from the "leadership." For example, public media were to avoid the word "refugees" and refer only to immigrants, and to show images of adult men rather than women and children. To support its decision to build a razor-wire fence along its border with Serbia and then also Croatia, a fellow EU member, the government plastered the country with posters declaring "The People Have Decided: We Must Defend the Country."

During this period, Hungary remained on the front pages of Western papers, mostly in negative terms. The *Washington Post*, for example, demanded in an editorial that the EU apply sanctions to Hungary. The Hungarian government called this coverage biased and ignorant, insisting instead that Hungarian police deserved to be commended for its restraint under a "brutal and organised attack by illegal migrants." Police beat and detained European and Australian journalists covering the confrontation at the border (one of them later won a World Press Photo award). The Organization of Security and Cooperation in Europe and the International Federation of Journalists condemned this; the foreign minister called their statements, and protests by European leaders and the United Nations secretary-general, lies and hypocrisy that "hurt the feelings of the Hungarian people," the preferred formulation of the Chinese government in similar cases. Those who followed the events on public radio and television heard only the government's statements and its rebuttals of foreign criticism. While a vocal minority protested the government's actions, the ruling party's popularity rose by a fifth. The prime minister, who according to a party slogan turned "a weak country into a strong homeland," remained the most popular politician. As Hungary became more isolated, conspiracy theories of an ever wilder kind circulated on the Internet to explain foreign hostility and domestic liberal treachery.

On its own, Hungary's case may be discounted as an oddity. But the trajectory of my native country from its days as the forerunner of reforms under state socialism and of peaceful transition to electoral democracy, the first country to dismantle the Iron Curtain and to lift the visa requirement for Chinese citizens, to the construction of this new iron curtain meant to defend it from foreigners is part of a broader context in which young Chinese journalists go out into the world. The rapid collapse of a worldview in which Hungary was part of a family of nations in Europe and beyond, with which it shared basic values—a view that was dominant in the 1990s and early 2000s—with one in which Hungary is a lonely fighter facing a cabal of enemies parallels similar shifts spearheaded by ruling parties in Russia, Turkey, Thailand, and Egypt, as well as more contested ones associated with the rise of isolationist movements in the United Kingdom or the United States. Next to the rise of a new generation of affluent media consumers in an authoritarian China that has long adhered to a similar ideology, these shifts are, perhaps, the other big story that frames the overseas expansion of Chinese media.

Chinese journalists, whether they realize it or not, are part of that story. The single most important factor behind the growth of Chinese foreign correspondent networks abroad is the government's desire to project its view of the world more convincingly, abroad and at home. As it does so, it plays close attention to other governments with similar goals, particularly Russia's, whose global television channel, Russia Today, some Chinese media producers envy for its punchy style and ability to recruit Western talking heads. But Chinese journalists do not necessarily and fully share the government's goals. Like others involved in similar processes elsewhere, they can and do assist, resist, go along with, or even ignore them. Much of this book is about their choices and motivations. But unless we make an effort to understand how individual actions and aspirations interact with shifting political frameworks, revealing their complexity neither diminishes the significance of the overall trend nor helps understand it.

"We construct horizons that determine what we experience and how we interpret what we experience."[14] Journalists construct horizons not just for themselves but for others, so their responsibility is greater also when horizons fail to open up or, having opened up, close again. The capacity to construct wider and different imaginative horizons is closely related to some readings of cosmopolitanism. The idea of cosmopolitanism has been criticized for prescribing a normative ethic based on a privileged First World experience, irrelevant to the plight of the majority and, at worst, repackaging the precepts of neoliberal globalization in morally desirable terms.[15] Others defend cosmopolitanism as a programmatic project to uncover the relationship between humankind and individuality "so that it is not obscured or distorted by cultural prejudices, social structures or historical contingencies," and thereby allow "Anyone [capital in original] the space to live according to the fulfilment of his or her capacities to author an individual life".[16] From this perspective, a "cosmopolitan anthropology" is one that endorses the ethics of expanding aspirations and stands in opposition to the policing of boundaries, rather than merely seeking to explain it while remaining agnostic about their ethics.

There is a difference between the call for a "cosmopolitan anthropology" and anthropological explorations of cosmopolitanism, which are empirical rather than programmatic. Nonetheless, anthropologists tend to treat feelings of solidarity or responsibility across predefined group boundaries, particularly those of the nation-state, or simply "awareness and appreciation of diversity in modes of thought, ways of life, and human products" as inherently positive.[17] Therefore, social structures and cultural processes that enable the emergence of such views, too, are implicitly judged in a positive light. Some anthropologists have chosen to sidestep the debate around cosmopolitanism as an ideological orientation and focus, instead, on practices of socialization across boundaries, or "cosmopolitan sociability".[18] They, too, however, regard such cross-boundary interactions as ethically and humanly preferable to their lack, without explicitly engaging in a normative debate.

In this book, I followed the footsteps of these scholars as I attempted to understand how foreign correspondents for Chinese media construct their own "imaginative horizons" and work to shape those of their audiences at a historical moment that is characterized, for Chinese, by tensions between unprecedented international mobility, rising nationalism, and increasing political repression. I set out to tell an anthropological story of complexity and diversity in the media, to document that while journalists, for a variety of reasons, often conform to a set of constraining rules and ideologies, they also make choices. Choice, as ethnographic studies of urban professionals and secondary school students have pointed out, is a technique of governing in contemporary China, where, as elsewhere under neoliberalism, individuals are increasingly encouraged to take charge of their own fate as long as the decisions they make are deemed to be positive for the nation.[19] The availability of choice within blurred but nonetheless strictly policed boundaries can be seen both as a sign of room for individual agency *and* as a manifestation of state biopolitics. Of course, the choices foreign correspondents make should be seen against the wider background of career paths in which being posted abroad in the first place is often not an active choice but rather a necessary step towards greater existential security back home. In this sense, they are just one reflection of the insecurities that powerfully shape young middle-class Chinese lives, the same insecurities that can drive others to take up, for example, engineering jobs in Africa as a way to accumulate capital to buy an apartment and start a family.[20]

The way foreign correspondents make choices and talk about them can be read, and largely is read, as a story of discerning the limits of space for individual action, either embracing or rejecting the impossibility of choice beyond those limits, and then being rewarded, punished, or, as it were, ground down by the system. "Dancing in chains" is how one of the correspondents put it to me, using a popular metaphor. In studies of Chinese media, such a story, and the expression itself, are commonplace. But does it distract us from a more important, though simpler, story of oppression? How important is the complexity of correspondents' motivations or the cosmopolitan views they adopt if they make little difference to the image of the world that media texts and images ultimately project? The correspondents I talked to certainly did not see themselves as an outstretched arm of the state, but they were not necessarily freer than that image would suggest. And media institutions, required to be both the "throat and tongue" of the Party and competitive market players offering high-quality professional news "products," appeared to have rather less difficulty in managing their staff in the midst of these contradictory imperatives than one could have expected. Was I, as an astute interviewee suggested, in essence kidding myself, pleasing my own liberal sensibilities by focusing on contradictions and dissent that replicated the Western understanding of what good journalism was, but which were essentially unimportant to Chinese journalism? Was the situation, from a liberal perspective, hopeless, as another correspondent who had quit working for a Chinese publication and moved to a Western media company suggested?

But if all of this means that we must come to grips with a decentering of journalistic standards and an acceptance that good journalism in China might mean something else, then it remains unclear just what that might be. It is similarly unclear whether cosmopolitanism, in the sense of empathy for people elsewhere, is conceivable without reflexivity about narratives that dominate one's own society, which, in China's case, are largely set by the government. It would seem that genuine concern for people whose lives or beliefs do not fit with those narratives is eventually bound to collide with them. It is by intimating that unfamiliar ways of life can nonetheless be valid and coeval, and inviting readers to experience them vicariously, that foreign correspondence can cultivate "cosmopolitanism, making audiences feel more realistically at home in the world."[21] Bracketing off those ways of life as belonging to a different culture and therefore worthy of respect but fundamentally incomprehensible and incompatible with one's own does not have that effect. This is as true of Chinese journalists as of those who write about them. The position of some Western commentators that Chinese media, or Chinese politics, follow a different cultural script and cannot be interpreted outside it is convenient but ultimately disingenuous, like the insistence of China's officials that foreigners follow Chinese media to find out about the "real China" while simultaneously believing that there is no agenda-free media. To be sure, the task of the anthropologist is to understand the frameworks in which actors see their actions, but also to step outside those frameworks to understand how they are created.

The anthropology of journalism is a relatively new pursuit, but most of those engaged in it recognize the similarities between the work of anthropologists and that of journalists—at least, investigative journalists who tell stories based on "being there."[22] Journalists exemplify forms of mobile and potentially cosmopolitan sociality that seem particularly prominent among today's elites, but they also mediate experiences, stories, and agendas in complex ways. It is this process that has attracted the attention of anthropologists, resulting in studies of how editors at a news agency in Germany make rapid-fire decisions that end up determining what is news and how behind-the-scenes collaborations between American and Palestinian journalists, technicians, and "fixers" produce the reporting on the Israeli-Palestinian conflict that American audiences see and read.[23]

The roles that journalists play in mediating the world to a changing Chinese audience were highlighted by the debate that surrounded the disappearance of a Malaysia Airlines plane en route from Kuala Lumpur to Beijing on 8 March 2014. The overwhelming majority of the passengers were Chinese. This reflected the shift that has taken place in the distribution of wealth and leisure in East Asia, and many in China saw the Chinese government's handling of the incident as a test of whether its diplomatic weight and agility are commensurate with its new economic status. Eager to show that it cares for its citizens as much as the next great power, and probably also keeping in mind its interests in the South China Sea, over which it has disputes with Malaysia and other states, China mounted the most extensive search operation in history, involving scores of ships and airplanes. Passengers' relatives, brought to Beijing hotels to wait for news that was not forthcoming, were mobbed by journalists eager to file tear-jerking stories. The government criticized the Malaysian investigation. Online public opinion blamed Malaysia but also castigated the ineffectiveness of Chinese media—and of the government. Record numbers of Chinese reporters, aboard the ships and planes and at press conferences in Kuala Lumpur, were suddenly caught in the limelight, waiting for editors' instructions, mindful of having to defer to the Chinese government line but unprepared to satisfy audience interest in the background of Malaysia's government moves, international law, and aviation safety. Although the story was in China's backyard and not considered politically sensitive, Chinese journalists failed to come up with "scoops" of their own and largely reproduced Malaysian government news releases and Western news stories. Their audiences thought they failed to mediate the world, and were angry with them. Journalists, like the government, seemed to be lagging behind their readers' expectations in the effectiveness of their engagements with the world.

CHAPTER 1

The Worldwide Expansion of China's Media

THE lackluster performance of the Chinese media in investigating the Malaysian Airlines incident resulted in a lively debate on the Chinese Internet, within the news profession and beyond. Had the country's investment in expanding its media overseas been worthwhile?

Seven years earlier, the Shanghai-based financial newspaper *21st Century Business Herald*, launched in 2001, had sent a correspondent to New York. (Prior to that, foreign news stories had been written by China-based journalists who occasionally traveled abroad on reporting trips or based on Xinhua agency reports.) This was the first overseas correspondent for the so-called commercialized (*shichanghua*, i.e., non-state-subsidized) Chinese media, soon followed by others working for the business magazine *Caijing*, *First Financial Daily,* and Caixin Media. Recalling the context of the decision, Zuo Zhixian, *21st Century Business Herald*'s foreign desk editor at the time, wrote that China's economic expansion into Africa and South America and its competition with the United States was "a transformation unseen in three thousand years" that was an "irresistible temptation for journalists, the writers of history's first draft."[1]

For both Western and Chinese observers, the social significance of this development has been overshadowed by concern with the government's intentions behind its support for this global expansion. At the same time as the commercial media began sending correspondents abroad but on a much larger scale, the news organizations funded by central Party and government organs—Xinhua News Agency, China Central Television (CCTV), CRI, *People's Daily*, and the English-language *China Daily*, often referred to as "central media" in Chinese—began receiving large amounts of extra funding, whose amount has not been made public but is usually said by journalists to have been ¥45 billion (around $5.5 billion at the 2008 rate), to expand their foreign networks as part of a broader government effort of creating internationally competitive media conglomerates in China that would make "China's voice heard internationally."[2] *People's Daily* now has around seventy foreign correspondents spread over thirty bureaus, possibly the largest number of any daily newspaper in the world, compared to around thirty before the expansion started. According to its website, Xinhua had 102 bureaus outside mainland China in 2014; the largest, regional bureaus have twenty to thirty Chinese staff as well as local employees, while the smallest have just one Chinese correspondent. In sub-Saharan Africa, Xinhua has twenty-seven bureaus, the largest coverage of any news agency. It has a bureau in nearly every European country, and in some countries, several bureaus, including three in Germany and two in Poland. CCTV has around seventy foreign bureaus and regional hubs in Washington, London and Nairobi; the largest one, in Washington, has around one hundred staff. It has seven bureaus in Latin America, as against CNN's three. CRI has 32 bureaus abroad, as well as some studios producing local-language content, with over one hundred Chinese staff in total. Even *Guangming Daily*, the Party's "theory" newspaper regarded as a domain of tweedy ideologists and obscure debates, has built a network of bureaus that numbers eleven in Europe alone. Unlike commercialized media, these networks have not been constrained by falling advertising revenues and the digitalization of media consumption, which unfolded in China later than in the West but, by 2013, was taking on dramatic proportions. By 2015, twelve mainland Chinese media organizations had correspondents in Brussels, from their perspective a relatively unimportant station on the global scheme of things.[3] Only one of those twelve organizations was commercialized, and after its correspondent went home he was not replaced. In contrast, for some of the smaller central media like *Guangming Daily*, setting up bureaus in places like Helsinki or Prague may have been a means to generate extra income through government funding more than anything else.

As another component of this initiative, the Ministry of Education and the Party's Central Propaganda Department funded the creation of master's programs in global journalism at five leading university media schools. A graduate of the first such class at Tsinghua University, launched in 2009, described its objective as training journalists who can write well in English, are familiar with international communication, and are able to express "China's voice." The focus of the program was on English news writing, "national conditions," and some financial journalism. Students also did "field research": her class went to southern Gansu province to write about Tibetan students who were learning Chinese.

In 2012, the government set the goal of "creating a group of . . . internationally competitive . . . corporations for expansion abroad" and one hundred thousand "internationalized news media and publishing personnel" by 2015, using "developing countries as a base."[4] This call was again consistent both with economic and with political goals: it was seen as important to sway public opinion in the countries in which Chinese companies are engaged in extractive and infrastructural megaprojects to create, in Hu's words, a "harmonious international environment," particularly in Africa where both media and audiences were seen as overly reliant on Western wires unfriendly to China. But at the same time, Africa was an emerging media market: a place where market penetration of Western wires was relatively low and there was room for a lower-priced news agency product; it is here that Xinhua had had the most success in selling its news. It was also a market poorly served by new, particularly mobile media. So, as with other emerging Chinese multinationals, Africa was suitable as a place to pilot Chinese media's international products and learn. "We don't need money—we have that. But sales are important because they are a measure of influence," a Xinhua reporter explained. As a CRI bureau chief put it, "If you are not able to influence people here, then how could you influence" other audiences in richer countries?

In 2011, CNC World, the English-language TV channel of the Chinese State news agency Xinhua, reached cable television audiences in Africa. The following year, CCTV, *Beijing Review*, and *China Daily* all set up or upgraded their regional bureaus in Africa. *China Daily*'s Africa bureau chief explained that they, like CCTV and Xinhua, chose Nairobi for the regional bureau because Kenya was both politically stable and open, with a strong presence of other major international media whose operations they could learn from. CCTV America and CCTV Africa, both of which launched their own programming in 2012, each have about one hundred journalists, some recruited from CNN, NBC, Fox, and CBS in Washington and from popular

Kenyan TV shows in Nairobi. CCTV International now claims to reach some forty million viewers, and CCTV-4 another ten million Chinese speakers. Chinese journalists have become a formidable presence at major international events: at the annual meeting of the International Monetary Fund in 2013, around seventy of them were in attendance.

Western scholars' and policy analysts' attention to the expansion of China's media abroad has focused on the state's strategy of soft power behind the global spread of institutions such as Xinhua and CCTV, on the propagandistic image of China that these institutions seek to project in their foreign-language programming, and on the potential damage to media freedom in poorer countries if these media were to be embraced as models by governments with authoritarian leanings. This debate is still unfolding, with scholars disagreeing on how successful this soft-power building effort has been and may become, how central it is to the actual operation of Chinese media abroad, and whether or not there is a link between it and dangers to free expression worldwide.[5] Yet the impact on these processes on how audiences in China see the world is potentially more important.

While the full extent of that impact can only be measured in a few years from now and will require extensive audience research, this book approaches the question through conversations with Chinese correspondents abroad.

CHINA'S MEDIA IN THE WORLD

For the financial media, associated with free-market liberalism, the decision to set up overseas bureaus was driven by the evolving needs of their readers: businesspeople, managers, and economic policymakers affected by China's entry into the World Trade Organization and a growing upper middle class interested in reliable information on investing abroad or sending their children to study overseas. It also had to do with growing competition as these media, set up in the early 2000s, matured. But the overseas correspondent networks of these papers remain very modest. They are typically limited to a few reporters in the United States—without a question the most important beat for any Chinese media organization—and one or two in Europe, totaling no more than five to six journalists. They operate on a shoestring, mostly without offices and trying to take advantage of scholarships for staff at foreign universities or journalists whose spouses get jobs in foreign countries. (In 2013, US correspondents' monthly salaries tended to be around $3,200, higher than at central media, but insufficient to cover rent in New York, so journalists had to share apartments and often wrote at cafes.) This means that foreign correspondents rotate often and long-term strategy—beyond the imperative to have someone on the ground in New York or Washington, DC—is largely absent and unaffected by the Chinese leadership's decision in the late 2000s to push for a worldwide expansion of Chinese media.

The motives for that decision were a characteristic mix of the political with the economic. Expanding China's "soft power" had been increasingly important for China's leaders since the early 2000s. As the director of the State Council's Information Office, Wang Chen, said in 2010, "a leap in our country's international media development . . . is a necessity. The purpose is to improve international society's understanding of China . . . actively participate in international cultural competition; recognize the necessity of enhancing our country's soft power; defeat the Western monopoly on public opinion."[6]

But though Wang was taking his cue from a 2007 speech by former Party chairman Hu Jintao, actually allocating a budget to the media—as well as, for example, to publishers producing books and periodicals for the foreign market and to universities running degree programs in international journalism—was likely to do with China's WTO entry, which created the specter of international media groups entering China's domestic market.

Xinhua, *People's Daily*, and a few other central media had maintained foreign correspondent networks for many decades and undergone an earlier expansion in the 1980s, but their visibility and impact had been limited because, as *21st Century Business Herald* foreign desk editor Luo Xiaojun quipped, they had focused on the question "What do leaders like?" rather than "What do readers like?" Now, they were being told to think about readers, both foreign and Chinese, and find ways to become credible sources of information and opinion about the world, capable of setting agendas rather than merely reacting to those set by the West. In the words of a senior *People's Daily* foreign correspondent: "In the past, *People's Daily* followed the *New York Times* and other Western media too much: whatever they thought was important we wrote about too. On many issues, we had no stand of our own; we unconsciously reported the Western position. This is why people didn't take us seriously, why *People's Daily* had little credibility, and Chinese media have little voice [internationally]."

People's Daily's market-oriented offshoot *Global Times*, which had been complaining about Chinese media following Western agendas for at least ten years, made much the same point in an earlier editorial: "Not many people around the world are willing to listen" to Chinese media; "its international credibility is pitifully low. . . . In this, Western prejudice towards China is a factor, but we ourselves are a factor too."[7] Yang Qi, a former head of Xinhua's international department, criticized foreign correspondents for merely translating foreign agency materials but added that they were only partly to blame: it was true that their sources tended to be too limited and their efforts to investigate insufficient, but even when this was not so, political sensitivity meant that journalists often "could not or dared not" delve into what was behind the news.[8]

Conclusions from this frank admission were not only to be felt in the resources invested in creating a more convincing foreign-language media, although that was and remains the top priority. Under its director from 2008 until 2014, Li Congjun, a former Propaganda Department official, Xinhua has made "professionalization" and global market share a priority while undergoing what the director-general of Xinhua Europe, Wang Chaowen, described as a "strategic transformation" with the purpose of "getting closer to the reader." As in the case of *People's Daily*, this has involved a cautious shift to a more colloquial language and building up a presence in social media. While the news doctrine of "three getting-closers" (*san ge tiejin*, i.e., getting closer to reality, the masses, and life) was announced by Hu Jintao back in 2003, after 2012, the trend to "speak human language" was bolstered by the "mass line" espoused by the new Party leader, Xi Jinping.[9] *Global Times*, which became one of China's best-selling papers in part by enforcing the use of plain language, must have served as an inspiration. Some prominent Xinhua correspondents—like Liu Hong, a former longstanding foreign correspondent and later deputy editor-in-chief of Xinhua's *Globe Magazine*—were increasingly adopting a style close to that of *Global Times*, especially in their writings outside the news wire. Liu's 2012 book *The American "Conspiracy"* contains a number of commentaries (*shiping*), a type of editorial Xinhua has recently developed as a new product. Commentaries are produced with the understanding that they would be read as a reflection of what Chinese officials think and are therefore written by trusted journalists and signed off on by senior Xinhua officials. Many commentaries and other articles in Liu's book are concerned with rejecting what he describes as Western pressure on China in a plain and sometimes strident language that has become a hallmark of *Global Times* editorials.

For *People's Daily*, expanding its foreign correspondent network was one of the ways to bolster its credibility. But for other central media, the primary goal of that expansion has been to increase China's influence in the global news market. For example, 90 percent of the stories filed by Xinhua's Zimbabwe bureau are in English and are typically sold to media in African countries. How successful Xinhua, CCTV, *China Daily*, and the others actually are in this effort to expand China's soft power is too early to tell, although most observers, including the journalists I interviewed, tend to conclude that the results so far hardly justify the investment, and perhaps never will.[10] Some anticipate a withdrawal of funding, which could potentially result in the reduction of foreign correspondent networks.

The impact on the internal dynamics of Chinese media, however, is already tangible. Until the mid-2000s, overseas bureaus were mostly manned by senior journalists, generally men: the postings paid well compared to domestic salaries (although very poorly by local standards) and were relatively stress free. These posts were often seen as a reward for years of work in China for those who posed no risk of defection because they had families at home. Studies of Xinhua and *People's Daily* based on research in the 2000s paint a picture of staff whose main job was rewriting stories published in local news.[11] When a thirty-six-year-old *People's Daily* correspondent was posted to Brussels in 2000, he found himself the youngest Chinese reporter in town. Today, most overseas correspondents are around thirty and often female—even in the Middle East and Africa, where Western media, out of safety concerns, rarely send young women. Many posts are now filled by fresh graduates after a half-year stint at headquarters, or, in some cases, filled locally after applicants have graduated from a foreign university. *People's Daily*'s Paris bureau, for example, recently expanded from two to four staff, all of whom except the veteran bureau chief are in their twenties. At the Washington, DC, bureau, considered the most important, the oldest of five journalists apart from the bureau chief is in his early thirties.

The change in foreign correspondent demographics is dramatic not only compared to the past but also compared to the practice of Western news organizations, where foreign assignments are often offered to experienced reporters, sometimes as a reward for past performance. Xinhua's and CCTV's regional bureau chiefs, who oversee entire continents, are relatively senior in both age and rank, but they, too, now tend to have track records as former foreign correspondents, rather than, as in the past, administrative cadre parachuted in from headquarters. Xinhua's Africa chief, Yuan Bingzhong, for example, was by his own account very active both as a White

House correspondent and as a United Nations correspondent in Geneva, and served as frontline correspondent in Afghanistan.[12]

Because overseas postings are typically for around three years, Xinhua replaces two hundred to three hundred correspondents every year. The international department, which used to have a monopoly on foreign posts, is far short of these numbers; therefore, for those working in other departments but with a good command of a foreign language, it is relatively easy to go abroad. The same is true for CCTV and CRI. The dramatic demographic change among foreign correspondents is not only due to the shortage of language-proficient senior staff, however. It is also related to the latter's reluctance to be away from headquarters, as it may mean weakening of important personal networks or worse, missing promotions to positions of leadership. Furthermore, many foreign correspondents agree that, from the perspective of Chinese audiences, there are simply many more important news stories in China than abroad. The strengthening of foreign correspondent networks has, therefore, ironically coincided with a weakening of foreign correspondence as a career path. It has also brought the sociodemographics of central media correspondents closer to the commercial media. But because commercial media do not offer job stability, and foreign postings are often contingent on the momentary financial position of the paper, their correspondents often leave journalism altogether for more lucrative jobs. The decreasing attractiveness of foreign correspondence may be one reason why so many correspondents are unmarried women: they may be under less pressure to seek a stable, high-earning career. "If it weren't for my daughter studying in Brussels, I wouldn't have wanted to come either," said a middle-aged male correspondent for a central newspaper in Brussels.

Nor are overseas postings leisurely any longer. As a CCTV correspondent explained, gaffes or delays would nowadays be immediately commented on in social media. A reporter who makes a mistake would be lampooned online and embarrass his superiors. All news organizations, except some dailies like *Guangming* and *Science and Technology Daily* that have limited room for foreign coverage, now implement a point-based bonus system, in which points are calculated on the basis of the number, type, and sometimes quality and audience data of the stories filed. Apart from CCTV, most require correspondents to operate across media: many Xinhua and CRI journalists are expected to produce photo and video reports as well as texts for online publication. Each month, Xinhua produces a chart for every bureau, showing how many clients picked up each story and photo. CRI issues a point-based monthly ranking of all journalists. Bonuses can make up 50 percent of a journalist's income, and laggards who do not meet the minimum standard also face criticism and sometimes fines. Foreign correspondents for commercial media have far higher workloads—sometimes they are expected to file several stories a day—but get low bonuses. In 2013, a *21st Century Business Herald* foreign correspondent in New York received $2,000 per month plus a $1,000 housing allowance, while a domestic reporter made between ¥10,000 and ¥20,000 ($1,700 to $2,300). Most foreign correspondents still make more money abroad than they would at home, but since living costs tend to be higher and access to supplementary incomes and non-monetary benefits (free or cheap meals, health care, etc.) lower, this no longer makes foreign postings attractive. In the early 1990s, a *People's Daily* foreign correspondent's salary was ten times that of a domestic correspondent; today, it is two times that. A Xinhua bureau chief commented that, in the early 2000s, she had made $600 a month as a junior correspondent in Europe—so she had to think before she bought a coffee or a bus ticket—but felt lucky to be a foreign correspondent.

Today, young journalists feel disadvantaged as they compare themselves to peers in corporate PR, particularly if they work at expensive locations: since housing and meals are provided, salaries are fixed regardless of how high living costs are. Nonetheless, young journalists in the central media still consider themselves lucky compared to those in commercial media, who, in the words of a CCTV correspondent, "struggle to survive." He added that there was a very stable support structure behind them that would not let them down as long as they did not make a "political mistake." Recently, Xinhua and CCTV have even taken steps to make careers in foreign correspondence more attractive by promoting more reporters to the status of senior correspondent, which carries the same rank and salary as mid-level leadership positions.

The strengthening of foreign correspondent networks has had another unintended effect. Most new correspondents for Xinhua, CCTV, and CRI were hired for the foreign-language services. Some correspondents pointed out that—despite their political tasks—these tend to be more commercially oriented, have more relaxed controls on content, more open-minded editors and, overall, a more laissez-faire atmosphere than the Chinese services. As one CRI editor put it, people at the English service tend to see themselves as more objective than their colleagues in the Chinese service, whose thinking is often more nationalistic. But many foreign-language correspondents end up filing as many or more stories in Chinese than in English or French, raising the possibility that their usually more cosmopolitan attitudes may have an effect on the stories Chinese audiences are exposed to. Indeed, some of the more ideologically or nationalistically minded older journalists believe that, in the future, foreign correspondents should be recruited from among international relations or foreign service graduates, who are, according them, more likely to prioritize national interests.

CHINESE MEDIA IN THE 2010S: COMMERCIALIZATION, CONGLOMERATION, PROFESSIONALIZATION, CENSORSHIP, AND THE DIGITAL CHALLENGE

Recent studies of China's media landscape have pointed out several fundamental and mutually constitutive tensions that underlie it. The first tension is between its continued propaganda function and growing commercialization to suit increasingly diverse consumer demand.[13] The second is between its propaganda function (known as "guiding public opinion," *yulun daoxiang*) and its watchdog function ("supervision by public opinion," *yulun jiandu*), now also harnessed by the central government as a way to gauge public sentiment, offer a controlled outlet to discontent in a society where the political system offers no channels for it, and keep tabs on unpopular or corrupt local officials.[14] The third is between the unchanged requirement of absolute loyalty to the Party and the quest for professionalism, undergirded not only by market imperatives but also by a government that wants official media to be more credible and "close to the masses."[15]

With the single exception of Hong Kong-based Phoenix Television, all print and audiovisual media in China are in one way or another state-owned, state-controlled, and rather heavily censored. This does not mean that all are crude mouthpieces for Party propaganda. There is, or has been, considerable variation that depends, roughly, on four factors: how much a medium is seen as representing the Party; how central or peripheral it is in terms of audience size, geographical location, and the position of the government organization that controls it within the national hierarchy; what share of the income it is able or supposed to generate from the market; and its top managers' political and professional agenda and ability to see it through. The more closely a medium is associated with the national leadership, the more visible it is, and the more state subsidy it gets, the less room it has to deviate from the Propaganda Department's line. These factors can of course work at cross-purposes: CCTV, for instance, is closely associated with representing the national government and watched by almost all Chinese, but needs no subsidy, whereas CRI is a lower-ranking and less visible organization but depends heavily on subsidies. As a result, some of CCTV's programming can be livelier, but in other ways it is more controlled than CRI's. At the two extremes are Xinhua and *People's Daily*, both of which are high-ranking party organs that survive only thanks to government-mandated subscriptions, and financial media that are highly market-oriented and typically controlled by relatively minor state media companies away from the capital. But even a profitable niche medium distant from the political center attracts greater scrutiny if it has a large audience.

COMMERCIALIZATION

No Chinese media has been completely exempt from the pressure of economic self-sufficiency that began in the 1980s as part of a broader reform of state-owned enterprises. In the print media, this first generated a spurt in so-called "metropolitan newspapers" (*dushibao*), tabloid spinoffs of official papers, designed to generate revenue that would keep their mother ships afloat. Next, media organizations were separated from the government organs they belonged to and registered as businesses. Beginning in the 1990s, they were gradually consolidated into "media groups," with the aim of making them commercially viable. Some of these groups have attracted private investment, although the state retains majority ownership of all media. This has allowed an effective differentiation between media corporations: depending on the province or city whose government controls them as well as the background, personality, and acumen of their executives, some are seen as more market-friendly and independent, while other media—especially national ones—are more closely monitored by the Communist Party's Propaganda Department.

Increasing dependence on advertising revenue has raised the risk that advertisers, whether state-owned or private, may want to influence content. Such worries came to the fore in 2014, when State Grid, the power monopoly and one of the wealthiest and most politically influential companies in China that is highly unpopular with pro-free market economists, bought stakes in *21st Century Business Herald* and other leading financial papers, resulting in a sharp drop of negative coverage. Later that year, the publisher of *21st Century Business Herald*, Shen Hao, an iconic figure among liberal journalists, was taken into custody on charges of extorting businesses in exchange for positive coverage and appeared on CCTV confessing to his crime. Many journalists commented that while the choice of target may have been politically motivated—the paper had run stories about the likely involvement of relatives of powerful officials in major companies, including Internet giant Alibaba—the charges were unlikely to be trumped-up, as such practices were widespread in media and had gotten worse as advertising revenues in traditional media shrunk. Foreign correspondents would have had relatively little exposure to them, although a freelancer for one of Xinhua's European bureaus said that her chief would often make decisions about reporting stories involving Chinese companies based on whether he had been approached by the company's boss. A correspondent for *21st Century Business Herald*, in a conversation before the arrests, recalled that her editor asked her to drop a story about problems with the overseas expansion of one of China's leading multinationals after a call from the company's PR team; on another occasion, a different corporate giant asked the editor to be shown the story prior to publication. "I didn't like being controlled," she said. "But we have to compromise for the sake of long-term contact." By the end of 2014, *21st Century* was rudderless.

Within each media group there remains a differentiation between more official and more market-oriented papers, and even the commercial papers may show very different degrees of political risk-taking. Regional differences play a role, too, but not a straightforward one. While it is sometimes believed that the Southern Media Group, based in Canton, could for a long time—until 2014—remain a liberal bastion because of its distance from the central government, Caixin Media, based in Beijing but until 2014 majority-owned by a Zhejiang media group, has suffered fewer repercussions because of its financial profile and narrower readership, and its publisher's close ties to high-level economic decision makers.

Conglomeration has most strongly affected the print media, although there are media groups that have film studios and television stations in their portfolios. The government—particularly provincial governments, which compete against each other—encourages further mergers between groups to enhance competitiveness. In 2013, Shanghai's media groups merged into just two, one of which, Shanghai Media Group, controls 95 percent of the city's print media. In other words, market share and political reliability cannot be simply seen as antithetical forces: governments have an interest in both. Staff employment conditions and incentives mirror this duality: only some central media continue to maintain what amounts to lifelong employment along the lines of government personnel, while at most official media, including CCTV, only a minority of staff has long-term job stability, and most incomes heavily rely on bonuses. Yet the careers of the top management of all official media depend on the Party-state's system of promotions and punishments rather than market performance as such.

CENSORSHIP

Much has been written about China's extensive, complex and sophisticated media censorship, part of the "thought work" or "propaganda work" that has retained its importance for the Communist Party as a tool of governing, even as it has shifted away from Leninist-Maoist ideology and embraced a brand of conservative nationalism that combines state capitalism with socialist elements.[16] As Chinese society has increasingly become one of market and consumption, the government has had to invent new, more flexible and less crude tools to ensure its interpretation of events remains dominant. Since Xi Jinping came to power as general secretary of the Communist Party in 2012, he has reintroduced some of the more heavy-handed methods of restricting the freedom of opinion, including the jailing of bloggers critical of the government and the promotion of Document No. 9, a Party directive that forbids the public discussion of "Western values" such as constitutional democracy, universal human rights, civil society, and media independence. Still, China's "authoritarian resilience" has largely depended on popularizing the Party's message using methods that are more credible and appealing.[17] China is one of the most wired societies in the world, and even with strict Internet controls and other ways to spin online discussion, gaffes in official communication attract instant ridicule.

Media censorship includes a mix of explicit gag orders; regular verbal instructions to editors from the Party's Central Propaganda Department; several levels of pre-publication vetting that relies mostly on self-censorship but sometimes, in the case of recalcitrant papers, on a censor seconded from a more compliant organ of the same media group; and post-publication punishments that can include dismissal or, in rare cases, closure of the paper. On the whole, there are no signs of the state losing or letting go of its grip on media content or of greater leniency towards those deemed to have transgressed against it seriously. On the contrary, the government keeps adding new instruments to keep up with the spread of technology, such as bans on posting original news items on websites and WeChat accounts of media that are not registered as news agencies or news sites: a regulation that is commonly flouted but nonetheless functions as a Damocles' sword that can strike at any time to punish or shut down an offending outlet, and therefore encourages self-censorship. Furthermore, in the mid-2010s, the number of foreign websites blocked in China was rapidly expanding after a period of relative relaxation, and the virtual private networks (VPNs) journalists had used to access them were being increasingly blocked as well. A foreign desk editor complained that, in combination with the blocking of foreign-based Google searches, this was making access to foreign media so difficult as to be impracticable.

At the same time, since 2008, after widespread anger at perceived bias in Western reports on the rioting in Tibet, which Chinese media initially kept silent about, the government has abandoned its longstanding policy to routinely ban reporting on sensitive issues and switched to a more proactive media strategy. Although one prong of this approach has been the hiring of paid online commentators who were to spin public opinion in the government's favor, it has also meant that censorship has become more selective and targeted. The Propaganda Department has become invested in increasing the journalistic professionalism and credibility of the media that were politically reliable. Moreover, the government has formally endorsed the "right to know" (*zhiqingquan*), and although this has no clear legal consequences, the concept has entered popular discourse just like "discursive power" (*huayuquan*).

As a result, "China's media policies are an inconsistent amalgam of improved transparency and responsiveness on the one had and huge investments in more effective censorship on the other."[18] While many journalists, especially in the commercial media, continue to push the limits, most have also deeply internalized the rules of the system, which now offers depoliticized discursive niches—for example in television or the burgeoning magazine market, room for professional development, and urban middle-class lifestyles for staff at both leading commercial and official media. (This is so even if incomes are now highly differentiated and, for many, strongly depend on bonuses and moonlighting.) Journalists appear to value the skill of pushing political agendas while displaying professionalism and remaining within the system more than the maverick "speaking-truth-to-power" journalism that attracted admiration—and persecution—in the 1990s and early 2000s.[19]

A prominent foreign desk journalist for *Southern People Weekly* commented: "According to estimates by some of those working in the field, there are currently fewer than eighty investigative journalists in China. The emphasis is on lifestyle stories rather than hard news, gossip rather than muckraking, flattery rather than analysis."[20]

Outright reporting bans and orders limiting reporting on particular topics to the mandatory reprinting of Xinhua press releases are still used to steer public debate, but less frequently to gag breaking news. For example, in August 2013, journalists reported that they were no longer allowed to discuss the debate on constitutional reform, which had rallied liberal intellectuals on the Internet and previously also in mainstream media, and the credit crunch that raised fears of bank defaults. Overall, the potential consequences of falling out of government favor in a shrinking advertising market are playing a more formidable role in enforcing self-censorship, as do journalists' and editors' existential fears of retribution.[21] Some journalists choose to file stories that make officials happy in order to gain privileged access to information, which can result in more articles, higher impact, and therefore higher bonuses. A former *21st Century Business Herald* journalist suggested that editors in the commercial media like to keep a mix of government-friendly and more critical journalists on staff as a hedging strategy against crackdowns.

As a result, while some formal restrictions are commonly flouted, this does not necessarily result in greater latitude for interpretation. Many journalists never pass the state exam needed to get a press license, and some media even employ foreign citizens without official permission. Most media routinely use translated, edited, and rephrased material from foreign wires or the Internet to report on news, although formally, all news reports must come via Xinhua. Yet, in 2012–13, journalists at commercial papers with a liberal orientation reported that room for views that diverge from the government's was shrinking and that senior editors were increasingly unwilling to take risks. This was in line with Xi Jinping's increasingly repressive cultural politics. Although Caixin had always steered clear of critical reporting on Zhejiang, in 2012, Zhejiang Media Group seconded a senior editor of *Zhejiang Daily*—the official paper of the provincial Party committee—to Caixin's Beijing offices with the task to read and "correct" every article. Foreign correspondents, who were not accustomed to direct censorship, were reporting increased tampering with their texts: for example, an editor removed a reference to Japan being an important partner for Singapore from a feature in early 2014, saying that otherwise the censor would do so. At *21st Century Business Herald,* the internal censor—a member of the Southern Group's corporate editorial board—cut an interview with a senior US State Department official by half at around the same time.

Meanwhile, *Southern Weekend,* the flagship paper of Chinese liberals, introduced mandatory pre-publication vetting of all "major stories" by the provincial Propaganda Department. This, and the censoring of a new year's editorial in January 2013 that called for press freedom by a new editor-in-chief, Huang Can, seconded from the provincial Party paper, *Southern Daily,* precipitated a public protest by staff that became known as the "*Southern Weekend* Incident." Although the protesters' demand that the final vetting be removed from the Propaganda Department and returned to the media group's editorial board was initially met, soon it was tightened again. In 2014, Caixin editor-in-chief, Hu Shuli, thought it prudent to decline an invitation to meet visiting US secretary of state John Kerry at the US embassy out of concern about possible repercussions. Later that year, Caixin book review editor Xu Xiao was arrested on charges of "endangering state security" related to the crackdown on Liren, a network of independent rural libraries, which Xu supported. In 2015, a reporter for *Caijing,* a financial journal also founded by Hu Shuli but now Caixin's competitor, was detained and paraded on television for having written an "irresponsible" article about the crash of the Chinese stock market.

What truly shocked liberal journalists and signalled a new turn in media control was the fact that the central Propaganda Department, under threat of suspension, ordered the Southern Group's popular Beijing newspaper *New Beijing News* (Xinjingbao) to reprint an editorial by another commercial paper, the nationalistic and antiliberal *Global Times,* condemning the protesters and accusing them of acting in foreign interests. Since *Global Times,* a highly profitable offshoot of *People's Daily,* has been allowed to editorialize on matters technically subject to gag orders—the Dalai Lama, Taiwan, Tibet—this was a sign that the government was now taking active sides in a clash of opinions: rather than forcing all parties to stick to anemic official statements, they were clearing the playing field for some but not for others. As a journalist on *Southern Weekend*'s international desk put it, the Propaganda Department was handing a murder weapon to the assassin. When this journalist denounced the case on his microblog he was in turn harassed by State Security agents. By 2014, he and most of his experienced colleagues on the international desk had left *Southern Weekend,* and the style of its international coverage—according to an editor at another news magazine—began to resemble that of *Global Times*. In October, the paper appeared with a new design and announced the expansion of its international content "to keep pace with China's rise." Huang Can's vetting expanded to *Southern Weekend*'s sister publication *Southern People Weekly*, which has its own international coverage. Increasingly, journalists from both central and commercial media were reporting that articles were being directly planted in their publications on orders from the Propaganda Department (although there have also been cases of editors-in-chief refusing these); at other times, they were given mandatory lists of experts to interview on particular subjects.

At a conference with writers in October 2014, Xi Jinping openly praised thirty-three-year-old blogger Zhou Xiaoping, an IT entrepreneur and occasional *Global Times* contributor, known for his stridently nationalistic online essays and denunciation of liberals as "running dogs" of the Americans. *Global Times* rejoiced in an editorial, but Xi's endorsement caused an uproar on the Internet, not only because of Zhou's politics but because the country's top leader turned someone derided by professional literati as a scribbler of rants into a literary paragon.

THE DIGITAL CHALLENGE

The rise of social media has changed China's media landscape in many ways. The appearance of blogs created an alternative to tightly controlled traditional media. While blogs, too, are censored, they nonetheless offer room for "citizen journalists" to report official malfeasance, protests, environmental disasters, and other news that mainstream media does not report on. Some bloggers have become hugely influential and, despite frequent struggles with censors and occasional detention, command a clout. This has been amplified by the rise of microblogs, the most popular of which, Sina Weibo, claims over five hundred million users, and its popular accounts may have millions of followers, and most recently of the mobile social network WeChat, whose users have already exceeded that number and which is becoming the most important channel of targeted news and advertising. Perhaps the most significant effect of social media has been to render news blackouts ineffective: even if posts are deleted in a few minutes, they are immediately archived and reposted by other users elsewhere. This is also true for events abroad. As several correspondents pointed out, ten years ago, if Chinese media did not report on an event, or reported badly, few people would know or care. Today, they face criticism and ridicule—a point brought home amply by the scorn Internet users heaped on Chinese journalists' coverage of the Malaysia Airlines story. While the blocking of foreign websites has not been relaxed, today a sufficient number of Chinese Internet users, both abroad and in China, translate and post news reported abroad that state media has little choice but to keep up and appear credible. The propaganda authorities' 2008 decision to back away from blackouts was triggered by the fact that Chinese students abroad had seen Western media reports on rioting in Tibet and asked relatives in China about it.

Journalists have embraced social media to various degrees and in various ways. Some use Weibo to champion social, environmental, or anti-corruption causes; a few, like *Phoenix Weekly* investigative reporter Deng Fei, to such effect that they have quit their jobs and become "professional philanthropists." Others, including some foreign correspondents like Xinhua Finance's Yu Liang in New York, *21st Century Business Herald*'s Lu Zhenhua in Brussels, or Sina Finance's Angela Hao in London, use it to disseminate their reporting and comment on current events related to it. Caixin automatically opens a blog and an "official" Weibo account for every journalist. (So does Sina, which is the provider of the most popular Weibo platform.) Journalists in China also use Weibo to preempt gag orders by getting stories out on the Web before the Propaganda Department has the time to ban them, but I have not encountered such cases among foreign correspondents.[22]

Unlike, for example, Associated Press, Chinese media organizations tend not to have explicit policies on staff use of social media. Even Xinhua, whose regulations tend to be among the strictest, has no policy that requires staff to separate their personal opinions from their status as Xinhua staff: the rules are only that journalists are not allowed to post elements of a story before the story has been filed or to negate something they asserted in a story. Han Song, a former head of Xinhua's China Features department that produces in-depth feature stories and currently deputy head of the agency's international affairs department, is also a popular science fiction writer who often posts views critical of the government on his Weibo account. Liu Hong, a senior editor at Xinhua's *Globe Magazine* and former Israel and US correspondent, uses Weibo to post regular comments on current international events, including in ways that don't entirely conform to the official interpretation of events, though never stray too far from mainstream Chinese views. For example, the copious commentary he posted on the 2014

WORLDWIDE EXPANSION OF CHINA'S MEDIA [37]

Russia-Ukraine war refrained from taking sides but described the Ukraine as the victim of a proxy war between the West and Russia. *Southern Weekend* foreign desk journalists used microblogs to protest the process against their colleagues who took part in the 2013 New Year's protests.

But most journalists, it appears, prefer to keep their professional and private personae separate: they use their microblogs to keep their friends updated about their lives and avoid using their real names or affiliations. A European correspondent for CCTV stopped blogging after just five posts after she arrived at her station, in part because she did not want to create controversy among colleagues by expressing her personal views that some might not agree with. A Caixin correspondent in the United States has largely stopped posting on his "work" Weibo account after being "flamed" by nationalists for some comments about Taiwan.

At the same time, although most foreign correspondents are not very active microbloggers, virtually every journalist, editor, and Propaganda Department official uses Weibo to keep up with the news. This means that decisions about news agendas for the day are to some degree based on microblog posts that senior editors and executives pick up on that morning. For some journalists, this can be a nuisance. A UK correspondent for a central news organization complained that her editors routinely ask her to report on stories from the tabloid *Daily Mail* that frequently find their way onto Weibo in Chinese translation but in her judgment are not necessarily newsworthy or reliable.

Media companies, too, have been scrambling to exploit the opportunities offered by online uses, anxious not to be left behind in the market and attempting to challenge each other's dominance in text, audio, and video. Caixin's publisher, Hu Shuli, has been the strongest proponent of transforming newspapers into multimedia companies: its correspondents write more for its website than for the company's flagship weekly *New Century* (Xin Shiji), and for a while had to supply videos for a partnership with a Hong Kong-based Asia TV to produce three hours of English television every day. The venture, however, has not been successful and proved an excessive burden on journalists. Meanwhile, a number of former and current staff at financial media like Caixin and *21st Century Business Herald*, including a former New York correspondent, have launched websites that offer specialized financial and business information. One of these, www.morningwhistle.com, which focuses on investment opportunities abroad, is partly owned by *21st Century Business Herald* and was previously run by its deputy editor-in-chief. The paper's foreign correspondents are expected to contribute to the site, and not all are happy with the added workload. *People's Daily*, Xinhua, and CRI correspondents are also expected to produce online text and video content as well as video material for their new TV channels: CRI's online Huanqiu Qiguan (Global Curiosities), also available as a cable channel in Beijing, and Xinhua's Chinese- and English-language satellite television launched in 2010. (Xinhua's larger bureaus have specialized television reporters.)

Many print media post video content, including studio discussions, on their sites, and some use social media to enable readers to ask journalists questions. On the eve of the second round of the 2012 French presidential election, Ying Qiang, Xinhua's then deputy Paris station chief, took part in a Weibo Q&A session organized by *International Herald Leader* (Guoji Xianqu Daobao), a newspaper owned by Xinhua. (To the question which candidate he would vote for if he could, he replied that he would vote for Nicolas Sarkozy, the conservative incumbent who ended up losing the election. Despite the fact that Sarkozy had been the target of online furor in China when he mooted boycotting the 2008 Olympics in response to human rights violations in Tibet, Ying said this caused no controversy at Xinhua.) All mainstream media outlets have official microblog accounts, and many have developed mobile apps. Xinhua has been particularly active in this area, first launching an English-language mobile news service in Africa in 2011 and then several specialized apps, both in China and abroad, that send top stories and multimedia content to users' smartphones. CRI also has a mobile TV app. Most recently, media organizations have started providing news feeds via WeChat. In 2014, Caixin launched several WeChat feeds, including one on energy and another on foreign affairs; *People's Daily* began using an unofficial WeChat account for chatty reportages of Xi Jinping and his wife Peng Liyuan's overseas visits in an apparent attempt to approximate society-page stories on British royalty's foreign trips; and *Global Times* launched a WeChat opinion feed, vowing "to provide a platform for ordinary people's thoughts"—although contributors have been well-known pundits rather than "ordinary people."

Until recently, the encroachment of digital media on traditional media markets has been the subject of intense discussion but failed to push traditional journalism into the kind of transformational crisis that it has been undergoing in the West. The impact has been delayed and dampened by the role of the state in financing and managing media; by still high, though falling, newspaper circulation figures; by the continued importance government officials attribute to the printed press; and by the sheer size and continuing growth of the advertising market. It was the meteoric rise of WeChat in 2013 that appears to have pushed print media over the brink by causing the collapse of the print advertising market. WeChat groups, unlike Weibo accounts and groups on other social media, are not open but private: readers have to be admitted as members of the group and are therefore likely to pay closer attention to messages within it. This allows companies cheap and highly effective targeted advertising. Caixin's advertising revenue dropped by 30 percent in 2013, according to an editor, and he expected it to fall even more dramatically in 2014. "Last year, I thought that paper media still had a few years in China, but now I think they will be finished soon," this editor said. He expected the weekly *New Century* to shrink from its current 120 pages to perhaps as few as twenty in the long term, eventually becoming a bulletin of exclusive investigative material that readers could not get elsewhere. This implies a much smaller staff than the current 300, and some have already left: a former journalist started a WeChat service that had gained 100,000 subscribers by early 2014; another, after going on maternity leave, launched a WeChat group helping Beijing mothers find child-friendly places, attracting seventy thousand followers. A third former reporter started *TMT Post*, a platform for the emerging TMT (Telecommunications, Media, Technology) profession. A former web editor moved to the *Wall Street Journal* as managing editor of the online Chinese edition. (The *New York Times*' Chinese edition is also managed by a Caixin alumnus, but an ex-Xinhua reporter is in charge of the *Financial Times*' Chinese site.) By 2016, some media were reportedly relying on the sale of their online users' lists to advertisers and on event organizing as their principal sources of income.

SQUEEZED BY THE GOVERNMENT AND THE MARKET

The perception that the room for journalism, especially investigative journalism, was shrinking, combined with a declining market for print media, had already prompted a number of journalists in the commercialized media to resign or contemplate resigning before the WeChat crisis. By late 2013 to early 2014, this trend was accelerating. Most of those I spoke to were planning to move, or had already moved, to corporate PR, online startups and web-based news providers during my research, or else were going to study abroad. Western news organizations with localized online Chinese editions, such as the *Wall Street Journal*, Bloomberg, and Forbes, hired some of the more accomplished journalists. Now that the weight of online content was poised to rise, Chinese business media would have to compete directly with these services, as well as with online news portals such as Sina, NetEase, and Tencent. The government realized that maintaining a strong position in dominating public opinion now required more innovative ventures into new media than merely expanding traditional official media's online presence. The launch of *The Paper* (Pengpai), a new online news and analysis portal and application by Shanghai Media Group, in mid-2014 was widely seen within the struggling market-oriented media as a move backed if not initiated by central government officials wanting to create an outlet through which messages favored by the state could reach a younger, urban, educated audience—the audience that upmarket commercial media depended on. Indeed, shortly after *The Paper*'s launch and its recruitment spree among journalists working for commercial media in Shanghai and beyond, the Party's Leading Small Group on Deepening Reform issued a "Guiding opinion on advancing the integrated development of traditional and new media" (*Guanyu tuidong chuantong meiti he xinxing meiti ronghe fazhan de zhidao yijian*). At the group's meeting, Chairman Xi Jinping spoke of the need to "create a competitive mainstream new media" in the form of several influential and well-capitalized new media conglomerates.[23] Journalists from *Oriental Morning Post*, the main news daily taking part in the new venture, were transferred to *The Paper*, and 80 percent of their time was now supposed to be spent on online content. Two years after the launch, advertising incomes only covered one-third of the paper's budget, while the rest came from an investment fund linked to state enterprises.[24]

Some journalists speculated that the choice of Shanghai for the new portal was meant further to weaken the positions of the Southern Group; all agreed that it would draw more advertisers and readers away from the commercial papers. This was soon followed by the arrest of the publisher and editor-in-chief of *21st Century Business Herald*, Southern Group's flagship, Shanghai-based business daily, in September 2014 on charges of extortion. They were replaced by two editors from *Southern Daily*, the provincial Party paper. Suggesting high-level political will behind the affair, *People's Daily* reported the matter immediately, and CCTV broadcast an interview with a contrite Shen Hao confessing to his crime in a setting that resembled a televised trial and was designed to turn public sentiment against Shen and his paper. The affair suggested that the combined pressures of a shrinking market for print media, renewed financial support for official media outlets, and diminishing room for publishing muckraking stories had made extortion or blackmail—referred to as "remunerated lack of news," *you chang wu wen*—more common as a source of revenue for commercial papers. By the end of 2014, the balance of commercial versus central media appeared to have shifted dramatically in favor of the latter, flush with cash and vastly expanded foreign networks while the former were in disarray. "The next decade, if there is one, will be precarious" for commercial media, predicted journalism scholar Hu Yong.[25] Readers who persisted in seeking alternative sources of foreign news were increasingly switching to articles from English-language media translated and posted on WeChat or cloud-based servers by like-minded readers who accessed them. The room for Chinese international journalism seemed to be shrinking even as its infrastructure expanded.

It is often said that the 1990s and the early 2000s were the best years of journalism in China. In those years, maverick journalists gained fame for muckraking that angered the authorities but propelled their papers—such as *Southern Metropolitan Daily*—to fame.[26] All Chinese journalists interviewed for a study in the early 2000s aspired to be investigative reporters and work for the Southern group or the CCTV show *Focal Point*, a program that a *People's Daily* correspondent remembers "was like a god" to him as a student.[27] At the time the base pay for journalists at the commercial papers was very low, and remuneration largely depended on bonuses that in turn were determined by their stories' sales impact. While the work of famous investigative journalists is still admired, a deteriorating climate for press freedom since the 2008 Olympics has combined with the spread of a discourse of professionalism that focuses on objectivity and rejects any form of advocacy by journalists in their reporting work, seeing the models of investigative reporting from the previous decade as having an anti-government bias and an intolerance for alternative interpretations.[28] While this discourse of objectivity is inspired by standards set in Western texts, it can lead to very different consequences in the conditions of government censorship than in a relatively free press environment.[29] Thus, ironically, this globalized discourse of professionalism understood in technical terms sometimes ends up colluding with official narratives that discredit political criticism as driven by agendas that undermine the national interest. Some journalists swear by objective standards and condemn "propaganda," although this does not necessarily mean either that they refuse to engage in what they see as such or that they oppose the system that requires them to do so. Others dismiss the idea of such a thing as objective, agenda-free reporting as an illusion, but may still use the standards of professionalism in judging whether reporting is good or bad. And though some journalists switch between discourses of professionalism and partisanship seemingly without reflecting on the contradictions between them, others admit to being confused or troubled.

Thus, the notion of journalistic professionalism is in practice often reconciled with accepting or even supporting government restrictions on reporting. There is another sense, however, in which Chinese journalists can more justifiably be described as professionals than a decade or two ago. An increasing number of them now write for a plethora of glossy magazines and Web portals devoted to a variety of subjects, from fashion to cars and technology, that cater to an expanded middle class with far more demanding and differentiated tastes.[30]

Notwithstanding their sense of being underpaid compared to peers in the business sphere and lacking security compared to those in government, as well as the considerable income differential between media and between individual journalists, journalists increasingly lead what can be called middle-class lifestyles in terms of their housing status and quality and consumption practices, including foreign travel. And as a Caixin editor told me, a number of new recruits are willing to take on jobs that he sees as not very well remunerated for the amount and quality of work they are required to do because they have wealthy parents and thus need not be overly concerned about money. (A *People's Daily* correspondent once interviewed for a position at Caixin, but, being freshly married, he felt he simply could not take such a poorly paid job.) While a survey of journalism students at Chinese universities found that students rarely mentioned the urge to "make a difference" or strive for social justice as a motivation, but rather tended to have chosen journalism out of strategic calculation among limited available options and advice from parents,[31] it is likely that ambition and curiosity are strong driving forces behind the career choices of young people coming from privileged family backgrounds. Overall, however, the journalistic profession in China today is characterized by improving technological and material conditions in the central media, existential insecurity in local and commercialized media, and a sense of political uncertainty and demoralization pervading most of the media landscape.

CHAPTER 2

How Stories are Made

"**P**ÁL, you are still looking for those things you want to hear. . . . You still think that we should look at ourselves [China] critically, and then we are OK," an exasperated official media correspondent once told me. Like many other correspondents I spoke with, he resented being typecast in the role of the brainwashed or cynical Communist Party hack, a stereotype he believed that Westerners held about journalists like him. But he also bristled against the somewhat more nuanced view that he suspected I harbored, one that pit Party hacks against the independent minds that criticize censorship and inhabit the liberal Chinese press. With an upper-class British accent picked up at elite universities and a man-of-the-world demeanor, it would have cost him little effort to play the part of the sympathetic character, the "good guy" in a book that reaffirms the sinister nature of Chinese media as a whole. But he did not want the part. He wanted me to accept official media journalists on what he regarded as their own terms and stop cajoling them into expressions of resistance that might redeem them in the eyes of the liberal Westerner. Looking for resistance, he implied, might be a way for Westerners to reassure themselves that their models of the world still work, and a few Chinese journalists would be happy to oblige; but ultimately, it does not help understand Chinese journalism. His comment came in the context of a conversation about a mutual acquaintance who had set up an independent website for Chinese reporting on the world that often criticized state media. A reporter from another central media organization interjected angrily: "He isn't even worth talking about! [But] you find one person like this and you treat him like a hero!" A bureau chief for a third large Chinese media organization in town admitted to sharing her colleague's dislike of the man. He "and his friends are too young, they don't understand the situation, how things work. . . . [Also,] they lack access to key information. Do you think the [Chinese] ambassador is going to meet with these kids?"

While for some, journalists retain the aura of solitary warriors for the truth, others see them as pawns of an impersonal media imperialism.[1] This is especially so when it comes to China, except here, the latter view replaces media conglomerates in search of ever increasing profit with an even more fiendish, oppressive state. In the more optimistic reading, this Leviathan is always one step behind in the "cat and mouse game" with the warriors of the keyboard, but in the years of this book's writing, the number of imprisoned journalists and bloggers was growing. The prevailing view of Chinese media in the West is that it is a propaganda monolith in which journalists just do officials' bidding, while scholarship that does take journalists' agency seriously, rather than seeing them as mere accessories to a machinery of spin and censorship, has focused on those willing to challenge the system or at least to critique some aspects of China's contemporary reality. Hence, there is a disproportionate interest in investigative reporting and in the ways that journalists constantly push the limits of what they are allowed to report.[2] In more sympathetic accounts, focusing on such behavior redeems, as it were, Chinese media—particularly official media—professionals from the blanket stigma of being witless accomplices of a propaganda apparatus and humanizes them by suggesting not only that Chinese media are not a monolith that parrots the Party's slogans but also that at least some of the people who work in it share at least some of the central values of Western news work, such as a belief in the watchdog function of the media, and implies that without the constraints imposed by the Party they would probably take the media in a direction that is aligned with these.

But, in the same way as a number of *lingdao* and editors in the central media are dissatisfied with what they see as Chinese media's inability to set global news agendas and instead reacting to those set by the West, the correspondents quoted above reject a line of questioning they rightly see as aiming to produce empathy on liberal universalist terms. What they demand is recognition of Chinese journalism as professional even if it has no critical edge but, for example, follows the tenets of what has been called "positive reporting" or—particularly in the context of anticolonial struggles and "third world" Marxist movements in the 1960s and 1970s—"development journalism." While this term has various interpretations, its Chinese advocates, following earlier usage by leaders of African anticolonial movements and authoritarian or nativist Southeast Asian politicians, typically use it to mean journalism that promotes national cohesion and stability and conforms to putative African or Asian (as opposed to Western) values, rather than journalism focusing on development needs.[3] *Global Times*, in particular, has been described as practicing development journalism for its unswerving advocacy of what it perceives to be the national interest and the centrality of great power competition—sometimes indistinguishable from Samuel Huntington's view of the world in which conflict is the inevitable result of a "clash of civilizations"—in its news analysis.[4] Its editor-in-chief, Hu Xijin, has said that if media in China attacked the government in the way some Western media do in their own countries, "it would undermine the very foundation of the state," and he requires his newsmen to "anchor their articles in China's rise."[5] Indeed, the paper has published an editorial titled "Media Should Be Watchdog of National Interest."[6] While *Global Times* is distinguished by its nativist ideology—reflected not only in its insistence on serving the national interest but also by its anti-elitism, colloquial language, and advocacy of a specifically Chinese approach to most anything, including journalism—the goal of projecting a "Chinese voice" is, as we have seen in chapter 1, state policy.[7]

CENTRAL VERSUS COMMERCIAL MEDIA

We must be careful not to see Chinese journalists in the dichotomous optics of Party hacks versus resistance fighters. Both individual journalists and organizations, in the central as well as the commercial print media, tend to be driven by a variety of motives and operate in a range of ways, from highly conformist to risk-taking, depending not only on the organization's position but also on the circumstances and topic of reporting.[8] The most admired journalists and editors are usually not open rebels but those who consistently succeed in pushing the boundaries of censorship without getting their stories banned or themselves or their organizations punished. Nonetheless, when I began my research, I was expecting to see a clearer division between "hacks" and "rebels," if not across the official/commercial media divide, then between individuals. In a way, the reporter quoted at the beginning of this chapter—I will call him John—was right. I was not prepared to meet Western-trained journalists who cultivated worldly-wise, cosmopolitan personas and Oxbridge accents, were critical of Chinese media conditions at times and embraced the goal of journalistic professionalism, yet often produced one-sided, propagandistic journalism and could in turn become defensive, cynical and impassioned about going along with this state of affairs.

But was John also right in that to look for critical journalists wishing to subvert China's media control was a sort of self-deception, a fundamentally misguided view of Chinese media because these journalists were mostly putting on a show for their Western allies and would never amount to a serious force? This was the message that *Global Times*, with 1.6 million copies China's second-largest daily by circulation and the nemesis of the liberal press, liked to convey in its barrage of editorials and opinion pieces that portrayed China's public debates as beset by a cabal of irrelevant intellectuals parroting Western ideas and out of touch with the majority's views and needs. *Global Times*, while pursuing a self-described Chinese approach to journalism and rejecting Western values—whatever these may be—has reported on events no other mainstream media dared to touch. In 2008, it was the first to report that China's Olympic torchbearers were attacked during the Paris leg of the torch relay. (Official media at first reported that the Paris leg of the relay had been "successful.") In 2010, it reported and commented on imprisoned dissident Liu Xiaobo's 2010 Nobel Peace Prize. In 2014, it published the leaked allegation by Poland's foreign minister that Russian president Putin had proposed to carve up Ukraine among its neighbors years before civil war broke out in 2014. (China's official media were sympathetic to Russia in the conflict over Ukraine and avoided mention of any evidence that would point to Russia's responsibility.)

In Hu Xijin's words, *Global Times* "wants to tell Chinese people about the world's real views of China. In the past," official media made it look like "foreign reports said that China was good, praised China; now, you can hear all the world's criticism of China in *Global Times*."[9] Instead of treating foreign visits of Chinese leaders as manifestations of "eternal friendship," *Global Times* offers analyses of bilateral relations that include conflicts of interest. In 1998, its cover story of Bill Clinton's visit to China was headlined "To China with Pressure" (*Daizhe yali lai Hua*). Yet, criticism of China is usually just mentioned as a foil for a repartee, rarely explained. A popular adage circulating on the Internet put it this way: "*Reference News*: The Whole World Praises Us; *Global Times*: The Whole World Envies Us." Hu

Xijin denies getting special dispensation from the government and attributes his ability to get away with taboo topics and opinions at variance with official foreign policy to *Global Times'* determination to "defend the interests of the people and the state by being vocal rather than staying silent."[10] In a preface to a collection of *Global Times* editorials, *People's Daily* deputy editor-in-chief Mi Bohua endorsed this claim: "No matter how sensitive a topic," the question is "whether elucidating such-and-such a stance is in the national interest, in the interest of development broadly seen, or not. If it is, then there are no reasons to be concerned."[11] In fact, the foreign ministry and other government departments have placed pseudonymous articles in *Global Times* under various bylines, and the Central Propaganda Department has given it several awards for facilitating foreign policy.[12]

The fact that *Global Times* editorials' tone on particular topics—for example, Japan—varies from strident to soothing appears to support Hu's claim that the paper wishes to reflect "China's complexity," but the timing of these changes in tone suggests that they are sensitive to the government's momentary strategy to amplify or to restrain nationalistic discourse, as well as to project a more hawkish or more restrained public opinion to the outside. "If you look closely," a CRI journalist commented, "*Global Times* cooperates with the government; it does not sow chaos (*peihe er bu shi tianluan*); it just does it by different means, just like in an orchestra there is both a soprano and a bass." A *People's Daily* correspondent recalled a talk Hu Xijin gave to the staff in which he used a more risqué simile: he likened *People's Daily* to the Party's senior wife, more mature and responsible, and *Global Times* to a secondary wife: more temperamental and willing to kick up a fuss. A journalist for a commercial weekly told me he had heard of meetings for op-ed page editors called by Propaganda Department officials where they were told that only *Global Times* was allowed to publish an op-ed on a particular issue. During the 2014 Hong Kong protests demanding universal suffrage, which the government perceived as a direct threat to the existing order, *Global Times* published opinion pieces that justified the possibility of sending the army to quell them and argued that the central government had no reason to protect Hong Kong's prosperity. These articles may have corresponded to the governments' interest in ratcheting up the pressure on the Hong Kong government, but they also contributed to a wave of anti-Hong Kong sentiment on the mainland.

By Hu Xijin's own admission, *Global Times* is a "patriotic newspaper."[13] The editorials and opinion pieces *Global Times* publishes—some by well-known "public intellectuals" such as political scientists Wang Jisi, Zhang Weiwei and Yan Xuetong or literary scholar Zhang Yiwu—almost always view the world through the prism of competing national interests, but while some are jingoistic, others are coolheaded and original. (The ratios seem influenced as much by Hu's judgment of the moment's political expediencies as by the divergent opinions of authors.) Yet, while Hu's figure fascinates the press—as evidenced by the number of interviews and in-depth articles on him and his paper—most foreign correspondents eye *Global Times* with distaste. Reporters for liberal, commercial papers relish collecting evidence of pro-government sycophancy, sloppy reporting, and outright misreporting of the news to fit the editors' agenda. In one instance, described in *Phoenix Weekly*, *Global Times* cited Japan's foreign minister as saying at a press conference that Chinese aircraft violating Japanese airspace could be targeted by missiles, but other journalists present at the conference denied his having made the statement.[14] Qin Xuan, a former reporter for *Southern Weekend*, now at *Phoenix Weekly*, described *Global Times'* position as a "vulgar realism" that "reduces the international relations system to great power competition for hegemony and glorifies conspiracy theory." He went on to conclude that "nationalist foreign news reporting and reflexive-cognitive foreign news reporting are fundamentally opposed to each other" and have no room for reconciliation.[15] Yet, in fact, my interviewees include correspondents who, at one point, wrote for *Global Times* and *Phoenix Weekly* simultaneously.

Despite the tailwind *Global Times* has received from the government, central media reporters' views of it are not much kinder. A China Radio International reporter dismissed its reporting as "exaggerated" and "not very truthful," and a China News Service journalist said it was "not really international news. It's using international affairs as a platform for popular opinion." He also accused *Global Times* of deliberately distorting foreign media reports to the extent of falsifying news. "It misleads and incites people," a Xinhua correspondent said, adding that he "particularly could not stand their articles on Japan." Another Xinhua reporter noted, however, that other papers have picked up the tendency to "collect stories about the maltreatment of Chinese people abroad, in order to stir up emotions."

Over the course of this writing, the position of critical journalists within Chinese media, including those Qin Xuan described as "reflexive-cognitive foreign reporters," has progressively become more marginal. By the end of 2014, departures of international desk reporters and editors at liberal commercial media for PR jobs, online startups, and graduate study abroad, high at the best of times, accelerated. Those who had not left yet were contemplating the possibility. In addition to tightening censorship and worsening finances, their work was made more difficult by the complete blockage of Google and the frequent shutdowns of virtual private networks (VPNs) they used to "scale the Great Firewall" to gain access to blocked sites. All of this made following foreign media, a routine part of keeping up-to-date with current events, increasingly time-consuming. "Every day, I think: does what I do have any meaning?" one foreign-desk editor said.

Even so, John's advice to stop looking for instances of resistance, subversion or even discontent among foreign correspondents seems premature. First, at least some liberal journalists, like Qin Xuan, are warning against complacency. Yang Xiao, a prominent foreign affairs journalist for *Southern People Weekly*, reflected:

> When I worked at the state-run Xinhua News Agency from 2004 to 2008, I . . . used puns, metaphors and homophones—any kind of linguistic trick I could think of—to express my approval or disapproval. Later on, at Southern People Weekly . . . I wrote a lot of sensitive features that relied on [these] skills. At first, I enjoyed the cat-and-mouse game with censors. I thought, "There will always be someone who can read between the lines." But now, I worry that this kind of expression will create in me a vicious circle of complacency, in which I know my efforts to speak freely will be fruitless but can console myself with at least having tried. I fear that, in China's increasingly complicated and ambiguous media environment, *chunqiu bifa* [language tricks to convey hidden criticism] may be changing from a means of dissent into a tool of inadvertent self-censorship that may ultimately deprive us of the ability to face the truth.[16]

Second, there are attempts to organize online platforms for alternative voices of reporting on foreign countries. The best established and most successful is Overseas Wind (Haiwai Lai Feng), a network of stringers writing for the finance "channel" of Sina, China's largest online news portal.[17] In 2013, the platform had twenty-four contributors across all continents, usually Chinese graduate students or young professionals, most of them not professional journalists. The stories are largely on economy and lifestyle, but occasionally, there are in-depth stories that elucidate aspects of politics not usually covered by correspondents and do not always have an obvious "China peg." For example, a United States–based stringer, Zhuang Qiaoyi, one of the few professional journalists on the network, contributed stories on the public role of women in the election campaign and on the Boston Marathon bombing.[18] In 2014, the veteran journalist Zhao Jing, known under his blogosphere pen-name Michael Anti, began collaborating with Caixin to organize a similar global network, called Globus (Caixin Shijieshuo), which was to operate independently of Caixin's foreign desk. Anti had long been known as an outspoken liberal critic of the Chinese government, and in 2006, he had started *Foreign Affairs Weekly* (Zongheng Zhoukan), an unaffiliated website devoted to international news analysis, to which journalists contributed on a volunteer basis. The site went inactive in 2010, but many of its contributors became prominent international journalists at various commercial papers. World Talk recruited stringers with profiles similar to those at Sina Finance—some still undergraduate students, others, like Zhuang Qiaoyi, already writing for Sina or even for Xinhua or *People's Daily* Online—but the output has been geared towards fewer and longer pieces of news analysis, from the elections in Nigeria to Chinese dramas on US television and profiles of young European politicians. Globus stays away from topics that are likely to run afoul of the censors, but it differs from the mainstream press in its in-depth local reporting and, occasionally, represents a distinctly liberal perspective that may be at odds with the official one. For example, unlike mainstream Chinese media, Globus' reporting on the 2015–16 European refugee crisis focused on its human rights aspects and included voices that criticized the agreement that allowed the EU to return refugees to Turkey.

Third, some central media correspondents, including those working at Xinhua and *People's Daily*, explicitly challenge official views of China and even applaud Western reporting on it. Upon learning of my research, a young *People's Daily* correspondent in Europe forwarded the 2014 report on "the State of Journalism in China" by Harvard's Nieman Foundation, entitled *Censored*, which unequivocally condemns the increasing limits on the freedom of the press. He recommended it as "a very good report" and complained that his paper was a "propaganda machine" and "not truly a newspaper." (Perhaps not coincidentally, his colleague, in a separate interview, said that it was necessary for overseas correspondents to be "firmly partisan" [*you jianli de dangxing*], otherwise it was easy to "slip over to this side," meaning the side of the Europeans. "Some of our foreign correspondents don't fully understand this point.") A Xinhua correspondent prefaced a query about European perceptions of Xi Jinping's war on corruption in China by asking whether it was seen as another "attack-style" move by an authoritarian regime. Others appear conflicted. A CNS correspondent fumed about Xi Jinping's cult of personality and, as a small sign of disagreement, did not sign his name when he had to report on overseas Chinese organizations' opposition to the 2014 demonstrations in Hong Kong demanding free elections. And a CCTV correspondent who played down the current tightening of press freedom in China nonetheless praised an analysis of CCTV's overseas expansion by an American journalist, which saw it as threatening to media freedom worldwide.[19]

Admittedly, central media journalists who publicly voice such views are a small minority, in part because a number of those who think in this way quit their jobs after a few years. Others may hold critical views privately. The editor of a Xinhua news magazine, a self-described liberal, assured me that "all Xinhua senior editors are much more liberal than I am. They have a clear idea of what's going on. But in their work, they toe the line" or pander to the market for which nationalism sells. It would be simplistic to fall back on the dichotomy of "public lies" versus "private truths," as many journalists are clearly genuinely passionate about defending what they see as the national interest.[20] Still, this view is held by a number of liberal journalists and probably does characterize at least some of those who work within the official media.

While the position of international journalism explicitly challenging the official view of China's place in the world is increasingly precarious, the landscape of Chinese foreign correspondents remains complex. The demographic difference between reporters for commercial and official media is shrinking. Increasingly, graduates of the same programs, with similar age, haircuts, and Weibo personae, work in the overseas bureaus of both, and some move from one to the other. One disillusioned Xinhua correspondent, for example, quit and joined *Phoenix Weekly* just before her first posting abroad. Another became an assistant for a foreign journalist in China while still working at Xinhua, and then moved to the Southern group. In the opposite direction, a stringer for *Caijing* returned to China to become an assistant for a Western correspondent, then moved to *Global Times*, and eventually became the director of its op-ed department.

Closeness in age, education, and lifestyle habits should, and sometimes does, make friendships between the two groups possible. (It also creates a divide between them and older journalists and editors in central media, particularly the more conservative ones who sometimes distrust their younger colleagues or view them as falling short in the necessary skills of writing or analysis. As one *People's Daily* correspondent put it: "They do have professional quality, but they fall way short on thought awareness.") Yet their circumstances of work are very different. Official media bureaus, particularly larger ones, operate with a daily regimen much more akin to a state enterprise in China. Concerns about internal politics, "leaders'" instructions, and evaluations at headquarters are paramount as they determine future promotion and structure daily routines. At commercial media, which rarely have more than one correspondent at any given place and do not have formal bureaus, correspondents have more freedom to structure their lives and create more diverse social networks, but their workloads are even heavier.

Even more important is the psychological sense of distance between commercial and official (sometimes called *tizhinei*, or "of-the-system") media. A United States–based Caixin correspondent said simply: "We do not consider ourselves the same media." An editor for *Phoenix Weekly* was more dismissive: "What Xinhua does isn't media work." And an international journalist at *Southern Weekend* wrote with some bitterness: "A certain international news media organization boasts of having hundreds of journalists in over a hundred foreign countries, but their level of knowledge and awareness still causes ridicule and sometimes even deliberate distortion or fabrication. . . . Having arrived abroad, journalists tend to rely on a day's superficial observation, or at most on interviews with key personalities."[21]

The independent Nairobi-based reporting website whose mention elicited such bile in the conversation recounted in the beginning of this chapter is similarly critical about reporting by official media, although it does not come down on them as hard.

> Many first-hand news reports are not properly transmitted to China. On the one hand, Chinese actors in Africa, such as companies, often monopolize the power to interpret events; on the other hand, Chinese government bodies in Africa, such as embassies and central media, bring their own baggage of epistemological frames while being concerned and uneasy about "negative reporting."[22]

Privately, a contributor to the site suggested that most official media correspondents are not very interested in Africa and have never visited a slum. "Their job is propaganda rather than reporting."

On the other side of the divide, among official media correspondents, emotions towards the commercial media vary. Quite a few admit to being readers of the commercial media; others are wary, dismissive, or display a sense of superiority. As a former Xinhua correspondent in a Middle Eastern country put it: "The quality and standards of the journalists at official media are higher than at the market media. This includes political quality as well as professional quality. In terms of objective and truthful reporting, official media can be believed more. We may not talk about certain things, but [at least] what we do say is not false."

A *China Daily* correspondent in Africa, who was ambivalent about Xinhua's and CCTV's "positive" reporting strategy there and shared much of the criticism of central media reporters—"They don't know anything about Africa until they come here, and after two years they begin preparing to leave and hope they can next go somewhere better"—was nonetheless even more critical of the reporters occasionally dispatched by Caixin and *Southern Weekend* because of what he saw as negative bias. "Those media don't report on CSR [corporate social responsibility efforts] and don't care about the sacrifices that Chinese companies here have made. They have no idea how hard [the companies] have worked; they are opportunists who follow Western media."

Very often, unless they are stationed in a city where they regularly meet commercial media correspondents at news conferences, official media journalists are simply unaware that they exist in the first place. But at those stations where they do—that is, Washington and London—some become socially acquainted with a few commercial media correspondents, although rarely close to them. As a Europe correspondent for China News Service explained, commercial media correspondents "follow completely different paths."

Central media reporters have a close relationship with the Chinese embassy: a *People's Daily* correspondent who worked in Paris in the early 2000s wrote that foreign correspondents were supervised both by their *lingdao* at the newspaper and those at the embassy. "When there are glitches in the bilateral relationship, reporting on it is particularly sensitive; at such times, we can play the smart alec even less. . . . Regarding interviews with some sensitive personalities, it is also best to ask for the embassy's opinion first."[23] In my interviews, embassy officials and correspondents denied having a formal supervisory relationship, but correspondents who are Party members are attached to the embassy's Party organization and pay their dues there (except at large regional bureaus that have their own Party cell). More importantly, embassy staff would often call meetings for correspondents to inform them of the government's view on a particular matter or to prepare them for a visit by Chinese officials. In addition, central media correspondents regularly meet the same crowd at embassy receptions, which rarely includes commercial media journalists. A CRI correspondent wondered how they even secured visas. "Doesn't the Chinese government stop them?" Being excluded from embassy activities gives commercial media correspondents more freedom, but also deprives them of access to important insider information.

Among themselves, central media correspondents at any given location tend to socialize regularly and to be familiar with each other's bureaus. While there are many casual friendships, there is also gossip, gentle rivalry and some mutual stereotyping. Correspondents for *China Daily* and China News Service (the smaller of the two news agencies, with a mandate to cater to Chinese-language media outside China) see themselves as least fettered by institutional rules and sometimes make fun of how Xinhua journalists at large bureaus are required to ask for permission to go out in the evening and encouraged to marry within the agency, which some of the staff at the smaller media also see as overfunded and inefficient. CCTV is envied for its advertising-generated wealth. Of the three media with the largest networks— Xinhua, CCTV, and CRI—China Radio International staff see their agency as freer but also poorer than the other two. One former CRI correspondent suggested that Xinhua correspondents are least free to report on a given event, and those for CCTV and CRI are progressively more so—although a Xinhua reporter at the same location denied this.

It appears, then, that the upbeat vision of an expanding network of Chinese correspondents who gradually become more professional and better at their jobs as their institutions learn and adapt but do not question their role as "voices of China"—a vision articulated by many central media reporters and managers, none better than John—is inaccurate. More reporters, even young, English-speaking reporters with international backgrounds, does not necessarily mean more critical reporting; that much is true. Among young Oxford graduates I have come across in my research, there have been both vocal critics of the Chinese media system and staunch "realists" like John who dismissed Western criticism as holier-than-thou. In fact, critical reporting may be further marginalized even as foreign correspondent networks grow. Even so, larger networks do mean greater diversity of opinions among correspondents. Even within official media, there are various degrees of impatience with the system and sometimes, rarely, outright contempt for it. At one major European bureau of a central media organization, I talked to a correspondent who defined correcting the falsehoods propagated by

Western media as her goal and another who—while agreeing to an extent that Western media was biased—felt that making Chinese society more tolerant was at least as important, although she felt she had to be cautious to avoid attracting the attention of colleagues who didn't share her view. At a smaller central media organization, also in Europe, I spoke to a correspondent who felt that writing politically motivated stories ordered from above was embarrassing (*diulian*) and said he tried to sabotage such tasks as much as he could.

In the end, however, the stories that are printed, broadcast, or posted online rarely reflect reporters' views alone. As in all media, they are refracted through the preferences of editors and *lingdao*, formal or informal editorial policies, and ad hoc considerations, all of which reflect a complex mix of considerations regarding the organization's style and profile, audience interest, and commercial and political risk. The state's media control regime means that the potential repercussions of misjudgment can be grave. For that reason, all media operate with multiple layers of approval and a longer gestation time for a story than their Western counterparts—a disadvantage particularly for Xinhua, as it tries to compete with the Big Three (AP, AFP, Reuters) at the "who reported it first" game. But given the divergent size, nature, and orientation of the organizations for which correspondents work, there is variation in negotiating the process whereby a story is prepared for publication.

After the deployment of a corps of correspondents to report on the vanished Malaysian Airlines flight in March 2014 failed to produce any original stories, Chinese media came under unprecedented fire by online commentators, journalists, and media scholars for failing to investigate the event and merely waiting for Malaysian government communiqués and Western reports. One commentator on the online forum of the Shanghai daily *Oriental Morning* called the incident "Chinese media's 9/11," while a journalist accused foreign correspondents of pursuing no more than "Here I am!" photo ops.[24]

Some contributors to the debate argued that Chinese correspondents' lackluster performance had more to do with China's still insufficient global clout—which limited both China's role in the rescue operations and journalists' access to Western sources such as aircraft manufacturers—than with the media itself, and could therefore be only remedied by more Chinese power. Others pointed out that, to the contrary, the inaccessibility and secrecy of China's aviation and satellite-imagery industries, closely linked to the military, meant Chinese journalists had no experts to turn to at home.[25] Yet others blamed Chinese media's reflex to wait for government instructions when it comes to major events, insufficient technical knowledge, and a habit of stirring up emotions instead of investigating.[26] But *Southern Metropolitan Daily* commentator He Xiaoshou suggested that Chinese correspondents were out of their depth because they were overly specialized in China-related issues, and People's University media scholar Ma Shaohua wrote that their propaganda responsibilities prevented them from accumulating the necessary experience and resources.[27] Reuters's former senior China correspondent Doug Young pointed out that Chinese journalists' lack of personal networks that could serve as information sources has to do with their heavy writing quotas, lack of financial support for expenses such as meals and transportation, and insufficient local staff.[28] Many others, however—both central media journalists and liberal critics—dismissed these arguments as excuses to cover up journalists' lack of professional skills.

When I asked a Caixin correspondent why no Chinese media has attempted to specialize in quality international reporting for a high-end market, she responded:

> I think the more entrepreneurial among the Chinese journalists have already tried many things out to have more informative international reporting, and it's largely due to two things that so far there is little success: one is the competency of Chinese journalists, which up to now is still in deficit but may be quickly improving; the other is, ultimately, censorship. Once you want to write about the most attention-drawing topics, i.e., Japan, US, North Korea, you quickly hit the "red line." Unless one can find a way to bypass censorship, the ceiling is bound to be low. *Global Times* became so popular for a reason: their voice on the most concerning issues is the only voice allowed to be said in public.

How does the negotiating process between journalists, editors, and *lingdao* actually work? How do ideas about potential stories appear, turn into approved topics (referred to as *xuanti*), then into filed stories or "packages?" How are these then edited and shaped until they take their published or broadcast form, and how are they, in some cases, subjected to post-publication censorship? To some extent, the process is defined by the uniform system of political control over Chinese media; yet there is considerable variation across media organizations, influenced by their position within the state media system, political orientation, management and editorial policies, and personal relations.

CORRESPONDENTS AT *GLOBAL TIMES*: PROVIDING AMMUNITION FOR THE "NATIONAL INTEREST"

Foreign correspondents have the least autonomy at *Global Times*, the popular nationalistic daily that focuses on international affairs and hovers around second place in the circulation rankings of Chinese newspapers. (Circulation figures published by media are widely considered inflated, but a senior editor gave me the figure 1.5 million in 2013.) *Global Times* was an innovator in foreign reporting in the late 1990s. Set up as a money-making venture of *People's Daily*'s international department—which was so cash-strapped it could no longer pay bonuses—it struggled to increase circulation and turn a profit. In doing so, it relied on *People's Daily* correspondents, who, back then, had time on their hands (before 2011 *People's Daily* had only two international pages, so any one correspondent's articles except those based in the United States appeared only infrequently).

People's Daily reporters were expected to meet reporting requests coming from *Global Times*. In exchange, *Global Times* paid *People's Daily* a lump sum every year in exchange on top of generous honoraria paid to the journalists: one hundred yuan per thousand characters was an "astronomical sum" in 1997.[29] But writing for *Global Times* was not part of correspondents' annual performance review (*kaohe*), and some shirked it as much as they could: not all *People's Daily* reporters were pleased with what happened to material they supplied at the hands of *Global Times* editors. A correspondent who reported from Japan in the early 2000s recalls that *People's Daily* reporters there tended to write little for *Global Times* because of what they perceived as its imbalanced stories about Japanese attitudes to atrocities committed in World War II. For example, a series of stories reported on a history textbook that denied the massacre of the civilian population of Nanjing in 1937 took place, but failed to mention that fewer than 1 percent of schools adopted the book. Japan is a very particular assignment for Chinese journalists, as it is not unusual for Japan-based reporters to complain about the pressure to file negative stories that then place them in an awkward position with their local news sources. But even for this correspondent, who dismissed that such a thing as objective reporting existed and strongly identified with the view that Chinese media should represent national interests, *Global Times* took too many liberties with his stories. Another *People's Daily* correspondent says that, during his posting to India in the early 2010s, he was among the top three contributors to *Global Times* and made "tens of thousands of yuan a year" from his honoraria but was "very annoyed" with what the editors did with his material in order to "whip up stuff about Chinese-Indian relations," which were quite tense at the time.

Global Times was launched in 1993 as a weekly eight-page supplement to *People's Daily* with an initial circulation of twenty thousand. At first called *Huanqiu Wencui* (Global Digest), it focused on international gossip and glamour: half of the first issue's front page was taken up by a photo of Gong Li, China's most famous actress at the time.[30] In addition to *People's Daily* correspondents, *Huanqiu Wencui*, with its generous honoraria, also built up a wide network of stringers, often relying on staff of Chinese embassies, students, Chinese staff at foreign companies, and sometimes their wives. When England's Princess Diana died in 1997, a Paris correspondent for *People's Daily* who happened to be visiting London filed a story on it that made the cover and propelled *Huanqiu Wencui* to record sales. Nonetheless, in the same year, *Global Times*, relaunched under its present name, shifted its focus to international politics.

The next sales leap occurred in 1999, when *People's Daily*'s Belgrade correspondent was the only one of the three Chinese journalists there to survive the bombing of the Chinese embassy in Belgrade in a NATO air raid and took photos of his dead colleagues. (That journalist is now the head of the international department.) The photos could not be published in *People's Daily*, but they were in *Global Times*; no other paper dared touch the story. From one day to the next, the paper's circulation jumped from 445 thousand to 780 thousand (Lu Yan 2013), and by the end of the year it reached 1.49 million. Some see this as evidence that the paper practices what detractors in China call "commercial nationalism": the editors discovered that patriotic fervor sold, and created more of it. More likely, however, this success only strengthened a course that had been initiated earlier. Two years later, buoyed by detailed reporting on 9/11, circulation reached a new peak of two million.[31] Although the numbers declined to 1.5 million in 2013, the paper has, according to its editors, consistently remained in the top three dailies by circulation. Since 2009, *Global Times* has also published an English edition, which receives a government subsidy and, apart from the editorial page, is edited separately.

In the Chinese edition, much of the selection and putting together (*cao-*

zuo) of the stories is done by the editors, who are much better paid than their colleagues at *People's Daily*. "The reporters' role," as an editor puts it, "is mostly to provide material. Most of the writing is done by the page editor. Of course, reporters are not happy with this, particularly if they write 1,000 characters and an article uses only a few lines, but this is just the way it is. They have to adapt." Every morning, the editors look at foreign media and social media headlines and decide on the stories for the next day, picking the headlines, which are chosen to be eye-catching and often provocative. Between 10:00 a.m. and 11:00 a.m., there is a pitch meeting (*xuantihui*) at which page editors propose stories and the "leader," editor-in-chief Hu Xijin, decides. The editors then write outlines for stories and send them to a number of foreign correspondents—often a combination of *People's Daily* correspondents and their own stringers—simultaneously with requests to fill in details and provide evidence to support particular points, for example, by 7:00 p.m. Beijing time. This may include interviewing people in the street or "experts." Some correspondents respond, others do not. Sometimes the editors also ask "enthusiasts" in China to find material on foreign- (English-, Japanese-, Korean-) language websites and translate it. Then the editors write the lead and, if necessary, ask the correspondents to supply more details. The byline in the paper lists the editors first, then the correspondents, and finally the unpaid "enthusiasts." In some cases, *Global Times* also dispatches correspondents abroad for reporting trips; in recent years, they have sent reporters to Syria and Libya several times. Contributors do not see the transformations their material has undergone until the story is published.

For example, when former British Prime Minister Margaret Thatcher died, a correspondent in England was asked to interview people and experts. She had been taught in China that Thatcher was viewed as an iconic leader and was quite shocked to find that a lot of people were quite happy with the news of her death; one even compared Thatcher to the archvillain Voldemort in the Harry Potter novels. This quote didn't make it to the article, because this wasn't what the editors wanted to emphasize: the focus of the reporting was to be on ordinary people's hankering for a strong hand. On another occasion, when this correspondent wrote about Prince William's wedding, she found that people were generally positive about it; the royal family's popularity was lifted, and those she interviewed in the streets thought it was good for the economy. But in this case, the editors wanted to focus on the protests, so she was pressed to find negative comments. She tried to argue, but the editors told her these were instructions from "the leader." Editors, in their turn, readily acknowledge that Hu sometimes has preconceived opinions. "Then," one editor said, "it is up to the duty editor's ability. He should tell the leader that reality is not like that. But some editors don't have a good grasp of the issue and just follow whatever the editor-in-chief says, and force the reporters to write accordingly." The editors described occasional factual mistakes as a sort of growing pain, due to the fact that "our [professional] level is not high enough." In the report on Lady Thatcher's funeral, for example, the *Daily Mail*, a notoriously right-wing tabloid, is mentioned as a left-wing newspaper.[32] Describing security at the funeral, the article mentions that a young man who was holding the "left-wing newspaper *Daily Mail*" was stopped and searched, conveying the implication that, just as in China, it is accepted practice for British police to target government critics.

How, then, does the editor determine the angle from which a story should be written? According to one editor, "We are called nationalists . . . but in my view our stance is statism (*guojiazhuyi*)." The editor-in-chief stresses two principles: "complicated China," meaning you cannot simplify things to the point of everything is good, like the government says, or everything is bad, like the liberals say, and "rational criticism," meaning this is a world of nation-states, and their actions are determined by their interests rather than their values.

> We say we represent the nation's interests as we understand them, but that is not always the government's interest. The foreign ministry may have other considerations. . . . *People's Daily* has defined us as "a representative voice of China's popular opinion," and therefore the government leaves us greater room. Sometimes the Propaganda Department tells us to keep our voice down, but we don't. We have carved out this room little by little. Of course, there is a bottom line: that the [Party/state] leaders are right, that they want the best for the country, so we have to support them. Other papers may not have the same guts, but this is a matter of ability. And then, they may have the wrong stance; they may be rejecting or wanting to disrupt the existing political order.

Correspondents' contacts are page editors. After the pages are typeset, they are read by the editor-in-chief, who may require more or less serious changes. If the changes are major, the page editor may have to break up and re-edit the page. Sometimes, stories deemed to be sensitive are submitted for vetting to the *People's Daily*—which, uniquely, has department rank within the Party organization and is therefore formally not subject to supervision by the Propaganda Department—or to the State Council's News Bureau for approval.

Global Times stories do occasionally get deleted. For instance, after the anti-Chinese riots in Vietnam in May 2014, an editorial that referred to the 1979 China-Vietnam war was removed from the paper's website, probably because it was deemed too provocative. Yet a much more explicitly worded opinion piece, which directly threatened Vietnam with a repeat of the war, remained on *Global Times'* military page, perhaps because it was part of a specialized column rather than a high-profile editorial.[33] Editorials and op-ed articles are the most widely read and most contentious content in *Global Times*, and when it comes to foreign affairs, they have an almost exclusive focus on the "national interest" and strategic competition between the West and China, particularly in relation to disagreements with the United States and Japan and regional security in East Asia.[34] A rare editorial about Europe, entitled "Will Western Countries Go Bankrupt One After the Other?" argued that rich and powerful Europeans force the poor and powerless to lend them money and finance their lifestyles, but this would be impossible in China where rich and poor were equal. Once there was no place left to plunder, this welfare regime would be finished along with its pretensions about the pursuit of happiness and human rights.[35] But news stories sometimes deviate from this optics and report on issues that other Chinese media dare not touch. One story described how the lawn outside the Chinese Embassy in Pyongyang was stripped bare by starving North Koreans.[36]

Many critics of *Global Times*, both in the formerly liberal and the official media, accuse it of peddling nationalism because it sells. The paper's evolution bears out this argument to some extent, although of course nationalism could not have become as popular as it has without the government's efforts.[37] But the personal backgrounds of the paper's two editors-in-chief may have played an important role in shaping the editorial line. The founding editor-in-chief of *Huanqiu Wencui*, He Chongyuan, spent the first twenty-four years of his life in a village, before being admitted to Shanghai Foreign Languages College in 1977 to study Arabic. He set the tone by requiring that everyone write in a simple way that workers and peasants could understand.[38] His successor and near contemporary, Hu Xijin, was admitted to an army college in 1978 to study Russian. He later described the experience in this way: "All of a sudden, I read the world's greatest works of literature: Tolstoy, Chekhov, Pushkin; those rays of humanity immediately illuminated me . . . not yet twenty years old, I suddenly saw the light. This was what he world was like! This was how great literature was! . . . Humanism, the search for freedom, determined my values for the rest of my life."[39]

In 1989, Hu obtained a master's degree in Russian literature at Beijing Foreign Languages College. Although his actual military service lasted no longer than six years, Hu likes to include his years in college and refer to eleven years in the army. "My time in the army laid the foundation of how I see the country. . . . People who have served in the army have a sense of responsibility for this country. . . . Today, when we compare China's various strengths with the West, discursive strength (*yulun liliang*) is the weakest link. Sometimes, consciously or not, I'll think about protecting the state through discourse (*yulun baowei guojia*)."[40]

Yet in the same interview, Hu also asserts that his current views developed *after* he left the army. In 1989, as a fresh graduate, "I was out in [Tiananmen] square every day, shouting like everyone else." Then he joined *People's Daily*, and two years later he was shaken by the collapse of the Soviet Union. In 1993, Hu was posted to Belgrade. He recalls encountering two Russian street musicians from the science city of Novosibirsk, one playing the accordion and the other singing in a cold Belgrade street. Shaken by what he saw as a sign of how low great Russia had fallen, he took them home and gave them dinner. Hu's three years in wartime Yugoslavia made him wary of the costs of adopting democracy and cemented his belief that "China must not descend into chaos."[41] In 2012, he returned to Belgrade to find that prices in the country whose living standards and level of modernity had been far ahead of China in the early 1990s were now a fraction of those in China. "They had had chaos for twenty years, they had stalled for twenty years, and China developed; its per capita GDP already surpassed theirs."[42] Hu has reported from the frontline in the Bosnian and Iraq wars, and a photo taken with Bosnian Serb commander Ratko Mladić, which he provided for an interview with *Southern People Weekly*, may be an indication of his sympathies, or at least of the sympathies he wants to display.[43] (At the time of the interview, Mladić had recently been arrested and dispatched to The Hague to stand trial for war crimes.)

Hu Xijin—along with the "other Hu," Caixin's publisher Hu Shuli—is one of the most scrutinized media personalities in China today. (With over four million followers on Weibo, he is also among the most influential.) But there are indications that a number of senior international journalists in China's central media who speak out for the "national interest" from positions of authority have, like Hu, undergone some formative experience early in their careers that appears to have alienated them from liberal universalist ideals. Xinhua's Africa regional bureau chief's career as foreign correspondent included time in Geneva in the early 1990s, a posting in Washington, DC, in the late 1990s, and a short stint in Afghanistan just after the US invasion. In his book *I Was a White House Correspondent*, Yuan, while praising the professionalism of the White House press service but noting its function as a spin machine, is miffed by what he perceives as the deliberate silencing of Chinese journalists. He also complains about their discrimination by the Western press corps in Geneva, but here the charge is more serious: "I attended one after another of President Clinton's press conferences. Almost every time, I raised my hand very high . . . he still did not call on me. So throughout my years of work in Washington, I felt constrained, I always felt second-class; I deeply felt the relative nature of America's freedom of the press. . . . News does have boundaries, and so do journalists."[44]

Yuan—five years Hu's junior—then goes on to describe how, during a European trip in 1997, AP forbade its journalists to ask Clinton about the sexual harassment charge Paula Jones had made against him. While elsewhere he writes contemptuously of the Washington press corps' obsession with the president's sexual transgressions, here he concludes: "When it really matters, American journalists, much as they worship freedom, pay attention to protecting the image of state leaders. News may look objective, but what questions are asked, when they are asked and who is allowed to ask them shows that they are not. When different journalists, with different nationalities and different backgrounds see the same event or describe the same person, they will write completely different news stories that will at the same time all be completely objective. . . . The objectivity and fairness of news are entirely relative."[45]

Eight years later, as Africa bureau chief, Yuan is an outspoken advocate of "positive reporting" as a hallmark of Chinese journalism. When I put it to him that some Chinese journalists, like their Western counterparts, say they simply want to report truthfully, Yuan responded: "I think this is incorrect." Pressed about how conflicts around Chinese companies in Africa may be reported constructively, Yuan said: "Whatever helps solve the problem. Whatever is best for this [African] country."

One of the earliest and best-known exponents of "development journalism" in China is Li Xiguang, former dean of Tsinghua University's School of Journalism. As a Xinhua editor (and later director of its politics department),

Li became famous after he co-authored *Behind the Demonization of China*, one of the first manifestos of contemporary Chinese nationalism. The book urged Chinese intellectuals to "liberate themselves from 'modern' Western speech and thought patterns, and acquire a new understanding of modern nationalism and nativism."[46] *Behind the Demonization of China* purports to be an exposé of a deliberate misinformation campaign against China conducted by those putative bastions of Western journalistic professionalism, the *New York Times* and the *Washington Post*, as well as the Voice of America. The book was written fresh on the heels of Li's internship at the *Post* as an Alfred Friendly Press Fellow in 1995, and it makes clear that Li felt slighted by his treatment there. At a Chinese-African media conference in Nairobi in 2013, Li told African journalists that they should "learn how to propagate the interests of their people and learn that every media outlet, whether private or public, is essentially a tool of propaganda." He urged "African and Chinese journalists to cooperate and tell the true story behind the uprisings in North Africa" lest they be "outsmarted by their Western counterparts and the story [be] told from the perspective of Western journalists."[47]

Of the younger generation, the career of Liu Hong, a deputy editor-in-chief of Xinhua's international affairs newsmagazine *Globe*, appears to echo Yuan's. Born in 1975, Liu volunteered to go to Afghanistan as a frontline reporter in 2001, at the same time as Yuan. Subsequently, he was posted to Jerusalem and then to Washington, DC, from where he returned in 2010. One of Xinhua's most prolific writers, with a strong interest in war journalism, Liu joined the agency in 1998. Shortly afterwards, he was assigned to edit two books: a collection of dispatches from the Kosovo war and *China Will Not Be Bullied* (Zhongguo bu ke qi, 1999). The latter was a collection of articles responding to NATO's bombing of the Chinese embassy in Belgrade, an event that catalyzed the emergence of Chinese nationalism and its media representation and, as we have seen, proved important for the development of many journalists' personal views. Liu then went on to author or edit nine books, including two on the Afghan war and one on Israel and the Palestinians.

In the preface to one of the books Liu wrote after his return from the United States, *The American "Conspiracy"* (Meiguo "yinmou," 2011), Yao Bin, editor-in-chief of *Oriental Outlook*, another Xinhua newsmagazine, echoes Li Xiguang and Yuan Bingzhong: "The intangible power of "national interest trumps all" forces those Western journalists who keep trumpeting "objectiveness and fairness" to make choices that are not in line with their news ideals. . . . Once you have understood this . . . it is not hard to understand the various maladies of today's world that have been called a "clash of civilizations."[48]

Echoing the book's subtitle—*Defending the Truth*—Yao warns readers not to believe the falsehoods spread by Western media, because "once one's worldview becomes confused . . . it will result in misplaced and confused moral values."[49] Although Liu told me his goal as a journalist was promoting understanding and dispelling misconceptions in both Western and Chinese media, the first part of *The American "Conspiracy,"* entitled "Nothing Wrong with China" (Zhongguo meiyou cuo), walks in the footsteps of *Behind the Demonization of China* in taking aim at American media and politicians for their distorted views of China. The remainder of the book is a collection of reporting on American politics and society and occasional encouragement for Chinese officials to be more assertive in representing China's interests. Most of the book's contents were originally published as Xinhua commentaries or articles in the agency's publications: *Reference News, Oriental Outlook, Globe,* or *International Herald Leader,* but their style and message would not have been out of place in *Global Times.* It is perhaps not a coincidence that the very first article in the book describes the difficulties Liu experienced in accessing the White House. Unlike Yuan, he never received full accreditation at the White House, and was subjected to restrictions that Japanese or German correspondents were not. Given such conditions, Liu wrote, it was hard to blame Chinese journalists for superficial reporting: a point of view diametrically opposed to that of the Caixin reporter we encountered earlier.

To be sure, stressing the underside of American freedoms, along with negative social phenomena such as mass shootings, is an expectation central media correspondents are probably aware of in a general sense. The view that the United States does not offer journalists a level playing field is in line with that expectation, but this does not mean it cannot be genuinely held. When I asked a former Washington reporter for China News Service whether there was anything she particularly wanted to tell her readers about, she replied: "Censorship in the US." She explained that Fox News journalists were banned from the Obama White House—she had heard this first hand from a colleague at Fox. Also, it was hard for foreign journalists to get a spot at press conferences; for example, Reuters was not as welcome as AP or AFP. Because of America's centrality for foreign news—one correspondent estimated that it accounts for about half of them—a posting there carries prestige and increased visibility within the network, and implies chances for promotion. Therefore, the views of former US correspondents, who may now be influential editors, carry weight in media organizations.

CENTRAL MEDIA: FOREIGN NEWS AS A FOIL FOR CHINA

Not all of central media's influential foreign desk editors consider defending China's interests their main duty. Prior to her promotion to deputy director of China Radio International's Chinese-language news channel in 2012, NewsRadio FM 90.5, Wang Shanshan worked in CRI's English service and was its Washington bureau chief. Despite being at a station many colleagues would envy—and then becoming a "leader" while still in her mid-thirties—she echoed a common refrain among correspondents that her editors were interested not in understanding (*liaojie*) America but in using it as a reference (*canzhao*) for China's own problems and policy choices. What was road quality like in the United States? What was the pension system like in the United States? Every day, the editors would send a series of orders (*mingling*). From the perspective of domestic audiences, this made sense. What they wanted to hear about was not an American America (*Meiguo de Meiguo*), but really, China. They wanted to hear about the economy and Hollywood, not about spending cuts, court challenges to same-sex marriage, or the bankruptcy of Detroit that were the news in American papers. Wang, however, wanted to report on these. So she had to maneuver. The risk was that her ratings (*shoutinglü*) might drop, but as long as they remained high, it was easier to convince her editors to accept a story.

According to Wang, who, early in her career at CRI, had spent some time in Sydney as co-host of a music show—one of the earliest Western pop shows on Chinese radio—and later obtained a master's degree in public administration at Royal Holloway, University of London, the station wants to be "as independent as possible," even though it has to serve as the Party's "throat and tongue." As an editor, she would like to see more analysis and discussion in the programming:

> US news radio, like WTOP in DC or NPR, would discuss the same story six
> times a day, each time in a different way, whereas for us, discussions are a
> formality. For example, for the Thatcher story [when Thatcher died], we could
> have used Chinese, American, British, European, gender, and all sorts of other

perspectives, but we didn't do enough. The show has to respond to the demands of the man in the street (*laobaixing*), so for example we talk about property tax in the US [since there was a debate on introducing a property tax in China]. Once we have the audience's attention, we can slowly tell them that the things they don't know about can also be very interesting.

NewsRadio 90.5 has begun experimenting with live discussions and other formats borrowed from the news radio model in English-speaking countries some years ago. Although CRI is heavily dependent on government financing and radio, as a whole, is mostly associated with an older and less educated public, NewsRadio 90.5 has been trying to gain influence and advertising by targeting a more affluent and younger audience, notably those who tune in while driving. International Online (Guoji Zai Xian), a two-hour news program loosely modeled on BBC's Newshour, has been on air three times a day since 2005. It combines foreign with domestic news and includes live linkups to foreign correspondents, interviews with experts, and recorded reports. All of CRI's news units propose stories for the program. An editorial committee, which consists of the leaders of the main organizational units within CRI's News Center, meets twice a day and decides which stories will go on air. Breaking news may be inserted by the editor on duty. The news of Margaret Thatcher's death, which came in at night, was one of those. Since it was viewed as major news related to Sino-British relations—particularly because Thatcher had been important to the negotiations about Hong Kong' retrocession to China—the editorial committee, in its meeting the following morning, had to decide whether and how to cover it in depth.

NewsRadio 90.5 also has weekly planning meetings with program producers, chaired by the channel's director (*zongjian*). At these, the director and Wang give feedback and suggestions. At one meeting I attended, the director admonished the producers to pay more attention to foreign media and present stories from more angles. For example, "let's do something from the Japanese perspective. Why does [Japanese Prime Minister] Abe pursue the politics he does? We can analyze Abe's career from the perspective of Japan's postwar history. You are too focused on whether the news is fun (*haowanr*) or not. Not enough depth. Too shallow. I keep repeating this."

"What do Japanese people think about the Yasukuni Shrine?" Wang added, referring to the Shinto temple honoring the war dead that is associated with Japanese militarism. Visits to the shrine by Japanese leaders always trigger Chinese protests, but Wang was suggesting that Chinese audiences should understand their local meaning better. "We need Japanese reporters to go out and ask, but the reporters also need more directions from us. . . . Foreign media go on about Chinese and Japanese public opinion, how 99 percent or so of Chinese people feel animosity towards Japanese. We need to have a variety of voices." "Is this too sensitive?" one of the producers asked anxiously. "Not too sensitive, but it needs time," replied the director.

About one-third to one-half of foreign correspondents' reports are commissioned by CRI's programming department (*cehuabu*). If editors would like a story on a particular topic, it is the programming department they need to talk to. Foreign correspondents send their proposals—including interview outlines and main questions—to the News Center. The editor on duty may then ask the reporter to add more material or change the structure of the story or, if in doubt, contact a higher-level editor. As in other central media, the duty editor's preferences are thus central to shaping the story, and those are by no means always identical to Wang's. In Wang's own words, editors from the Chinese service, in particular, sometimes think rather like *Global Times.*

She may have had in mind colleagues like the editor at International Online who told me that helping Chinese diplomacy was an important element of CRI's work. This editor, perhaps a few years Wang's senior, was another of a handful of journalists who were openly skeptical of the idea of professionalism. "Total professionalism" (*wanquan de zhuanyezhuyi*), she told me, was something she did not quite approve of (*bu tai rentong*), because no one could be completely objective, and those who claimed otherwise were "either fools or pretending to be" (*yaobu sha yaobu zhuang sha*). It is unlikely, however, that this editor would have appreciated the reference to *Global Times.* In fact, she complained that "new media made diplomats' work very difficult" by their interference and impatience on foreign policy issues such as relations with Japan. For her part, she wanted to help them as much as she could, and many times this meant being restrained.

It was from a CRI correspondent, whom I will call Xiao Song, that I got one of the few spontaneous discussions of government restrictions early in a conversation. When I explained that I was interested in what stories Chinese journalists wanted to tell their audiences, Xiao Song replied somewhat bitterly: "It doesn't matter what I want to tell if the government doesn't let me"—although she felt she still had more latitude to report than her colleagues at CCTV or Xinhua, because CRI had far less visibility and because transcripts of most broadcasts were not published, so if a story was aired but was then deemed offending it left no trace.

Xiao Song had recently returned from a posting in Jerusalem, and it had been a frustrating one. She had expected the assignment to be a high-visibility if perhaps onerous one in one of the world's news hotspots. Yet during her tenure, there were neither political breakthroughs nor major attacks in the Palestinian-Israeli conflict. The peace process had stalled. "We were in a quandary: there was little news worth reporting in China, but when there *was* news that was important locally it was not always reported in China."

In Israeli media, the main news story during her tenure, perhaps for the first time in recent decades, was one unrelated to the conflict: the 2011 protests against the high cost of housing. The Xinhua reporter, with whom Xiao Song was friendly, wanted to do a story on the demonstrations but was not allowed to. The correspondent knew that a story of a large middle-class movement against social inequality was sensitive, the more so that it took place against the background of a budding Arab Spring, reporting on which was closely controlled. Her duty editor also felt the subject was sensitive and forwarded her proposal for a story to a mid-level *lingdao*. The *lingdao* did not object, and the next time Xiao Song proposed a follow-up, the duty editor approved it on his own. Altogether she filed three or four stories, an experience she described as "playing with the edge." Luckily, this happened at a politically relaxed time in China; before a major party congress, they would not have allowed it.

The growing tensions between orthodox and secular Jews could have been a major unfolding story, but she could not report it because all religious topics were sensitive. She was allowed to do a story on Passover, but only as a cultural custom rather than from a religious angle. Even her reports on China-Israel trade were cut because of the topic's sensitivity for Arab countries.

So what was there to report? Xiao Song tried to cover everyday life. She did stories, for example, on science, environmental protection, and tourism. As she felt that Chinese views of Israel were overly focused on conflict, she wanted to show listeners that life in Israel was "normal" and "under control." If she had been completely free to report on what she wanted, she would have done more stories on culture and tourism. But there was also the issue of the audience: they were not all that interested unless it was breaking news. As a young correspondent at a relatively marginal station, she did not have the status, visibility or ratings to persuade her editors to air such stories.

A Xinhua correspondent, also young and female, was posted to India at about the same time and experienced similar frustration. She was initially enthusiastic about covering the proverbial "world's largest democracy" and felt deeply offended when her Indian interviewees asked if she was a spy. She was particularly looking forward to covering the 2014 elections. But her *lingdao* did not want too much election coverage, presumably because of the potentially negative contrast with China. Then, surely, there was a lot of reporting to be done on brutal gang rape and murder story that gripped India and the international media the same year? No, because Xinhua correspondents were not to harm Sino-Indian relations. Added to this were safety warnings that discouraged female reporters from going about on their own. Gradually, she lost her enthusiasm and became despondent and restless.

A *People's Daily* correspondent experienced similar frustration in Europe. He invested two months interviewing Muslims in a European capital for a story on Islamism, only to be told by Beijing that the paper could not carry it because if they did, readers would speculate that it might signal a shift in the Chinese government's policies on Muslims at home. In other words, somewhat paradoxically, freedom of reporting is affected not only by authorities' expectation that central media stories reflect government policy but also the anticipation of readers' assumption that they do so. (The story was eventually published by the Chinese edition of *Global Times*.) Sometimes, stories are not published because editors fear they might unintentionally draw attention to undesirable domestic developments. Thus, *People's Daily* did not carry a Europe correspondent's exclusive interview with a Red Cross official because it happened to come at a time when a Chinese Red Cross employee was embroiled in a scandal surrounding her lavish lifestyle.

Occasionally, correspondents are able to take advantage of contradictory instructions to push their case. In 2014, the head of an international desk at a central media organization asked his London correspondent to cover the referendum on Scotland's independence. Reporting on Europe is generally perceived as not very sensitive, as long as one does not paint Europe in such attractive colors that China begins looking inferior by comparison. In this case, after the correspondent arrived in Scotland, the editor-in-chief asked the desk chief to reduce coverage. "So what do you want me to do?" the correspondent asked the desk chief. The desk chief advised him to call the editor-in-chief. The editor-in-chief said that, although the Propaganda Department had asked not to cover the referendum too much, his personal opinion was that the correspondent could go ahead as long as he was careful with his writing and specified that the stories were not for release within China. The reporter ended up filing more than ten stories and added "not for release within China" to only one.

Sometimes, journalists try to increase their maneuvering room by submitting important stories when more sympathetic or broad-minded editors are on duty or by liaising with senior editors. One Xinhua correspondent filed a report based on a World Health Organization press release that stated that Chinese health authorities had identified possible human-to-human transmission of a new strain of bird flu. The story was approved by the duty editor and a more senior editor, but a member of the News Centre's editorial committee (*bianwei*), who read it subsequently, cut the mention of the Chinese case, so that the resulting story, in the correspondent's view, lost its news value. The next day she phoned and asked whether there was a clear guideline that this topic could not be written about, but was told that there was not. In fact, the editor she spoke to encouraged her to keep filing whatever she thought was important stories and let the editors sort it out.

But such negotiations are not central to correspondents' work. Most correspondents do not complain about stories being "killed" by editors, at least not without prompting. In fact, a more frequent spontaneous comment is that one has freedom to report on whatever one wants—certainly compared to the strict controls they were used to in their domestic reporting. Although upon further probing most of my interlocutors named a few instances when their stories were rejected, these were relatively marginal to their overall experience. Nonetheless, a common complaint among central media correspondents was that the line editors who deal with their texts are often very inexperienced and lack understanding of their beats. As one Xinhua correspondent turned editor put it, the agency's problem is "young editors, old journalists" (*xiao bianji da jizhe*). This is because new hires at international departments typically start as junior editors before being sent abroad on their first posting. The position of these editors differs from their colleagues at Western media organizations rather more strongly than the correspondents. For one thing, their responsibility is a political as well as a professional one: they need to be able to detect elements in stories that may attract government officials' criticism or displeasure and therefore pose a risk to their organization and their superiors, probably more than to themselves. Second, they have less independence than their Western peers in deciding what story to publish and in what form. Whereas at Reuters or AP, what is news is effectively decided by the desk editor who receives the incoming stories, at Xinhua, every item undergoes a three-step process. Incoming stories are first vetted by shift supervisors (*daibanren*), who select about half of them and assign them to desk editors for checking and correction. These pass the edited stories back to the shift supervisor, who in turn presents them for approval to a higher-level editor known as a "releaser" (*fagaoren*), a rank that requires a special exam, before it is sent to the wire. At *People's Daily*, a similar process is followed. The line editor submits the article to a higher-level editor within the group (*zu*) in charge of a world region (for example, the Europe group). If approved, the article goes on to a senior editor of the international desk, who signs off on the copy. The correspondent does not see the changes until the article is published.

A Xinhua editor described the releaser's job as follows: He (or occasionally she) checks whether the report is truthful and balanced, whether anything is missing, whether it "adopts the [Chinese] state's stance (*zhan zai guojia de lichang*)," and whether it is suitable for external release, and if so, decides on which of Xinhua's wires to release the item. In some cases, he or she will decide to release an item as a *neican*, for internal circulation only. Most of the time, the senior editor's vetting focuses on the political "safety" of the story rather than its professional merits. Indeed, more senior editors who do much of the commissioning may also have a poor understanding of foreign contexts. A CCTV correspondent in London complained that her editors kept picking up translations of stories from sensationalist British tabloids such as the *Daily Mail* and *The Sun* and took no time to reflect on their veracity. In one instance, they had seen pictures of Romanian Gypsies that were linked to a story on the recession and took them to be of Britons made homeless by the crisis. Although most of the time she was able to persuade them to drop requests to follow up on such "leads," they kept taking such shots in the dark, always asking her to "take a look" at this or that.

Another type of assignment correspondents generally lack enthusiasm for is the "round robin" or, in *People's Daily* parlance, the "clenched fist" (*zuhequan*), referring to how multiple fingers ball up into a fist. (Less martially, a *People's Daily* bureau chief likened such reports to the slices of a mooncake. CCTV calls them *peihe baodao*, "cooperative reports.") In this type of report, bureaus around the world are asked to contribute materials that either examine the way foreign countries deal with or view a particular issue—examples mentioned by my interlocutors ranged from punishing drivers who run a yellow light and the prospects of the United States defaulting on its debt to policies on air pollution, sustainable agriculture, rogue police officers, mobile taxi-hailing applications, and solar panels—or react to an important political event in China, a state visit by a top Chinese leader, or can be linked to a slogan launched by a senior state leader, like Xi Jinping's "China dream." Some of these materials were collated as *neican* reports for government departments, and a Xinhua bureau chief with experience in Europe and Africa reflected that—despite Xinhua's professed aim to become a global competitor to major Western wires—time spent on such "government work" appeared to increase in the mid-2010s. Such assignments are usually both highly prioritized and considered politically sensitive, so they come in the form of urgent and very specific requests that are often difficult to satisfy. Correspondents end up spending much time on them, yet the eventual output and hence their rewards are often minimal. Sometimes they succeed in rebuffing a request. For example, in 2013, *People's Daily* published a series of articles on "national character." So US correspondents interviewed Americans and reported why they were proud to be American. This was presumably in line with the editors' intention to suggest that national pride was normal and healthy. But the bureau chief in Germany explained to the editors that national character was a sensitive topic in Germany, and Germans were rarely willing to say they were proud of their fatherland. This did not conform to the editors' wishes, and they dropped the request.

In the same year, *People's Daily* launched another series on how Chairman Xi Jinping's slogan "Chinese dream" is conducive to "win-win" relations with foreign countries. A young correspondent at the Paris bureau spent months contacting Chinese and French companies trying to find an example of a "win-win situation" that she could write about, but most investment projects that could fit that rubric had not yet started. Finally she settled on a Chinese businessman who had started publishing Chinese comic strips in French. Yet her bureau chief viewed the story as not weighty enough and accused the correspondent of not having followed other leads diligently enough. On another occasion, foreign bureaus were asked to file stories about how Chinese companies welcomed the Spring Festival (the

Chinese New Year). This time she produced a story about a company that had purchased a bankrupt French factory, but her bureau chief and editors would have none of what she had written about the difficulties it experienced in turning the factory around: all they wanted was a moving story for the holiday.

Also in 2013, *People's Daily* asked foreign bureaus to report positive reactions to the Party's third plenary session the day after the plenum opened. "This could work in Africa or Pakistan, because they are friendly towards China, but I had no way of doing this," complained a bureau chief in a Western country. "Even if I could get comments, they might not like them. There is no point reporting negative comments; the editor will cut them out, so reporting them is just a waste of everyone's time, mine and theirs." In the end, he filed reactions from some local Chinese. A former intern at Xinhua's Paris bureau said that her dislike of such assignments—at the time of a highly publicized high-speed train crash in China, for example, she was asked to contribute to a story on how such accidents also happened in France—was part of the reason for changing her mind about becoming a journalist. Others express frustration but soldier on. "You always have to think about what people in BJ [Beijing] will think. You have too many bosses; you have no clear instructions; you always keep guessing. You have to make it look boring," complained a foreign desk editor at one of Xinhua's magazines. And some correspondents shrug the problem off: "If we get assignments from Beijing, we complain: 'Oh shit, they want us to do such-and-such.' But we have to live with that. We have to do 20 percent of stories that we have reservations about, so that we can do the 80 percent that we feel is valuable," said a CCTV correspondent.

COMMERCIAL MEDIA: MORE FLEXIBILITY, HARDER WORK, CORPORATE PRESSURES

At commercial media, the relationship between editors and correspondents is more personal as there are many fewer of both. While CCTV has about a hundred editors "in the rear" processing the "packages" sent by foreign correspondents, the entire international desk of *21st Century Business Herald*—the commercial media organization with the largest foreign correspondent network in the PRC—had thirteen staff members in 2013. Most of the foreign correspondents are in the United States, and a handful are in Europe. Even by the standards of the profession, they have to be highly flexible and ready to travel at a day's notice if a story comes up. On the other hand, compared to reporters for central media, they enjoy considerable personal freedom. Plans for stories are made in close consultation with the international desk editors in China, who are usually experienced journalists, and sometimes with the editor-in-chief. The formal process varies. *21st Century Business Herald* correspondents file their stories with one of two international desk editors, who then forward these for approval to the director of the desk, and then on to the *"lingdao* on duty" (the editor-in-chief or a deputy). At Caixin, the process is less formal, but all stories are ultimately read by the managing editor-in-chief.

Editors at commercial media tend to be experienced journalists; correspondingly, their authority and salaries are considerably above those of reporters. Generally, editors are supportive of correspondents' ideas. For example, Caixin's London correspondent spent about a month working on a story on the Chinese construction company COVEC's failed road construction project in Poland. The English version of the resulting report received an award from the Foreign Press Association in London. But such investigative scoops are the exception. And, as all commercial papers focus on financial and business news and all are short-staffed, the reporters have little time or budget to work on stories that fall outside these subjects. At Caixin, correspondents are expected to contribute at least one story per day for the website and around three major stories for the monthly magazine. "There is too much pressure to generate stories immediately," a Caixin reporter complained. Under increasing financial pressure, commercial media concentrate on countries with the highest reader and advertiser interest. This means that, unless journalists receive fellowships or go to study in other parts of the world, there are no correspondents in Africa, South America, the Middle East, or even Asia. Some correspondents travel to these regions on short-term assignments, particularly to cover stories seen as significant for China. Thus, most commercial media sent reporters to Libya, Egypt, and Syria since the beginning of the uprisings known as the "Arab Spring," as well as to Burma after the end of military rule several times.[50] The Brussels correspondent for *21st Century Business Herald* went to Egypt four times in 2012, at his own initiative, even though, as he noted, the stories he filed from Egypt generated much less interest than, for example, his coverage of the European Union's plan to introduce punitive tariffs on Chinese solar panels. But many correspondents feel that their professional standards are compromised by the fact that they are expected to report on vast regions without time or funding to travel. "I don't want to be a domestic reporter on international affairs—then I'll end up being a translator. Even though [my editor] is very supportive and does not limit me in any way, writing here about Egypt is ridiculous. I applied several times to go, but they said no," recounted a frustrated Europe-based correspondent for a leading financial media organization.

As with central media, disagreements between editors and correspondents about the newsworthiness and significance of issues do occur. The political sensitivity of stories is, in contrast, rarely a consideration. This does not mean, however, that commercial media correspondents are less aware of political limitations than their colleagues at central media. Rather, every commercial medium is a rather tightly knit community within which, under normal circumstances, the limits of the permissible are internalized and not much discussed. The editor-in-chief uses her judgment in sensitive cases, and shields her staff in case of attack. As one international desk editor put it, "the editors don't need to consider these things, only upper management does; the editors' and journalists' job is to step on the gas pedal and drive." If the Propaganda Department pressures the paper to cover a story in a way that its staff is not comfortable with, editors and correspondents work together to find ways to produce the story with the least damage to their sense of integrity. A foreign correspondent for a financial paper, however, mentioned instances when her editor asked her to drop a story because a major company mentioned in it "would really appreciate it." Indeed, corporate, rather than political, pressures appeared to be a more important constraint on her reporting, including instances where her editor agreed to stories being vetted by a corporate PR team before publication. "I didn't like being controlled. But we have to compromise for the sake of long-term contact. Our chief editor is now very, very conservative," as "he's had to handle a lot of lawsuits and disputes." So the paper had gradually become more and more conservative and less and less prone to muckraking. The same correspondent also complained of being asked to write for a private investment website in which her paper had a share.

The sense of an unspoken consensus about what was and what was not safe to write and of relative security provided by supportive managers, already gradually eroded in the 2010s, was upended by the 2013–14 crackdowns, in which the senior managers of *21st Century Business Herald* were imprisoned, other papers were saddled with censors, and even experienced editors found Propaganda Department's officials increasingly hard to second-guess. A reporter from a magazine specializing in interviews and "soft" stories was surprised when parts of his interview with the Burmese opposition leader Aung San Suu Kyi that were critical of the Chinese government and Chinese companies were cut, as he had expected his editors to shield him from political pressure. A reporter for a financial paper had a reference to Japan removed from a story filed from Singapore. A correspondent for another financial paper obtained an exclusive interview from the US assistant state secretary for Asia-Pacific affairs. The editor-in-chief was pleased because this was the first time this official had spoken to Chinese media, and wanted to run the story straight away on the cover page. But the editorial committee member (*shewei*) delegated by the media group to which the paper belonged to vet its major stories kept rejecting one version after another until all potentially sensitive content—such as references to tensions in the South China Sea and Chinese hacking of US websites—was excised and only half of the interview was left. In the meantime, a State Department publicist kept calling the reporter and asking when the interview would be published. The editor-in-chief asked the correspondent to explain the situation to her American sources and ask for their understanding. The reporter, however, was struck by this request as naïve and clumsy, evidence that her boss did not understand the danger it would mean to her to be on the record informing US officials about China's censorship regime.

*   *   *

Foreign correspondents in China today, unlike even fifteen years ago, tend to be young members of an increasingly urbane middle class, whose consumption habits and distinctions of taste they share in various ways, including via social media. Their exposure to the world outside China is incomparably wider than that of their predecessors. Many of them have studied abroad or interned with foreign media organizations in China (for my interviewees, these included AP, Reuters, the *New York Times*, the German news agency DPA, and the *South China Morning Post*) or worked as assistants or fixers for foreign journalists. A number encountered foreign journalists or academics as lecturers while at university; for example, Lee Miller, editor-at-large of Bloomberg News in China, taught the introduction to journalism practice at Tsinghua University in 2011. For some journalists, such encounters have led to a critical reappraisal of China's politics, but overall, there seems to be little correlation between such experiences and either journalists' job choices or their reporting. They certainly contributed, however, to their familiarity with foreign lifestyles. Moreover, many journalists of this generation have travelled abroad as tourists.

While young Chinese correspondents enjoy lifestyles that have, in some ways, more in common with Western peers' than the somewhat dour, almost entirely workplace-oriented lives of their older colleagues at the turn of the millennium, their sense of privilege associated with an overseas posting is nowhere near what it used to be. Living or studying abroad is no longer exceptional and, in fact, is sometimes associated with missing out on opportunities at home. As a *People's Daily* correspondent said, referring to central media employees, "For us, studying abroad gives no advantage." In the marketized world of today's China, where many foreign correspondents feel disadvantaged compared to peers working in the corporate sector, the most important asset of a state media job is its stability.

Some correspondents comment on this with open cynicism. A *People's Daily* reporter based in North America told me that he had a strong sense of responsibility for his job, but "if I enjoy it is another matter. I still enjoy some parts, like meeting people. But otherwise, it is just a job, not a vocation (*shiye*). How many journalists still have ideals?" His friend from CCTV chimed in: "If you work for Chinese media, you cannot avoid having a split personality" (*bu renge fenlie bu ke*). "So how do you cope with this?" I asked. "No need to cope, we are used to it," he replied. "It's based on self-discipline (*zilü*)," the *People's Daily* correspondent added. "It's in our genes," the CCTV journalist said. "We get this [the official view of the nation] in our history classes, in our literature classes . . . " "The whole school," his friend concluded.

Such cynical but nonetheless implicitly self-indicting reflexivity is, of course, not shared by most central media correspondents, at least not in public. But it is adopted by some of those with the most urbane and cosmopolitan personas, even as others opt for the kind of suave and self-assured, though by no means intellectually lightweight, relativism voiced by John at the beginning of this chapter. Both attitudes reflect, perhaps, a need to justify one's choices in a society characterized by a striking combination of belief in development—as attested by the phenomenal rise of Chinese people's fortunes in one generation—and abiding anxiety about one's individual future. Will I be able to afford an apartment that is often viewed as prerequisite to marriage? Will I be promoted? Will my child be able to get into a good kindergarten, a good primary school, a good university, a good job?

Will I become ill from adulterated food, and if I will, will the medical costs bankrupt my family?

*   *   *

Correspondents for the highest-regarded commercial media organizations still command a measure of respect among colleagues, in part because these organizations are seen as being more professional and meritocratic than state media. On occasion, official media reporters may even be sheepish in their presence. A Caixin correspondent recalled that a young CCTV reporter posted in the same city, in conversation with her, would often make remarks like "Oh, it's good that you guys working for independent media organizations can do these things. As journalists, we are not as good as you." He would complain that nobody cared how hard he worked or how well he wrote; the only way to be promoted was to be good at managing personal connections.

Yet existential anxieties are even greater for those in the commercial media. While jobs, at least for journalists who have proven themselves, have until recently been relatively secure despite the short-term nature of contracts, there was no obvious path to promotion, and without that, incomes were regarded as insufficient to provide for the financial security of a married person with a child. In the last two years, even this relative security has been upended by the precipitous decline of the traditional media market and the threat of political repression. Existential anxieties are only partially, and decreasingly, compensated by satisfaction taken from the job done. With the room for journalistic initiative shrinking, a senior international desk editor at *Phoenix Weekly* told me, "Every day, I ask myself: does what I do have any meaning?" A senior editor at another commercial media organization commented: "In addition to the media being in transition, everyone faces his own transition, everyone is looking for a way out." One of the longest-serving veterans in international journalism, he gave himself another year before quitting media altogether. He would have preferred to emigrate in order to let his child grow up outside China, but believed he lacked the financial means to do so. An equally senior journalist at another commercial media group put it even more plainly: "If I had a child, I would want to run away from China." An editor at another well-known commercial newspaper commented: "Being an international journalist in China doesn't really offer any career perspective. The first batch of our foreign correspondents had started as assistants to *New York Times* and *Wall Street Journal* reporters. But our paper's attractiveness has gone down, because it demands harder work than *Global Times* or Xinhua, while the salary advantage has decreased since salaries at other papers salaries have gone up." A number of my interviewees in the commercial media have quit and moved to foreign media, online start-ups, or to non-media jobs in the course of the research. Some have moved to domestic reporting. "You have to be in China to really impact Chinese society. If you report on mining deaths in Shanxi, that can change the lives of thousands of people," argued a former Europe-based stringer for an online news portal who now covers the Chinese economy.

Not only foreign correspondence but, more generally, journalism is rarely seen as a lifetime career choice. "In China, if you are over thirty, you are considered a senior journalist, and if you are over forty and still a journalist," then you must be a loser—you should have moved on: this is how a Caixin journalist described the mainstream view. High turnover at media organizations is the norm, to the extent that staying in one place, particularly in commercial media, makes a journalist the target of attention. On one occasion, a *Phoenix Weekly* editor described a mutual acquaintance as an "old man." I expressed surprise, as the journalist in question was just in his thirties. My interlocutor laughed: "Of course he is an old man! If you have spent five years at the same paper you are an old man, and how long has he been there—ten years?" A CCTV reporter related the following anecdote: When freshly hired US staff visited headquarters in China, an editor asked one of them, an experienced anchor recruited away from an American broadcaster: "How old are you? Forty-five? How come you are still a journalist?" The man was deeply offended.

Some media have launched initiatives to promote foreign correspondence as a career. CCTV has recently made it possible to promote correspondents to producers, deputy bureau chiefs and even bureau chiefs while abroad, without having to go back to China. At the same time, senior correspondents and editors can now, in principle, get higher salaries than a department head. In the words of the head of CCTV Europe, the company wants to "create a culture in which being a *lingdao* is not the only measure of success." If it is accepted for an anchor to be paid more than a bureau chief, then why not for an experienced foreign correspondent? Yet, as proponents of the system acknowledge, it will take time for it to take root as staff continue to associate *lingdao* positions with security.

In these conditions of existential insecurity, the most conservative central media institutions, *People's Daily* and Xinhua, where journalists' room to maneuver is the most constricted, offer the greatest sense of protection, not only because of their political "safety" but also because of having preserved some of the socialist ethos of the *danwei*, the state work unit, with its collectively organized leisure, factory-style mess halls and basketball courts, and superficially egalitarian treatment of both journalists and service personnel. As a former Caixin correspondent wrote in a thoughtful e-mail reflecting on her own choices and those of her friends who work at central media,

> I don't think they bother so much about [China's political climate and their relationship to it]. [Their] life is comfortable and yes there are uncertainties but that's shared by pretty much everyone. So there isn't so much incentive about giving up what they have.
>
> Somehow I totally understand. If I was not so lucky to meet those people that made it possible for me to work in Caijing in my first job, I might have ended up in some official newspaper doing the same thing as what they've been doing. I would have felt the same way about many things in the Chinese system, but I don't think I'd be so courageous to speak out or rebel. In a sense having worked in an independent media helped me feeling better as if I were on the moral high ground. But in reality I think I'm not so much different from these official-media journalists. What have I done to change things, after all?
>
> [Philip, a foreign correspondent at *People's Daily*] told us yesterday on our way back that when he first joined P[eople's] D[aily], he liked it so much there because he felt "*wennuan*" [warm] there. I was a bit surprised when he used that word because I would have imagined *PD* to be a cold and bureaucratic place. I used to use that word to describe Caijing because I have always felt it was a great workplace and everyone was so nice. Well, I guess *PD* was a "warm" place for [Philip] in a slightly different sense—it was like a typical socialist *danwei*, where people not only worked but actually lived together. The seniors might treat the juniors as their children and give them very good advice if they happen to be kind-hearted. I think that also partly explains why they are willing to serve in these places [like Africa] despite what they sometimes feel about the alienation. It's not just because of the vest[ed] interests they became part of, but also there [were] human feelings.

Foreign correspondents choose their ways to navigate these uncertainties in the hope of moral, professional or existential rewards. Whether they are employed by a central or a commercial media organization—a circumstance more often determined by luck and chance after graduation than by a clear sense of professional or political identity—narrows their range of choices, but does not eliminate it altogether. In the next two chapters, as we follow foreign correspondents through their work and leisure from New York to Harare, we will learn more about the circumstances in which these choices are made.

CHAPTER 3

How Correspondents Work

I WAS once allowed to stay in the flat of a young female Xinhua correspondent when she was away on vacation. The flat was obviously inhabited by a single, transient person: apart from a leather sofa, a large flat-screen television, and a Nespresso machine, it was cheaply furnished and full of boxes. Above the stove in the rundown kitchen there was a sticker that read LIVE HUMBLE EAT NOBLE.

The shelves housed an eclectic assortment of books. There was a novel by John le Carré, a brief history of the United States, a Michelin guide to Sri Lanka and the Maldives, and *The Little Prince* in French; *Hamas: A Beginner's Guide* and *China Business* in English; a French and a Korean grammar; Chinese guidebooks of Bali and Switzerland; a Taiwanese writer's popular book on the wounds of China's civil war; several volumes of classical Chinese dramas and poetry; a novel each by Danielle Steel, Louisa May Alcott, and Cecelia Ahern; *The French Revolution*; *The Corruption of American Politics* by Elizabeth Drew; *State of War: The Secret History of the CIA and the Bush Administration* by James Risen; two Chinese books on Tibet, one of them in French; *Snorkeling for All*; the catalog of a Christie's jewelry auction; and *A Farewell to Justice* by Joan Mellen, a book about the assassination of President Kennedy. This was a library, it seemed, of a person with not yet established tastes, but who was interested in a wide range of subjects and eager to experiment.

On the desks and shelves were a fax from Xinhua's head office agreeing to pay for her driving lessons; a receipt for fifty local souvenirs delivered to the Chinese embassy; a number of candles in red candleholders, mostly from IKEA; a stuffed bunny with the logo of an international humanitarian organization; and a large mounted print of a steamy Klimt nude. Of course, these various books and artifacts were not necessarily the young woman's: some of them would have been her predecessor's and others may have been lent by colleagues. But even this superficial and somewhat illicit glimpse of a private life revealed something about the tastes and preoccupations of a correspondent normally hidden behind the forbidding notion of the Chinese Communist Party's "throat and tongue," as Xinhua is still often referred to. How did Chinese correspondents live? How did they work?

SINGLES ON A SHOESTRING

In January 2013, I met Peter, then the UK-based correspondent of a respected Chinese commercial media organization, at the bar of a London hotel not far from New Broadcasting House, the BBC's headquarters. The son of workers who had not been allowed to go to university because of family connections to the Nationalist government that had been defeated by the Communists, Peter had graduated from a top journalism school in China some years earlier. While at university, he wrote about a Beijing Internet addiction clinic that, he found, made considerable profit with treatments of dubious efficacy. With his supervisor's endorsement, Peter presented his research at a conference in London, where it was received enthusiastically. Peter was invited to more conferences, first in Hong Kong, then in the United States, where he took part in a panel organized by scholars from the University of Pennsylvania's Annenberg School for Communication. Attracted to academic debates, Peter decided to pursue a doctorate in communication theory at the Annenberg School, but when he visited it he decided he did not like Philadelphia and, because of his favorable impression of England, decided to study in Britain instead. In the meantime, however, on the wave of foreign media interest in China that preceded the 2008 Beijing Olympics, he landed a succession of internships and freelance work with Western broadcasters in China. Simultaneously, he helped the American media scholar and Internet freedom activist Ethan Zuckerman gather data for a study on the Chinese Internet.

In 2009, Peter went to Oxford, where he was offered a master's scholarship in social science. His master's thesis was on the use of new technologies in foreign news reporting. He graduated in the following year and returned to Beijing for an internship with an American financial news organization, planning to become a financial reporter. But he found the work boring—"not journalism"—and returned to Britain, hoping to find a job. He was then offered a post as a Europe correspondent by the organization that he worked for when I met him. There was some debate about whether London was the best location to cover Europe, but the fact that Peter had a British residential visa that was valid for another couple of years decided the matter. Peter was not officially accredited by the British government. Nor was he, for that matter, officially a journalist from the perspective of the Chinese government; although all journalists in China are required to pass an exam and obtain a license from either the General Administration of Press and Publications (GAPP) or the State Administration of Radio, Film and Television (SARFT), Peter never got one.

By this time, Peter also had a job offer from a financial institution in China, but he wanted to work in Europe because "debates in a plural society" interested him more than money. So he accepted the London post with its relatively modest pay, without an office or local assistants.

His first assignment, a trip to Egypt to cover the unfolding protests that toppled Hosni Mubarak's regime, kindled Peter's interest in political transitions. Initially, the assignment included travel to other countries involved in the Arab Spring, but this did not materialize, as his editors had other priorities and funds were short. Nonetheless, Peter continued to cover the upheavals in Arab countries. In an article on Libya, he used the term *liberation* to describe the advances of rebels on Col. Muammar Gaddafi's army in Libya. Although the official Chinese view was largely sympathetic to Gaddafi, the story was not censored. His editor told him that the authorities did ask that one of his online stories on Egypt be taken down, but the organization managed to fend off the order.

Peter's intention was not to glorify the Arab Spring, but rather to document the difficulties of replacing an authoritarian regime with democracy. Liberal public intellectuals in China, he explained, tended to paint a simple picture: "We want democracy, and once we get democracy everything will be fine. I want my readers to understand how the process actually works." In other words, despite the tightening political climate in China, Peter's concern was with complicating what he saw as the overly simplistic hopes of liberal intellectuals.

On his desk, Peter kept a photo of Alistair Cooke, the legendary BBC correspondent whose series *Letter from America* was broadcast for fifty-eight years. For Peter, Cooke captured the essence of the foreign correspondent as someone who knows intimately the society he covers but always retains an outsider's view. He also—despite what he saw as her excessive idealism about the Arab Spring—admired Lyse Doucet, the BBC's long-standing Middle East correspondent; he once walked up to her to say hello when he saw her at an airport. His view of the BBC's foreign reporting overall was more nuanced: he was critical of what he saw as the company's overreliance on local assistants. For in-depth local knowledge, he saw the *New York Times* as the leader. In contrast, he had come to "hate" the *New Yorker* for stories that were overdramatized, "too interesting to be true."

In Britain, Peter set out to develop his local networks, making use of connections he had made at Oxford. Many of his friends were academics, and the discussions he had with them helped him understand current debates in more depth. But after a year, he was unexpectedly transferred to the United States to cover the 2012 elections, leaving it to a part-time correspondent to cover Europe. After the elections, he was moved to New York because his employer nominated him for a scholarship at a university there. His beat was now to cover financial markets and Chinese investment, an area he had less enthusiasm for. He could not pursue his interest in transitional societies, all the more because the United States gave Chinese journalists single-entry visas, which made it difficult for them to travel outside the country. But at least, from the perspective of the US government, Peter was indeed a correspondent. The Chinese embassy in Washington, however, did not consider him as such: only central media correspondents received invitations to official events.

Peter was increasingly frustrated by what he described as "pressure to generate stories immediately, without time to investigate what's really important for the audience to understand the complexity of American society." Sometimes, this left him relying too much on local media coverage, a practice he was deeply unhappy with. He proposed to write about poverty in the United States and its implications for the election, but his editors preferred more interviews with congressmen and their views of China.

Chinese correspondents in the US either want to show how good it is—and by contrast, how bad China is (this was the reason Sina and [Internet portal] Tencent sent so many reporters to cover the election)—or else they want to unmask US democracy as a fake. It looks like they send reporters with a very specific purpose, without caring much about what is really going on out there. So I am disappointed in all Chinese media. Part of it is that they are not willing to invest in reporters who stay abroad. It is true that most Chinese readers want to read about how the world sees us, but there should be at least *one* Chinese medium in the world that shows how the world really is, like the *New York Times*. We do this selectively, and the selection is determined by our publisher.

If this was so in the United States, by far the best-covered part of the world for Chinese media, it was even more so in Europe where there was only a token presence of Chinese commercial media, such that reporting was, to an even greater degree, defined by central media organizations. An article by the influential *People's Daily* opinion writer Ding Gang, in which he wrote that the European Union needed to ask what they could produce in the coming decades, was, for Peter, typical of the superficial and demagogic tone of the coverage of the European debt crisis, much of which highlighted how a "Western-style" democratic system was unsuitable to deal with it. There was little coverage of how EU institutions actually worked and why they looked messy—the articles were content with stating they were messy.

An additional burden was that Peter's employer entered into a partnership with a television station in China to produce three hours of English-language programming every day. On top of their other tasks, foreign correspondents were asked to contribute to this programming, and then the project was abandoned as abruptly as it started. While expressing his admiration for the way his organization's founder, who continued to lead it, pioneered the development of Chinese media, he was frustrated by what he saw as a lack of coherent strategy. "Yes, salaries are low compared to the competition, but I knew that when I joined. But the problem is that management is a mess. Strategic decisions are taken without any discussion, staff are asked to put a lot of effort into them, and then the strategy is abandoned without much explanation."

Despite his growing disappointment, Peter asked to be allowed to stay longer in New York so that he could develop new networks, and he was "more or less promised" that. Yet less than a year into his new posting, he was abruptly recalled to China because of his organization's financial constraints. He was replaced by a colleague who had received a scholarship from an American university, allowing the employer to pay only part of his

salary and no housing allowance. Peter understood the company's difficulties but felt he was being "thrown around," without anyone sitting down
with him and having a serious discussion. Finally, frustrated, he decided to
go back to Britain, where was offered a research assistantship. The following
year, he quit his Chinese employer altogether and moved to a European
broadcaster.

. . .

While Peter has changed locations four times in four years, Lynne has
stayed in New York since April 2012, when her employer, a well-known financial newspaper, chose her as their US correspondent after two years at
the international desk. She was offered a choice between Brussels and New
York, and although she prefers Europe to America as a place to live, for her
beat, financial analysis, the latter was more exciting. Lynne commutes to the
city daily from a New Jersey apartment she is renting; all our conversations
took place in various midtown Manhattan cafes. Although she has no office,
her salary and the extras are enough for what she describes as a "relatively
decent" standard of living. In her late twenties, unusually, Lynne is married;
she describes her husband, who lives in Europe, as a "Chinese who is a foreign citizen." Lynne hopes he will join her in America. Like Peter, she completed a master's degree in journalism. Unlike him, her degrees are from
Chinese universities, although she spent one year of her master's as an
exchange student in Europe. Like Peter, she was offered a job in the finance
sector—in her case, for a leading international accounting firm—after graduation, and, unlike him, she took the job rather than accept an offer from a
leading commercial media organization that came with a salary she considered too low. But international journalism was what she wanted to do, and,
after a year in the finance sector, she quit to take the job with her current
employer. "Men who could be finance journalists usually prefer to be financial analysts, which pays better. They are more likely to have families,"
Lynne reflects. "Women are more likely to take the challenge of a foreign
posting and not worry so much about the money."

Although Lynne's job has been more stable than Peter's, her paper's international strategy is hardly so. For reasons probably having to do with her
organization's financial difficulties, Lynne is now the sole US correspondent,
replacing three or four others who have quit or gone back to China for personal reasons. Nonetheless, and although a foreign posting is initially for
two years, the organization's preference is for a correspondent to stay in the
same post for five to six years so that she can build up a local network. Fur-

thermore, foreign correspondents are required to sign a commitment for five years, and if they quit earlier they are supposed to pay a fine, although in practice there has been some room to negotiate.

Compared to Peter, Lynne is decidedly happier about her job. She is concerned about the future of her company, as its advertising revenue is diminishing. This is affecting the budget she is allocated. In part, this is mitigated by the recruitment of Chinese students in New York as interns who help her transcribe and translate interviews back into Chinese, and occasionally do interviews. "For now, this is still the best among Chinese media," so she wants to continue working for it. In part, this is because her beat is what she is most interested in: in-depth financial reporting. It is a basic requirement that all her articles be based on first-hand information; in contrast, she says, Xinhua Finance or Sina Finance only offer short news, and often just translate local media reports. This, Lynne believes, is the basic difference between her work and the work of journalists for central media. She has many friends among central media correspondents and they spend much of their free time together, because "all of us are on our own here." She socializes much less with non-Chinese peers, who, she finds, are "all boys" and often have different interests, "like football."

Before her overseas posting, Lynne already travelled widely, covering important global business events such as the World Economic Forum in Davos and interviewing a number of high-profile personalities such as the former US president Jimmy Carter and the economist Nouriel Roubini. Her ambition is "just . . . to be a professional finance journalist who knows as much as a financial analyst does." In an online exchange in English, she added that many of her colleagues "think we should strive for a better China through our way of doing news, digging out more truth and becoming an independent force. But [another colleague] and I are more into professionalism in Journalism [sic]. . . .We all want China to be better, but I do not think journalist[s] should have too much [of an] agenda when reporting news, even [if] it is [a] very good agenda."

Unlike Peter, whose style departs rather markedly from China's official rhetoric—he says his publication "tries to get away from rubbish political rhetoric"—Lynne's stories, in terms of language, do not read very differently from those on the financial pages of central media. Although she reports on Chinese companies' investments in the United States, which are frequently at the center of political controversies, she rarely mentions these issues, describing them as outside her beat. Lynne's organization is known for its dry, factual reporting, and Lynne is comfortable with that: "I hate political news." Nor does she offer critical analysis of the strategies these companies choose. "I don't think I have enough knowledge to criticize them. A lot of them are great people; they want to create history." In some cases of critical coverage she got rapped on her knuckles by her editor because the companies involved, often powerful ones, called to register their displeasure. "Our chief editor is now very, very conservative. . . . [H]e's had to handle a lot of lawsuits and disputes."

Lynne's own political position is harder to pin down than Peter's, who may be described as a liberal universalist impatient with national narrow-mindedness. Lynne acknowledges that her focus on Chinese companies abroad is influenced by a Sinocentric perspective of the world, but "What's wrong with being nationalistic?" Yet when it comes to the "development journalism" theory that media should advance national interests, she is deeply skeptical. "I don't care about national power; I care about giving a voice to Chinese companies who are investing abroad. There is definitely no national interest reporting—only professional and unprofessional." For Lynne, public interest does not exist, only a multiplicity of conflicting interests. "So my job is to include as many interests as possible: that's what being objective means." Some of her recent stories she is most satisfied with include a series on quantitative easing by the Federal Reserve and one on international tax reform affecting companies operating in the United States. She also launched a new biweekly column on urban planning and how public spaces are changed to make people feel more comfortable. She wants to turn these into a book. But finance and mergers and acquisitions remain her main interests.

. . .

The first time I met Zhu Feng, it was in the company of two other Chinese correspondents at a café in a European capital on a spring weekend in 2013. China News Service (CNS), the smaller of China's two news agencies, had posted Zhu in the country a few months earlier. All of them single and dispatched from Beijing by central media organizations, the correspondents spent much of their free time together. All three lived in an area some way from the city center, not far from the Chinese embassy and the compound owned by the larger news agency, Xinhua, and conducted most of their social meetings at a couple of Chinese restaurants nearby. Unlike Peter or Lynne, they rarely met non-Chinese colleagues outside press conferences, did not have many social acquaintances among locals, and were not very familiar with the center of the city in which they lived. Our meeting was a relatively rare occasion for them to go there. Perhaps it was as a Xinhua correspondent said: "older people, those over thirty, often feel out of place if they are asked to socialize with locals."

CNS has around fifteen bureaus abroad, but, with the exception of the United States, they are each manned by a single correspondent. Zhu likes this: "There is no one looking over my shoulder." Correspondents have to file a minimum of twenty stories per month to get their base salary. For work above that quota, they get bonuses. About half of Zhu's stories involve some interviewing; the rest are based on local media materials. Unlike Xinhua, CNS focuses on Chinese-language news, as its primary mission is to supply Chinese media outside the PRC. Subordinated to the Overseas Chinese Affairs Bureau of the State Council (Qiaoban), CNS was founded in 1952 in order to communicate the achievements of the "new China" to overseas Chinese concerned about the country but distrustful of Xinhua as the "throat and tongue" of the Communist Party. Compared to Xinhua, CNS uses less official and more colloquial language and refers less frequently to Party directives. Since the government's 2012 directive on accelerating the expansion of Chinese media abroad called on media to "rely on the Chinese-language overseas market," CNS's traditional mission has received a new lease on life. CNS offers its stories to overseas Chinese media largely free of charge, and they provide typeset pages that are ready to print to a number of Chinese newspapers in Europe (see Chong 2015). Because CNS has the option of sending stories to Chinese-language media abroad without publishing them on the agency's domestic website, it can report some stories that would not be approved for domestic release.

Zhu derived satisfaction from doing a story faster or better than the much better-resourced Xinhua, noticing things that the Xinhua reporter did not or talking to people the Xinhua reporter did not interview. Although CNS is not a market-oriented venture, its domestic weekly, *China Newsweek*, is popular because of the comparative liveliness of the writing, and does turn a profit. Correspondents like Zhu are often asked to contribute to it, although this is not an obligation.

Zhu and his friends agreed that their aim was simply to report in a "truthful, objective, and balanced" fashion, not to try to influence readers one way or another or to change the way they saw the world or Europe. They were, after all, reporters, not commentators; that was a separate function that foreign correspondents did not have. Their personal feelings should not affect their reporting. If what they reported had an impact on their readers' view of Europe, that was something outside their control. The problem was, Zhu said, that there was not much happening in Europe that would be of interest to Chinese readers. Too many strange and fascinating things happened in China every day, and if people turned to foreign news at all, it was the United States they wanted to read about. So stories had to be presented for their reference value to China, rather than for their intrinsic news value. For example, Zhu reported on the meat adulteration scandal in 2013, when meat sold as beef in a number of European countries was found to contain horse meat. In China, this would not have been major news because such occurrences were common. Still, the story was interesting because of what it could be made to say about China. It could be interpreted as proof that such things happened in Europe too, and that by implication China's food safety problems were not as grave as alarmists would have it. Or, to the contrary, it could be seen as evidence that European authorities launched a thorough investigation even though the meat was not tainted by anything dangerous—horse meat was, after all, edible too—and, by extension, that European government was more efficient and less corrupt than Chinese. Although, Zhu and his friends agreed, a correspondent would not report the story with a particular spin, the editor who commissioned it would often spin it one way or another. Even so, interest in the meat story would not last for long. Stories that would sustain the interest of Chinese audiences over time were very few: the European debt crisis was one.

The three reporters agreed that British media's coverage of China was more in-depth than their own work. Audience interest was one problem, as were lack of resources, limited access to good sources, and political constraints on reporting, although none of these concerned Europe as such; it was more a matter of common sense. If the Dalai Lama was in town, Zhu might go and listen to him but he certainly wouldn't report on it. They would have to publish the ambassador's "severe criticism" of the visit instead. He is interested in culture but has not had the time to report on it, although he did do a story on an auction at which two items looted from the Summer Palace in Beijing by European troops in 1900 were sold, an event that aroused strong emotions and calls for repatriating the relics in China. Yet Zhu did not do any backgrounder on the auction house or the Yves Saint Laurent collection from which the relics came.

LIFE AT THE BUREAU

By the time I met Liu Ying in the European city where she was stationed, I had disabused myself of the stereotype of the Xinhua correspondent as a somewhat scruffy middle-aged man in a zippered jacket. Still, I had not been prepared to see a young woman with a daring, asymmetrical haircut verging on the punk and with nails painted green on one hand. Was this a sign of rebellion, and how did Xinhua, China's most conservative news organization, take it? Liu replied that she had once had a more adventurous cut, with one side of her head completely shaved. At that time, she had asked the bureau chief whether it was all right to attend a press conference with such a hairdo. The chief, whom she called "teacher," had joked that it was fine as long as she dyed it purple or white. (Another Xinhua correspondent suggested that the leadership made a conscious effort to promote journalists who helped counter the Xinhua stereotype abroad.)

Liu studied English and journalism at Peking University, graduating with a master's degree. She considered working for foreign media in China, but Chinese law did not permit Chinese journalists to work for foreign news organizations; those that did could only be called "assistants" and could not publish under their own bylines. During her studies she interned for three months at the Hong Kong newspaper *South China Morning Post*, and she wanted to apply for a job there, but her advisor at the university dissuaded her, arguing there was so much that was newsworthy in mainland China that it was a better place for a good journalist. Among mainland media, Xinhua seemed the best choice because it offered the closest access to the news itself: even though she may not be allowed to report everything, she would at least be there and witness, and this was what was most important for a journalist.

Liu joined Xinhua at a time when the rapid recruitment of new staff, fuelled by the extra state funding Xinhua received as part of the effort to expand the international influence of Chinese media, had just begun. Before her posting abroad, Liu mostly wrote feature articles in English. Among her stories, there was an interview with the famous liberal blogger Han Han, which she considers one of her better articles. For the sixtieth anniversary of the founding of the PRC, Xinhua produced a series of features on prominent personalities. She proposed Han Han, and the editors accepted. This was one of the first instances for the central media to write about Han, and it was not easy to persuade him to accept the interview. Although Liu thinks she did not capture his personality as well as a *New Yorker* story by China correspondent Evan Osnos, she rates it as more successful than a profile published in the *New York Times*—an evaluation that suggests she benchmarks her stories against those by foreign colleagues. The story then circulated widely and was extensively quoted in Western media, with commentators speculating whether a Xinhua story on Han Han was a sign of political change.

Liu describes the *New Yorker*'s past two China correspondents, Peter Hessler and Evan Osnos, as models of how she would like to write. Several other Chinese journalists—including one from *People's Daily*—also mentioned Hessler or Osnos as writers they like or admire, although I have also come across critical remarks. Liu actually sought Osnos's advice on how to prepare for her posting. She thought of herself as a skilled reporter with six years of experience, but she found that she needed a longer learning period reading up on the topics she covered than she had expected.

Liu did not apply for a posting abroad until her husband, a diplomat, had been posted in Europe, and she was unwilling to accompany him without her own work to do. In the event, she was offered a posting but was told that family circumstances had not played a major role; rather, the offer was based on the results of an exam that all Xinhua reporters have to take before their first posting abroad. This is essentially a foreign-language newswriting exam. Liu was given a statement by US President Obama and was asked to write a news item on its basis, as well as to write an opinion piece.

For a while, Liu considered applying for a one-year British government scholarship to study political science. This was because much of her reporting was on politics, but she felt she lacked the conceptual framework to reflect on it. "When you read a *People's Daily* article you know something is wrong with it, but it's more of a gut reaction, not something you can argue." Liu, the Xinhua reporter, wanted to equip herself with the conceptual tools to dissect the Party's view of the world. In the end, however, she returned to China after the end of her term, gave birth to a child, and quit Xinhua for a startup.

As a student, Liu had fantasized about becoming a frontline reporter. Then, when she started working, she saw her role as helping China reform and change by bringing some stories to light internationally. At first she had a strong sense of success every time an English story of hers was referred to in Western media, even if it was just one line. But after a few years she realized that these stories did not help change the things that she wanted to change. For example, she wrote about grassroots organizations in China, but this did not earn them more favorable treatment. Later, she came to find reporting news for Chinese readers more meaningful.

Liu filed an average two stories a day for the news wire and one or two a month for one of Xinhua's magazines. A typical day, during my visit, entailed a phone interview, one or two press conferences, and writing at home. Her focus was on breaking national news, major international organizations in the country, and China-related news. The bureau received its share of the usual tedious requests from editors in China, asking for endorsements of foreign "experts" for new policies of the Chinese government and the like. The bureau chief did his best to fend off or derail the most unreasonable requests. This left her with some time to pursue feature stories on her own initiative. Contrary to the disparaging stereotype of Xinhua reporters as journalists who sit in front of the TV the whole day and file their stories based on what they see, Liu, like most other Xinhua reporters, told me that most of her stories involved live interviewing of some kind. It was a convenient thing about Europe, she said, that one could easily find experts by searching the Internet. "If you see that it's a famous expert you can just contact him," and most of the time get a reply.

Liu's bureau—or "station" (zhan), as it is officially classed within Xinhua's structure—is medium sized: not so large or old as to have its own residential compound, but not the "mom-and-pop shop" (fuqidian, as the correspondents call it) that many African or South American stations are. The earlier employees stay in a block of adjoining flats, but more recent staff stay in rented flats in separate buildings near the office. The station chief did not generally keep tabs on the correspondents: sometimes he would distribute assignments, and he introduced a system of duty where someone had to be in the office every day, but at other times he was content to let staff divide their tasks and liaise with their editors in China. Although the station chief himself was somewhat old-fashioned—he took his place in the official system (tizhi) seriously and always spent a lot of time covering the activities of Chinese government delegations—he did not mind if his staff were interested in other matters and did not intervene with their writing. Compared to some other station chiefs who insisted on approving every event a reporter attended, this was a relaxed place. Nonetheless, it was very different from being one's own boss in the way Zhu effectively is. Correspondents' lives took place in front of their colleagues and superior, and their daily routines were structured by obligations related to the collective. Since station chiefs are responsible for the conduct and safety of their staff, they can and often do impose rules on reporters' private lives, such as prohibiting the practice of adventure sports.

· · ·

Zhao Juan, a woman twice Liu Ying's age and one of the oldest active foreign correspondents I interviewed, is one of those disciplinarian European bureau chiefs, but for *People's Daily*, not Xinhua. Bureau chiefs nearing retirement age are less common than before at central media—even some regional bureau directors are now in their late forties—but are not unusual. What is unusual is that Zhao clearly relishes reporting and, while conforming in some ways to the stereotype of a *lingdao* who expects obedience in all matters, remains a whirlwind of activity instead of sitting back in her armchair and issuing instructions, the way bureau chiefs of her cohort, mostly men, often will. Unsurprisingly, this leads to some grief among her staff, all in their twenties, to whom "Teacher Zhao's" ways appear outmoded, even though they respect her integrity. One of the reporters, after protracted fighting with her parents who thought it was foolish to abandon a steady income and stable career at *People's Daily*, quit shortly after my visit and decided to look for a job in Europe. She felt, she explained, "too unfree" in shaping the stories, referring not so much to political censorship as to the editors' rigid prescriptions for particular formats and positive ("win-win") stories, and pressure from Zhao Juan who accused her of not taking her assignments seriously enough. (In revenge, Zhao Juan reported her departure to the French authorities, causing the cancellation of her work visa and forcing her to return to China.) In comparison, this correspondent preferred writing for *Global Times* as they allowed a freer and livelier style, but Zhao insisted on vetting all requests from *Global Times* and assigning or rejecting them as she saw fit. The reporter's sense of a lack of freedom was exacerbated by living next door to the bureau chief. Although staff lived in different buildings, she clearly felt under the watch of the bureau, which adhered to *People's Daily*'s strict code of personal conduct, including a ban on romantic or sexual relationships with foreigners.

At the age of the reporter, Zhao Juan had just recently returned from the countryside where she had been sent for rustication as an "educated youth" during the Cultural Revolution. She was one of the first to complete a master's degree in journalism in China, and has held a succession of *lingdao* positions at *People's Daily*, although she never rose to the level of her husband, one of the top political cadres at the paper. Although Zhao trained to be a foreign correspondent, she did not have the chance to go abroad until

relatively late because her husband did not want to do so and she needed to look after the family. This, her final posting, is her third, and despite spending much time on reporting—often on standard topics such as local reactions to a Chinese Party congress—Zhao now sees her role principally in training her young staff. Every week, one of them is on duty for breaking news, and the others are assigned to longer stories. While other bureaus practice a division of labor, Zhao does not allow it.

> I want the young people to broaden their thinking. It's tiring but necessary. . . .
> This may not be the job you always wanted; liking it is something you can build
> up gradually. But you must have the ability to dig deeper, to see something new
> in what you observe. You have to be willing to run around: news is something
> you get with your feet (*xinwen shi yao paochulai de*), you can't just sit at home
> and read the papers. And you have to be able to accumulate insight, such that,
> for example, even if you are writing about sports or entertainment you should
> be able to see the politics in it; you have to move all the time (*yao buduan gun-
> dong*). . . . Young correspondents often lack the insight into local society; they
> don't know how to interpret news.

Like at Xinhua, the stereotype of "armchair reporting" no longer applies at *People's Daily*. All articles are required to involve at least one phone interview; none are purely *bianyi*. In 2011, the paper's international section expanded from two to four pages, and, in 2013, it introduced scannable QR codes, so stories can now be linked to online photos and videos. While, divided between all correspondents, this still makes for a relatively light workload—and at most stations, the formal requirements are impossible to meet because there is just not enough space in the paper—it is much heavier than in the past. Every month, data is gathered on how many "expert interviews" each journalist did, and these statistics become part of annual performances reviews. In addition, the paper's international department announces a list of "good articles" (*haogao*) every month, and then another list is announced for the entire paper. For every *haogao*, reporters receive a cash award, and they are also important for promotion.

Zhao sidesteps questions about how she interprets the requirement to be partisan and how that requirement squares with the professional ideal of objective reporting. "Partisanship is a very abstract requirement. Actually, in our work there isn't much politics. As for being objective, there are various ways to do it. Our reporting is completely different from Western media. . . .

We basically report positive things, like healthy nightlife or the protection of independent bookstores. . . . If we kept talking about the bad side, the thieves, the air quality, what would be the point?"

. . .

Much as Zhao Juan insists on keeping an eye on her staff, their lives are far less regimented than correspondents' lives in the self-contained compounds that Xinhua, *People's Daily*, and CCTV still maintain at some locations, either for historical reasons or because the environment is considered unsafe. This is the case in Nairobi, where all Xinhua staff have to ask for permission if they want to go out after 7:00 p.m., reporting with whom, where to, and for how long. At 10:00 p.m. the dogs are released, and getting back in becomes difficult. So most staff members confine their social lives to karaoke, cards, drinking, or basketball within the compound, and even practice evening walks within its perimeter.

Here I met Annie, a correspondent on her first overseas assignment. She had recently graduated with a master's degree from one of the new programs in "global journalism" co-funded by the Propaganda Department. After ten months writing features and a bit of "socialization," as the agency called it, in rural China, she joined some thirty Chinese staff in Nairobi. The regional bureau issues two hundred to three hundred English stories and eighty to one hundred Chinese stories per week, including those that are sent to the business wire called Xinhua08 and the mobile apps for African news.

In Nairobi, Annie's main job was to supervise the work of African correspondents at various locations, almost all of them far older and more experienced. Beyond the base pay and a small honorarium per article the African correspondents received, Annie was given considerable freedom in shaping their remuneration. She introduced a system in which articles that were praised by editors could receive a substantial bonus. This was in order to encourage better writing and cut down on stories that the agency was unable to use. "Some write very well, but not always what we want. For example, about banana, potato, or maize, or three times a week about mobile money." Most of the stories were for the English wire only: while she sometimes filed over twenty English stories a day, the number of Chinese stories did not exceed two or three a week. Annie was disappointed by the lack of interest in Africa back home. She thought Africa deserved more attention because it was important for China's strategic competition with the West, "as it is the last place where people are still friendly towards China and Chinese companies have a chance."

Every Monday, Annie went to a planning meeting, where all staff discussed the stories planned for the week and the director provided some "guidance," including about how to report certain stories positively. The director was generally supportive of staff plans and rarely stopped them from pursuing a story. Outside these meetings, Annie did not discuss reporting with her colleagues. "We talk about mundane things, like the dog being sick."

Although much of Annie's time was spent on editing English stories written by African staff, her own main interest was in writing *neican*, internal briefs for Chinese policy makers that are handled by a separate Reference Department (*canbianbu*) and used to be Xinhua's hallmark but have become less central to the agency's work. Unlike Zhao Juan, Annie talked openly and articulately about Xinhua's dual identity as a government mouthpiece and a competitive global news agency, and, unlike Liu Ying, she admitted to being confused about it but rejecting neither function. "We need to compete with Western media and criticize their negative reporting about China. But this is too weak, because it is still following Western media, rather than setting our own agenda." Competing with Western media, Annie continued, was a "stupid idea." Xinhua correspondents should "just do our job. . . . I prefer professionalism instead of propaganda. I hate that! But, of course, I have to do it. But I try to do [it in a] balanced [way]."

Such an attitude did not, however, mean adhering to a liberal universalist news agenda of speaking truth to power, whatever that power might be. Annie was very much committed to "developmental journalism." She concurred with the regional director that it was "quite necessary" to report positive things. It was true that Western media acted in the interests of their countries. During elections in Africa, Reuters and AP made the atmosphere tenser by their reporting. Annie, too, wanted to help China's goals, and reconciled herself, though not happily, to the reality that this may conflict with her pursuit of professionalism. "I prefer to tell the audience the truth," but since this could not be done in publications she often wrote *neican*, as it was "very necessary to update policy makers," and this was the only way to do so. To determine which issues might interest decision makers, she used informal contacts with Chinese diplomats. "When you have dinner with the embassy people, especially after a few drinks, you can ask questions."

When she arrived in Africa, Annie gave herself two tasks: to report on China-related events and on how Africans actually lived. In the previous year, Eric Gui, a Xinhua editor who had returned from Nairobi, published a book entitled *Shifeizhou,* with the explicit aim to counter Chinese stereo-types of Africa: "Are Africans really lazy and stupid? How do Africans see aid? Is African democracy a mess?"[1] Gui lamented that many of his col-leagues had done little to answer these questions, as some of them never even ventured into a slum. Annie agreed with Gui's criticism, and was particularly interested in reporting on the lives of the poor. Within the limits of how receptive she deemed her audiences and editors to be, she had written both published stories and *neican* on the subject. She thought of this as public interest (*gongyi*) journalism, so Chinese people might want to help Africans.

Annie also planned to write about a famous African chef who was born in poverty but eventually trained in Geneva and returned to his native coun-try in glory: this, she thought, would resonate with Chinese audiences. But although this format fit the "hero narrative" considered to be one of the techniques of "constructive journalism," editors did not support the story as they had other priorities.[2] Annie found the editors of the social and cul-tural news department unimaginative. "Last time they wanted a story on April Fool's Day in different countries. Is that news?" And she was thinking of a story about how Western companies deal with corruption in Africa. "Of course I can't write about Chinese companies. But I want to show that there is corruption everywhere, only the ways differ."

Outside the compound, the time window for my meetings with Annie was short. Dinner at the compound was at 6:00 p.m., and at 6:30 p.m., Xin-hua's "chef" called to see if she wanted him to keep her food for her. Al-though Annie was hardly a rebel, she found living in the enclosure hard. Xinhua encouraged staff to intermarry, but Annie avoided relationships with her colleagues as she found the idea of working and living with the same person twenty-four hours a day "awful." She broadened her social ac-tivities far beyond most of her colleagues'. She introduced herself to the other foreign correspondents in town; she frequented the foreign press club's lectures and occasionally had lunch with some American, British, and French correspondents she has made friends with, and with some Western expatriates who shared her interest in art. But the stress of the compound may have contributed to her decision to quit Xinhua about a year after my visit and embark on graduate studies in the United States.

. . .

"Sometimes we think he is a spy," a US correspondent for a financial paper said semi-jokingly when I told her about my meeting with Bai Qiang, chief of one of *People's Daily*'s US bureaus. I was curious why. "Because he looks like one." Many journalists believe that some of those on Xinhua correspondent lists are actually intelligence agents. Such beliefs are fuelled by the fact that some of those on the lists are hardly ever seen. But Bai Qiang was not difficult to find.

A quiet, unassuming man born in the 1960s, Bai studied English at university and graduated with a master's in international relations from a specialized college in Beijing in 1989. His thesis advisor encouraged him to pursue a PhD, but during that early period of economic reform, academia held little attraction. ("You are better off selling tea-dyed eggs than developing the atomic bomb" was a popular ditty at the time.) Bai declined and accepted a position at a State Council international relations think tank instead. He remembers that his first salary was 73 yuan. This was a time when foreign correspondence was a coveted source of extra income. "At that time, foreign correspondents made US $100 a month, which made you a rich man in China. In 1996–97, this was raised to $600."

Bai had wanted to go abroad since his days at secondary school, which specialized in English. After taking some more courses taught by US academics at a graduate center jointly established by an American and a Chinese university, he joined *People's Daily* in 1997 because a friend who worked there told him that the correspondent in a European city would be retiring in three years, and the post would become available. Bai started as an international department editor, and then was duly dispatched to Europe for four years; he remembers being the youngest Chinese correspondent in town. At that time, *People's Daily* had just started allowing family members to visit correspondents, but did not yet allow them to live together. This was allowed in 2002, and Bai's daughter then spent a year with him, going to a local preschool. Bai's wife stayed with them for shorter periods. His daughter also accompanied him on his current posting in the United States, which began in 2008. Bai was trying to prolong the posting to enable her to finish secondary school: her Chinese writing was not good enough to go to university in China. *People's Daily* did not provide any support for the school fees; he had to pay them out of his pocket.

As a result of increased staffing, Bai now has two other correspondents in his bureau. "It's to increase China's influence," says Bai, "even though this isn't necessarily the right way: it's not because you have a lot of people or put up a big screen in Times Square [like Xinhua] that you are necessarily going to have a lot of influence. CCTV in DC has over a hundred staff, but who watches them? I don't. What I watch is their reports on [China's] central policies, but I definitely don't watch their international coverage."

The bureau focuses on China-related news and produces some stories on culture, sports, and education. It also contributes commentaries (*pinglun*) and stories for some other columns, such as "Reporting Live" (*Di Yi Xianchang*). Usually, they file one news item (*xiaoxi*) a day and three to four stories per month, plus photos and videos. Bai does not write much for *Global Times*; when he does, it is mostly on issues he finds interesting, such as gun control and art. If he had the time, he would like to write about the American educational system: why it is set up the way it is, its positive and negative sides. But this is hard to report because you first have to spend time to understand it, read up on it. "American correspondents have a clear division of labor: some specialize in finance, some in culture, and so on. This is why they can write such in-depth stories. But Chinese correspondents are expected to write on everything. This is hard to change, because if we took two to three months to report a story, we wouldn't deliver our workload."

Bai's own tastes in journalism might appear unorthodox. Some years ago, he contributed to the Strong Country Forum (Qiangguo Luntan), an online discussion board established by *People's Daily* in 1999 that was an early gathering place of nationalist online discussion. He likes *People's Daily* and *Global Times* editorials: "They aren't as nationalistic as people think." But overall, he finds Chinese media too superficial, one-sided and biased compared to a paper like the *New York Times*. "It is perfectly normal for a paper like *People's Daily* to speak for the government. But you can only have a Chinese stance if you are very clear about the issues first. China's weight has grown too rapidly; nobody was prepared for it, including the media. The rapid change has resulted in an abnormal mentality, like a pauper who has suddenly hit it rich."

I asked Bai to explain what he meant. An example of one-sided reporting, he said, was how Chinese media reported on China's declaration of an exclusive flying zone over the Diaoyu Islands, which are disputed with Japan, in 2013.

> They said that this is the right thing to do—I agree—and reported that the Chinese government criticized [US secretary of defense] Chuck Hagel for saying that this is dangerous. But they didn't report what he actually said, whether it made sense or not, or why others oppose this move. Yes, it is normal that the media support the government, but the way they arrive at this conclusion

should be through analysis rather than just slapping a label (*kou maozi*), and this could help find a way to compromise. [Besides,] a Chinese stance may not be the same as the government's stance. The problem is that other media also want to represent China's stand. They should be a bit more independent. Old Hu [*Global Times* editor-in-chief Hu Xijin] says he represents a Chinese voice. I should say that *Global Times* has made a big contribution to the freedom of the press. But there should be other media representing other Chinese voices.

In other words, Bai tended to find the constraints of his own organization justifiable but reproached other media for not being enterprising enough. He regretted that *People's Daily* did not provide the sort of even-handed reporting he considered ideal, but he did not entertain any notions of doing so himself. He was candid and only mildly wistful about this. "This is a systemic problem (*tizhi wenti*). I can talk like this to you today, but tomorrow I'll go back to Beijing, and I'll have to talk in a different way. They [the *lingdao*] all know this, but there is nothing to be done about it: the larger framework can't be changed, because China has a top-down regime."

· · ·

"I've been here so long I sometimes forget why I am not happy," Zhang Gang told me, referring to CCTV rather than to his current posting at its major North American bureau. Though only a couple of years older than Annie, Zhang is already a chief correspondent, and this somewhat wistful comment—at odds with his confident and cheerful personality—may indicate the passing uncertainty of a successful *tizhinei* (within-the-system) journalist about his choices. After graduation and a brief stint as news assistant at a Western news agency, Zhang took a job with CCTV in the hope that their rapid overseas expansion would soon give him a chance to go abroad. His posting to one of the most important overseas stations and his rapid promotion after just four years attested to Zhang's image as a rising star, and his height and good looks add to it. One of about ten Chinese-language reporters at CCTV America, he is in a small minority compared to the 150 or so non-Chinese reporters, cameramen, and anchors who work for the English service and the Chinese editors and support staff. Accordingly, the English team has more resources and, Zhang says, also more leeway to report freely, including the ability to provide uninterrupted live coverage of important events such as the US elections. Giving up the controls that studio editing entails is still a rare occurrence at the Chinese service.

Zhang's beat is political news, including breaking domestic and foreign policy stories and relations with China. He has interviewed a number of important North American politicians. He appreciates what he calls "progressive" journalism—something he associates in part with the former crew of *Southern Weekend*—and notes that management at CCTV America recommended staff to read former *Southern Weekend* journalist Zhou Yu's book about the United States, *Democracy in Detail* (Minzhu de Xijie). But, as with many other correspondents, this appreciation for liberal Chinese journalism does not prevent him from feeling strongly about the lack of a "Chinese voice in international news," as he puts it. When US President George W. Bush gave the Dalai Lama the Congressional Medal of Honor, there was no "alternative version" of the story.

Every morning at 10:00 a.m., there is a meeting, which is led by the senior editor of the Chinese team that is in constant contact with CCTV's news center in Beijing. At these meetings about 60 percent of the stories are proposed by the head office, and the rest are proposed by staff. Most of the time the team leader approves these, and the reporters then feed them into the online approval system for formal approval by Beijing. The atmosphere in the bureau is relaxed and supportive. "Overall, we are quite free here. Everyone is very young and open-minded."

"My friends in China," Zhang says, "always ask me if what we do is produce anti-American propaganda. But that's not true." Yes, CCTV's reporting on international affairs "more or less reflects China's foreign policy road map," in the same way as the US State Department expects Voice of America or Radio Free Asia to reflect their priorities. China's current, more assertive foreign policy line, demanding a "rightful place for China in the international system," means that when CCTV reporters go to the State Department, "We want the United States to explain if they want to form a bloc around China. We ask tough questions." But there are also reporters who do soft news, including profiles of ordinary Americans that bring them closer to the Chinese viewer, like the one about a woman in New Orleans who picked up photos blown away by Hurricane Katrina and tried to get them back to their owners. "Actually, we are humble storytellers. These stories show the best of human nature." There have been stories on technological advances in Hollywood and on how farmers in Iowa preserve corn.

Zhang believes most Chinese have a love-hate relationship with the United States: a very negative view of American foreign policy—"stirring up shit"—but an overly positive one of life in the United States, as if copying it were a panacea to all China's problems. At the same time, Chinese people "are crazy about US TV dramas and absorb individualistic American values from them." Ideally, he would like to correct both sides of the picture. He is also interested in doing more long reports like the one on lobbying, to introduce US institutions, the independence of the judiciary, or the watchdog function of the media. But time slots longer than two to three minutes are hard to come by.

Also, as a CCTV correspondent commented, "it is smart to propose stories that will be approved, otherwise it can be very frustrating." In his early days in America, Zhang did a story that was not fully approved. It was a story on lobbying, one of the feature stories produced for the Labor Day holidays in May. (Such features are usually broadcast during longer holiday periods.) The studio interview with the convicted US lobbyist Jack Abramoff after his release from prison, in which he talked about how he bribed politicians, was well received by the *lingdao*. But the other half of the story, illustrating the positive side of lobbying on a case of people living along a planned oil pipeline successfully pressuring politicians to suspend construction, was cut. Sensitivity to stories on environmental protest is rather specific to Chinese media censorship, but Zhang's take on the intervention was that "in Western coverage of China, it is also conflicts and controversies that dominate." At the same time, and somewhat contradictorily, he suggested that CCTV, like other Chinese media, wanted "to set a positive tone for the US–China relationship," and in this way they differed from their Western counterparts.

If Zhang's views on news reporting seem somewhat conflicted, so are his ambitions for the future. He brushes off my query about his chances as a *lingdao*: "I am completely uninterested in becoming an official." Yet, in the next breath, he says he would enjoy being the press secretary to a future leader of China and help him "really engage" with foreign media, "the way Jen Psaki or Josh Earnest do" as spokespersons for the White House.

RUNNING YOUR OWN SHOP

Tom picks me up at 9:00 a.m. at my hotel in the capital of a small African country with a troubled history of relations with the West and strong ties to China. We end up spending the better part of the day together driving around the city. I remark that the place does not feel as sinister and the repression is not as obvious as I would have expected from Western media reports. Although I mean it, the remark is also intended as bait. Will Xinhua's local chief, in a city where no other major news agencies are present, rise to the occasion and complain about Western media bias in the way Annie did? But Tom makes a face and shakes his head skeptically. He acknowledges that there are opposition posters in the street, but says that many people are very careful of criticizing the government when he interviews them.

Tom joined Xinhua's Foreign Department in the mid-2000s as a fresh foreign language graduate of a prestigious Chinese university. His first job, as with most new recruits, was "translation and editing" (*bianyi*), a term that refers largely to the rewriting of reports in other media, with some occasional interviewing. He was posted to Africa as bureau chief—albeit at a bureau whose only other Chinese staff member is Tom's wife, for whom this is the first time overseas after a period of *bianyi* work. Like Annie, Tom's wife, Wu Fei, underwent six months of "socialization" at a Xinhua bureau in one of China's northern provinces as a "frontline journalist" (*yixian jizhe*), a term originally derived from the Maoist vocabulary of class struggle but that now means more something like "getting one's feet dirty." Such tours of duty have recently been made mandatory for all prospective foreign correspondents. Some appreciated theirs and saw it as a valuable introduction to real reporting work; others saw it as akin to the "rustication" of educated youth during the Cultural Revolution, designed, in the words of a critical Xinhua editor, to "get rid of the foreign bullshit" they had been taught in college.

Tom, as a journalist with some seniority compared to Annie, had some room to negotiate his posting. He chose this location over one in Northern Europe—which he was afraid would be too cold, empty, and lacking in news—and Cairo, which he decided against because that would have been at a regional bureau, "too close to the *lingdao*." Here, Tom is his own master, and, since it is considered a hardship post, he and his wife can apply to go home after two years instead of four. Another argument they can throw in for an early return is that they plan to have a child, and Xinhua has an unspoken rule against staff having children abroad. Once the child is born, foreign postings will become tricky because if he or she is to have any chance of success in university entrance examinations, the child will have to attend school in China.

Although making a correspondent report to her own husband as station chief seems awkward to me, Tom explains that at small bureaus in Africa it is common to post either a single reporter or a married couple, because two unrelated people sharing a house would inevitably get into conflicts. Sometimes, if the wife is not a Xinhua employee but is qualified to do the job, she helps out as a temporary reporter. The agency regards couples as one unit, so there is no formal division of tasks. And Tom and his wife appear much happier than another Chinese correspondent in town, in charge of a bureau that comprises, apart from himself, a female reporter who is there with her child, which is an unusual arrangement. He never expected to be posted to Africa and clearly cannot wait for his three-year term to end so that he can go home. "There are a lot of personal issues," he complains. "I am getting old, and work is just one part of life," a reference to his unmarried state.

One advantage of working in such a place is that the annual performance review is not very strict. Although all correspondents are evaluated according to a point system, Tom's bosses recognize that the couple has many other responsibilities, such as supervising the two local reporters (called *baodaoyuan*, rather than *jizhe*, the term used for Chinese staff), taking care of the villa that serves as office and residence, maintaining the rickety infrastructure, and ensuring security, which includes keeping three German shepherds. Still, every month, Tom receives a chart that shows how many times each story and photo filed by his bureau has been picked up by media. Most of the station's output, of which 90 percent is in English, is sold to media in the region as "Chinese readers are not very interested." As station chief, Tom also has sales responsibilities, and sometimes has to chase late payments. In addition, he has to monitor and report how many times local media uses Xinhua stories.

Reliance on local staff distinguishes Chinese media operations in Africa from those on other continents. Although Xinhua and CCTV bureaus have started to "localize" their operations, non-Chinese staff are typically employed to produce news in foreign languages, and, until recently, many local employees have been ethnic Chinese. Newspapers, so far, do not employ local staff; a *People's Daily* journalist said such plans existed but the procedures were too complicated. But while some correspondents wish they had local assistants, not all are enthusiastic. A correspondent for *Guangming Daily*, for example, said disdainfully:

> There is no way I am going to employ a foreigner and then have him pester
> me about human rights and freedoms all day. I have a schoolmate who does
> video reports for Xinhua, he went with a local employee to do an interview,
> then at 4:00 or 5:00 p.m., he says he has to go back because the [local] camera-

man wants to go back. I said if it were my employee I would have fired him a long time ago. Employees here talk to me about eight [working] hours or whatever! If I work till midnight you have to wait till midnight too. It's all rubbish. You have these problems if you employ foreigners.

Where there are local employees, their role is much more limited than at the foreign bureaus of Western media, where resourceful assistants and "fixers" are often critical to "scoops" and, to an extent, determine how events are framed. When local assistants are relied upon for sources—most frequently at CCTV—unfamiliarity with the local context can lead to misjudging the suitability of the sources they propose. For example, for a story on the commemoration of the sixtieth anniversary of D-Day in Britain, a cameraman, who happened to be Polish, suggested interviewing a compatriot who, he said, participated in the Normandy landing. The reporter he worked for did not ask why a Pole was in the expeditionary force but simply accepted the suggestion. In Africa, local staff is usually highly experienced and in a position to influence the framing of stories, but the stories they file are limited to foreign-language services and rarely make it into the Chinese news reports.

Although Xinhua is the only international news bureau in town, Tom is actually not sure that his operation is worth the investment.

> Maybe, but not necessarily, because Reuters and AP have very good, very experienced local stringers. AP's local correspondent is a veteran white journalist who used to be in exile together with the president [in colonial times]. The Reuters correspondent is a former top manager of the state news agency. They got the best journalists; our local staff is also OK, perhaps mid-level in terms of skills or slightly above. It's easy to get them because local media doesn't have money. So Xinhua can give some struggling local journalists a platform. So we need them, and they need us. But the help I can give is too little. Many of the better ones have left and are now freelancing elsewhere in Africa.

Like Liu Ying, Tom describes his work as that of a correspondent who strives to do professional work within the constraints of an institution that does not always provide the best conditions for it but, on the whole, is increasingly like other major news agencies. His personal favorite is AP, whose writing he finds better and the facts more carefully checked than Reuters'. He also finds the BBC's and the *New York Times* reporting on Africa "very professional." Liu Ying's comments implied criticism of the broader system, though not of Xinhua, and Annie was, in a conflicted way, both committed to and critical of Xinhua's mission. Tom, in contrast, just does not seem very interested. He tends to deflect questions about his agency's role as the Communist Party's mouthpiece by making light of it and emphasizing instead the importance of selling a good product.

> There may be temporary setbacks, but if you look at it over a ten-year period, then things are improving. Ten years ago, if Xinhua didn't cover an event in a foreign country, then Chinese readers didn't know about it. Now, if there is an important story by a foreign wire or BBC, then in five hours, someone will translate it and it will be on the *Global Times* or the CNS website, and if we haven't covered it the leadership will ask why. So we feel pressure. In this sense, there is real competition among the central media, including for budget allocations. . . . Xinhua has to keep its "throat and tongue" function because the Chinese government does not have a proper system of spokesmen and timely press releases like in the US. If that improves, then Xinhua can gradually shed this function. . . .
>
> I remember a veteran reporter told me when [I] joined the trade that as a reporter there is no *jinqu* [taboo]: file whatever you want to file as it does not really matter whether the angles and the content are appropriate—there are editors and releasers who do all the checks and considerations. Reporters just [have to] make sure they got the facts right. . . . [W]e can always keep the desk informed and they decide whether to publish, what to publish according to the Marxist news perspective [*Makesizhuyi xinwenguan*].

Tom's reply appeared to carry some dose of tongue-in-cheek irony and considerable self-distancing. He displayed a similar attitude when both of us attended a talk by a visiting scholar from China and agreed afterwards that some of his comments had been formulaic and condescending. Yet as station chief, and because a greater share of reporting from Africa concerned China's policies than in Europe, Tom appears more involved in Xinhua's ideological function, if only because he has to write, or approve, a number of reports on events organized by the Chinese embassy or visiting government delegations. Shortly after my visit, Xinhua's director, Li Congjun, in an article published in *People's Daily*, identified "enthusiastically promoting the policies of our Party and government, energetically criticizing the untruthful discourse of Western media, [and] strengthening [our] international discursive power"[3] as the main task for the agency's "discourse work" (*yulun gongzuo*). He pointed out that "insisting on the principle of partisanship is the most important condition of firmly grasping the initiative in discourse work,"[4] and stated that "the principle of partisanship must not be lost, must not be forgotten; there must absolutely not be a shred of confusion, aloofness or wavering about this."[5] The article said nothing of the previously much-touted effort to make Xinhua a globally competitive news agency.

It is true that Li's article was written against the background of the overall political and cultural tightening undertaken by the new Party leader, Xi Jinping, and thus could plausibly be read as an attempt to polish his credentials. In this, he followed Hu Zhanfan, the new president of CCTV, who reportedly said that "journalists who think of themselves as professionals, instead of as propaganda workers, are making a fundamental mistake about identity."[6] Seven years earlier, the editors of a volume entitled *How to Be an International News Editor* had also described correspondents as soldiers and editors as generals of an information war.[7] Nonetheless, Li's stridency seemed at odds with the discourse of gradual professionalization that Tom and many of his colleagues presented to me. Indeed, like many journalists who bristle at the suggestion that *People's Daily* is China's most authoritative news medium, Tom appeared miffed by the fact that Li published his comments there rather than choosing one of Xinhua's own outlets. Were his and Hu's statements just the usual obeisances to the "spirit of the Central Committee" or did they mark the end of the emphasis on building professionalism within the limits of loyalty to the Party that had dominated the previous two decades? Were they, as increasingly seemed to be the case with other kinds of cultural production, a declaration that the previous unspoken consensus by which media lived—the government will tolerate you as long as you do not attack it directly and perform certain expected tokens of obedience—was invalid?

Along with many other Xinhua reporters I talked to, Tom did not think so, at least at the time—although a series of trainings for journalists on the "Marxist news perspective" and attacking the idea of impartial objectivity was in full swing.[8] When I asked him about Li's article, he said he had not heard about it. He told me he got wind of the latest "spirit" at half-yearly work conferences that define work for the next half-year. These are first done at the head office and then at the regional bureaus, where the regional director interprets and operationalizes Li's remarks and translates them into a number of practical points, such as, in 2013, focusing on the end users and new media, specifically on mobile apps—another Xi priority. There were no political "study sessions" at the work conferences. The way he understood it, Li's political course seemed to be of little relevance to his daily work.

In the beginning of his time in Africa, Tom kept filing political stories in Chinese that were rejected by the editors as uninteresting for Chinese readers. Later he figured out what sort of stories were accepted: mostly to do with relations with China, or else social and cultural topics. By the time of my visit, his most widely read Chinese story, and the one he was most satisfied with, was on a poaching incident where a large number of elephants were killed. This story was used by wildlife protection activists China in an anti-ivory campaign and therefore had a high "pickup rate" by online media. Moreover, it corresponded to Tom's own interests in nature conservation, humanitarianism, and human rights, by which he meant not primarily political but social rights such as access to clean water, food, and medical care. "First of all, a journalist informs, but a good journalist also enlightens through his reporting and makes people think about issues such as environmental protection, water access and so on."

Tom's interests were visible in some of his interviewing that I witnessed. For example, in an interview with an African official, he asked whether he was worried about the environmental costs of industrialization and whether African leaders had the political will to manage environmental problems. But Tom has not done any in-depth stories on conservation or health, and his stories with the highest pickup rates tended to be about air crashes and other disasters. Stories on health or the environment are difficult to do, because travelling to rural areas is costly, locals do not speak English, and it is hard to build rapport. What about religion, then—a striking feature of public life in the country? There was no ban on writing about religion, Tom said, but no reporter or editor dared to touch it for fear of offending someone. It seemed, I reflected, that Xinhua was worried about offending nearly anyone except Japan and the United States.

As for national politics, apart from major events such as elections, only top stories such as an interview with top officials would attract sufficient interest in China, and although Chinese journalists may have more access to them than Western colleagues, local journalists have the most access, and the other big agencies use local journalists. In addition, whatever the country's leaders say about the United States, the president gave the *New York Times* the only exclusive interview before the last election, because of the paper's global influence. Tom himself relies on Google and Yahoo news alerts to keep up with what is happening in the country. Often, too, he finds something of interest in Britain's *Daily Telegraph*, which he then asks his local staff to check with their sources.

In line with Xinhua's effort to provide more business information for Chinese investors, he has also been doing more stories on new business regulations. Some of these stories, written for a mobile Chinese-language app on African news launched in 2013, are directly approved and posted by the editors at the regional bureau in Nairobi instead of being sent back to Beijing. Yet Tom has not done any major reports on Chinese companies active in the country, for reasons similar to those mentioned by Lynne in New York. "We do report on Chinese investments, but we can't talk about [the companies'] internal affairs—that's a matter of journalistic ethics. And they may not be cooperative; they are quite media-shy." After a few conversations in which I kept returning to the question why there aren't more in-depth stories on these issues, a somewhat exasperated Tom replied: "Investigative journalism should be nurtured by a proper internal management system of the media organization and specific editorial guidelines but not depend on individual Robin Hoods. . . . By the way, I know for sure that I am not a fearless investigative reporter. You may find others who are and can ask why they did not jump ship to Caixin under Madam Hu [Shuli] to pursue that career."

Once, Tom interviewed a Chinese researcher who had conducted a survey of attitudes to Chinese companies in Africa. The survey concluded that Africans' views towards these companies were mixed, but more positive than towards Western companies. Although much earlier research by African and Western scholars suggests the opposite, and even a local Xinhua employee insisted that labor conditions in Chinese companies in the country were far worse than in Western companies but "for obvious reasons we are not going out to get such information," the story did not mention this. Tom, however, did not refer to those "obvious reasons" when I asked him why. He replied: "I think there is no problem if I put the background you mentioned into the story. I just took it for granted that everyone who cares to read the story knows the criticism very well already." He added that while Western wires were more consistent about adding such background to stories, Xinhua did so only in some cases. "It has to do with professionalism and rigorous training. After all, adding background, explanations, framing stories should really be more the job of editors. Reporters send facts, quotes, ground information to the desk as fast as possible, before editors get off duty. I admit there are loops here and there to be fixed by editors. I would try my best to ensure Xinhua has a story. The desk's job is to make it a better story."

THE PECKING ORDER: STATUS, RANK, AND RATINGS

As the profiles in this chapter show, each correspondent faces a different set of local, institutional, and personal circumstances and finds different ways of dealing reconciling these with her ambitions or ideals. Although the lifeworlds of *tizhinei* versus commercial media journalists are rather starkly different, each state media socializes its correspondents in slightly different ways, which are again differently inflected depending on the location, the size of the bureau, and the personality of the bureau chief, among other factors. Across media organizations, a cohort of ambitious mid-level managers in their forties with experience either studying or working abroad and often an agenda of changing existing ways of working has been on the rise. CCTV's regional bureau chiefs, several of whom have been women with backgrounds in the English or French service, have generally enjoyed an "open-minded" or "progressive" reputation among like-minded young correspondents. An ex-director of CRI's African regional bureau, who had been an anchor of the English service, used to say that more criticism of China could sometimes mean more help, otherwise if people only heard praise they would not believe it and tune out.

Whatever journalists might think of their organization, their institutional identities tend to be strong, and intra-institutional personal networks within a cohort are a crucial resource for journalists to get things done. Some media organizations encourage and even help shape such networks. CCTV, for example, runs boot camps (*tuozhan xunlian*, literally "development trainings") for new staff with the express goal of forging close relations among them and teaching them to rely on each other. As a correspondent told me, without such connections it takes three days to get archive footage for a news story through the official channels, so when he is in a hurry it is crucial that he has a friend from boot camp working in the archive.

To be sure, cohort-based networks are generally strong in China, and friendships among former classmates, especially at the large journalism programs such as China University of Communications (CUC), can also cut across media divides. One CCTV correspondent I talked to has remained good friends with his classmate who became a commercial media journalist highly critical of central media and the government. The same networks can also run beyond media, into corporate public relations and government. A correspondent's college friendship with an army spokesman allowed him to involve his friend in live broadcasts. A young attaché in Africa, one of whose jobs was to write the ambassador's speeches, had a background similar to many journalists—a degree from CUC, an internship with a Western news agency—and her experiences turned her away from journalism. She found the expatriate correspondents she was helping were forced to deal with China because of its economic power, but had a distaste of the country and discriminated against Chinese staff because they felt they represented an authoritarian state. She had the ambition to represent China, but working for the central media would have made her just a propaganda hack in Westerners' eyes. "So instead of that, why not be on the inside and be a spokesperson for the government?"

Institutional identities are strengthened by a pecking order that is largely unquestioned. Circulation, audience ratings, and advertising revenues have created a ranking of media outlets that is roughly market-based, even though it is manipulated by government institutions in numerous ways, of which the channeling of advertisers and compulsory subscriptions are just some of the most obvious. Despite the subsidies they receive, central media organizations are expected to compete in this new ranking. But the political pecking order, which defines the closeness of media organizations to the center of power and was set down at or even before the founding of the People's Republic of China, has in no way been rendered obsolete. Not only are Xinhua and *People's Daily* institutionally higher-ranked and therefore in possession of administrative privileges compared to other media. The fact that correspondents of these two outlets always have privileged and sometimes exclusive access to top officials and the leaders of the largest corporations, including during foreign trips, means that they often have insider information others do not. Although they do not make that information public, they may, in principle, utilize it to access the ears of selected decision makers, or even to inform them of wrongdoings—a kind of internal watchdog function that is now diminished but not gone. Much as their competitors and friends from other media may make fun of their antiquated rules, stilted language and propagandistic obligations, this fact sets those privileged journalists apart. The political capital that such positions represent has, at least in principle, consequences for economic value. While commercial media generate revenue by preparing tailor-made reports on economic issues, Xinhua and *People's Daily* journalists "sit" on potentially highly valuable information they cannot market.

Moreover, these two organizations are also reputed to have the best welfare provisions among central (or any) media, since all correspondents are state employees, referred to as *biannei*, roughly corresponding to the old term *nomenklatura*: staff within the purview of the state and Party apparatus that can, above a certain level, in principle be transferred to any, including non-media, posts. At CCTV, many correspondents are now *bianwai* (non-*nomenklatura*), or as the station prefers to refer to them, *qipin*: employed by CCTV's corporate arm. *Bianwai* employees tend to believe, and resent, that the welfare privileges of *biannei* staff (medical care, pensions, bonuses, non-monetary rewards) are far above their own. Although some *biannei* correspondents dismiss this view as exaggerated and suggest that the resentment they experience from *bianwai* colleagues far outweighs the actual benefits, they remain administratively higher-ranked and psychologically more secure in their positions, a significant benefit in a society where insecurity about the future is overwhelming.[9] There is also some evidence that *biannei* employees' personal preferences are accommodated more than *bianwai* employees' when it comes to choosing or extending a posting. For example, the longest-serving correspondent at CCTV's London bureau is a *biannei* employee whose daughter has been studying in England.

On the other hand, no correspondent these days is completely immune to the pressure of performance ratings. This is heaviest on television, where audience figures are constantly monitored and broken down by news segment. In other media, there is a range of frequently adjusted and often complex performance assessment models, some of which focus more on quantity of output while others are more sensitive to the nature, depth, online traffic generated, or quality (as assessed by editors or internal evaluation boards) of the stories. In CRI's evaluation system, for example, so-called audio reports, which contain at least three sound bites and may be used by the company's other language services or channels, are worth between five and ten points. Short on-air news reports, equivalent to up to five hundred Chinese characters, are worth one to three points. Live call-ins by program hosts are worth five to eight points. Depending on the category, however, points are assigned by two different organizational units, and correspondents tend to believe that despite the differentiation, the system rewards quantity more than quality.

In recent years, CCTV has made adjustments to counter such criticism. "We used to give a point for any material the correspondents sent. Now, if it is useless, it gets no points. If it is something very basic, it can get 0.2 to half a point. Better or more complete material, but also material obtained at higher risk—going to dangerous areas, for example—gets more points. This is all to encourage people to report live," Director Pan Linhua of CCTV's international news department explained. "Packages" of footage and text earn between two and six points. The points are assigned by the producers of the channels. Based on whether the packages are deemed good, the bureau chief decides on the correspondent's bonus, which can be up to 50 percent of the base pay. But correspondents who do not respond to breaking news on time can be punished, both through fines and criticism. In addition, three special "reviewers" (*jiankanren*) watch every report and sometimes send back comments that land on *lingdaos'* desks and, along with periodical audience rating reports, may influence a correspondent's chances for promotion. Since 2013, CCTV has in part moved away from the process of online filing of "packages" to be processed by duty editors, which one bureau chief described as "completely mechanical" and resulting in waste, especially at busy times. Instead, foreign correspondents can now work directly with program producers under a framework provided by the Special Reports Group (Tebie Baodaozu). This means that correspondents can plan their reporting better and spend less time on short video bites.

People's Daily journalists generally face less pressure of this nature, in part because of the paper's limited capacity for international news relative to the number of correspondents. They, too, work with a point system, but one in which, according to one bureau chief, a story can get extra points for "promoting the Chinese stance." But, as explained earlier, pressures of a different nature mean they still have little room to pursue in-depth reporting. Until recently, the few senior international desk journalists at commercial media with an established reputation have had the most room to pursue in-depth reporting with the least pressure for deadlines or quantity, even if their opportunities to travel abroad were limited. One former *Southern Weekend* journalist travelled abroad twice a year, but on one of those trips he spent fifty days in the Middle East. He wrote only features, two or three a month, with no further obligations, an arrangement almost unparalleled in Chinese media. By 2014, however, as room for journalism outside the official line diminished simultaneously with printed media sales, such arrangements came to an end.

IN THE COMPOUND

The floor plan at CCTV's overseas bureaus has a definite corporate feel. The specificities of Chinese state media become visible only upon closer inspection. During my visit to CCTV America, in one corner of the open-floor workspace, an American producer was telling his team about the day's news program. The main theme was corruption and how China was fighting it. The producer was stressing that they were not to show any images of Zhou Yongkang, the former top security official who had just been expelled from the Party.

In contrast, Xinhua's regional bureaus—always headed by men—feel much more like socialist "work units." When I was invited to give a talk about my research at Xinhua's Africa bureau, I was asked to speak in Chinese because the kitchen staff would also be in attendance. Before the talk, I shared the staff's simple dinner. It consisted of kung pao chicken, cauliflower, rice, porridge, and leftover fish and steamed buns from the previous day, served in large enamel basins. Carrying their own enamel bowls, staff helped themselves, and no more than fifteen minutes later got up again to rinse their dishes. The scene would not have been very different in a 1970s factory.

Under the previous bureau chief, one night a week had been dumpling-wrapping night: all staff rolled, wrapped, and boiled dumplings together, in northern Chinese fashion. This was meant as a team-building exercise as well as a way to diversify staff diet and to alleviate homesickness. The new bureau chief discontinued it, as a young technician explains, because the "old comrades over forty" have left and the young people did not know how to make dumplings, so too much food went to waste.

Unlike CCTV, Xinhua's foreign bureaus have no *qipin* staff, so the psychological benefits of the "selective paternalism" afforded by a state work unit accrue to all Chinese employees.[10] In contrast, it is as if local employees inhabited a different world. Chinese colleagues usually refer to them collectively as "the locals," and African journalists, even those most enthusiastic about their jobs with a Chinese media outlet, refer to their bosses and co-workers as "the Chinese." Career tracks for Chinese and African colleagues are distinct. The former generally responds to more or less implicit rules and incentives that govern career advancement within and potentially across central media organizations, while the latter is framed in financial and professional terms and rarely points beyond Africa.

Although the bureau has about as many Kenyan as Chinese staff—around thirty each—the locals are absent from the compound after working hours, and even during the daytime, they work principally at a city office. Africa stays outside the compound's gates. Like the temporary settlements put up for Chinese workers on construction projects across Africa, the compound is a piece of China. But every now and then, as on the construction projects, some of Xinhua's Chinese support staff decide to go into private business. One former marketing employee now lives in a big house in the affluent Western suburbs of Nairobi and, along with a Kenyan partner, runs a business manufacturing and selling souvenirs to Chinese tourists. What complicates this is that her husband still works at Xinhua, and is thus technically required to return to the compound every night before the curfew. He is also involved in the business and explains that they want to help local craftsmen market their work. Many Chinese, he says, are not satisfied with the low-quality crafts they find at local markets and want something better, but "Western colonizers" either take the better materials out of the country or own the good workshops and have crafts made according to their designs. They commission beadwork from Maasai craftswomen and barter them for sun-powered LED lamps. The husband, an avid amateur photographer, has made a film about these settled agriculturalist Maasai. But, in fact, most of the crafts they sell are either imported or made in a workshop on their own premises.

My talk is attended by about ten people: everyone who is in the compound shows up. (The bureau chief and most editors are having dinner outside.) The audience is attentive, and there are many questions, including from the cooks. There is an atmosphere of curiosity and equal exchange. A correspondent says postings abroad are an opportunity for young people to open their minds and sit down and talk to people with views they would not have heard at home. A young man from the new media department, in charge of selecting stories for a newly launched mobile app, seconds her, saying this opening of minds is rare in China. Many people, he says, asked him why he wanted to come to Africa. "To be honest, I didn't. But now I am happy with it: look, I am even wearing their national dress," he says, pointing at his tie-died shirt.

By next morning, the compound would have a different atmosphere, dominated by the work of the English-language team. Incoming stories would be collected and assigned by the shift supervisor. There would be a brief informal discussion among the five English-language releasers about dividing tasks; this was largely ad hoc, except that West African stories were usually assigned to the same veteran editor. The releasers would watch the morning news on the newsroom's single television screen in the morning, and would then turn it to mute for the rest of the day. Most of the time, the TV was tuned to CNN, sometimes to the BBC, and sometimes to a Kenyan station. The releasers would also glance at the morning's *International New York Times* and the week's copies of *Jeune Afrique* and the BBC's *Africa* magazine. (Local correspondents often listened to local radio while driving, as radio usually quickly reported local news, and sometimes they would go to the scene if they heard something important.) Online, they usually checked Reuters, AP, and AllAfrica.com, a news aggregator, and if they saw important news that had not yet come in from Xinhua reporters they would alert them or the respective bureau chiefs. This was the releasers' other important task in addition to editing, following up and releasing the stories, and was called "mending tires" (*butai*), a pun based on the homophonous characters for "tire" and "TV station" (*tai*).

Every Thursday, the main planned topics for the next week were reported to Beijing, and a summary was printed out for the staff. Like at CCTV, the regional bureau chief would hold staff meetings to evaluate the stories of the past week. The bureau chief at the time, Wang Chaowen, had joined the French service in the early 1980s and was then promoted to senior marketing positions. Wang had the French news channel, France 24, running in his office, and kept a close tab on whether Xinhua stories were getting out fast enough. The three main indicators of success, he emphasized to his staff, were being the first to report a story, pickup rate by local media, and originality (as opposed to following other news sources). When he left Nairobi to lead Xinhua's European regional bureau, his staff presented him with a scrapbook containing clippings of Xinhua stories from African newspapers. Although Xinhua has made visible inroads in African media, some of Wang's former staff dispute not only the economic but also the political value of that fact, pointing out that most of the stories African media picked up tended to be lurid or fantastic (in the words of one journalist, "unnatural and antisocial") reports such as about a putative sighting of two suns or about an individual who had two sex change operations.

I caught up with Wang soon after he took up his new station in Brussels, an office building near the European Commission's headquarters that Xinhua built in 2006. There was no contradiction between Xinhua's market orientation and its partisanship, he told me. Xinhua represents China in the same way AFP represents France as it is funded by the French state. The Chinese Communist Party is China's ruling party, therefore representing China means representing the Party. At the same time, in order to build credibility, Xinhua had to be objective, fair, accurate, and timely. Wang stressed, in particular, that it was not acceptable to use materials from other media sources without indicating the source—a practice that had apparently not been uncommon in the past—and that all information had to be carefully verified.

Furthermore, Wang continued, "If we want to be influential, we need foreigners to write the stories" for the foreign-language wires. He attributed the inroads made by Xinhua into African newspapers to the hiring of local staff, and planned to promote the practice in Europe, even if some Chinese staff will miss out on postings in Europe. "Even if it means retrenching Chinese staff, we still have to do it, because a Chinese person simply cannot write as well as a foreigner in his mother tongue." Two years later, Xinhua had some two hundred local stringers across Europe, with two "polishers" and a senior Chinese correspondent in Brussels in charge of "guiding" their reporting and editing the stories they filed.

As for the requirement that Xinhua represent a "Chinese perspective," he continued, "naturally, as patriotic Chinese people, every single one of us hopes for the world to understand China and for China to understand the world better, regardless of any requirement." He did not elaborate on how he envisages accomplishing the former, except to say that "unlike some [Western] media, we definitely won't exaggerate small matters and reduce the significance of large issues." (The information on Wang's own reporting available on Xinhua's webpage states that he "interviewed world famous people, took risks to enter African jungles and war-torn areas multiple times, and visited the land of the African pygmies.") What Wang felt strongly about was the need for the world, or perhaps more specifically Westerners, "to understand China better. Western media's understanding of China is twisted, unfair, superficial; it never reports anything good. What if we only reported on the red light district or drug addicts in Amsterdam but not on Holland's economic successes? Western media always report that Tibet is not part of China. But these young journalists don't know our history. I can guarantee you that a European leader wouldn't even be able to manage one of China's provinces."

Back at the headquarters in Beijing, the editors of Xinhua's Chinese-language international department are divided into four groups: politics (*shizheng*), economy (*jingji*), society and culture (*shewen*), and review (*guancha*, also known as in-depth, *shendu*), a group in charge of longer, analytical articles. Their work is organized similarly to their colleagues in the English service in Nairobi. In the morning, there is a short meeting, led by the shift supervisors and releasers, about the key stories of the day. In addition to following up on the incoming stories, the editors' other main task is to translate stories from foreign wires Xinhua subscribes to, if these are important enough to release in Chinese. But the share of this work is decreasing as there is more original material, and if stories are translated, this is usually done by foreign correspondents. Sometimes, one of the duty editors is assigned to monitor the foreign wires and television (mostly CNN, but also BBC, Phoenix, and CCTV). What sources an editor ends up monitoring often depends on personal habits, such as whether he or she is used to American or British English. Work at the review group is different: much of it involves planning, contacting correspondents, and sometimes writing articles based on sources from different locations. Politics is the largest group: it releases forty to fifty stories every day and has two night shifts. At 6:00 a.m., the duty editor of what is known as the "long night shift" prepares a note for the day shift on the day's major anticipated stories.

POSITIVE NEWS?

It may be due as much to their relatively few years on the job than any specificity of Chinese media that most correspondents I talked to did not reflect much on just what constituted news for the purposes of their particular assignments. For news agency staff, this was perhaps the most natural: beyond breaking news, news releases of national governments and major international organizations, and the activities of Chinese delegations, there was generally little time for much else. Financial journalists reported on business, and that was that. But even correspondents for other print media did not have their own news agendas in the sense of following particular unfolding stories. This differentiated them from the experienced, older correspondents for Western media studied by Ulf Hannerz, but also from the senior China-based feature writers specialized in international issues, a number of whom have followed stories such as the Arab Spring, reform in Burma and Vietnam, and North Korean politics over a number of years.

Part of the problem was that many unfolding local news stories were considered insufficiently newsworthy for Chinese audiences, and more often than not, their place was taken by reportage that was deemed relevant for China but not necessarily related to any recent development. Yet these negotiations were treated as practical matters to be resolved, rather than issues related to the core of what news journalism means.

This fact was all the more remarkable since, as discussed in Chapter 1, many journalists, editors, media *lingdao*, and government officials recognized setting news agendas and remedying the hitherto overly reactive stance of Chinese media as a crucial task for its global expansion. Yet that task was not perceived as one for individual reporters. It is perhaps this fact that prompted critical comments from some central media correspondents about the general state of foreign news reporting. In the view of a few of these journalists, their colleagues used the lack of freedom as an excuse for a lack of initiative. Among others, I encountered such criticism from a CCTV and a *China Daily* correspondent in Africa, leveled principally at Xinhua journalists for "just translating from local employees and not doing anything" on their own. In contrast to them, the CCTV reporter insisted, "We are very good at dancing with handcuffs. We know what story we can tell and that at the same time we *want* to tell—in a way that the editors will accept." Yet while these two correspondents may have taken more individual initiative, they did not elaborate what a news agenda that goes beyond that of Western media, which both insisted were biased, might be. In this respect, there was little difference between those who saw their job as the objective reporting of news, those who believed that objectivity was impossible because all media had an agenda, and those who embraced both views at various times or at once.

A look at reporting from Africa can serve as an illustration of this phenomenon. One might expect new journalistic agendas emerge from reporting from Africa because here Chinese media presence is relatively heavy while that of their Western counterparts is fairly sparse, and because, on the other hand, the low priority assigned to and limited knowledge about Africa among China's media censors seem to offer journalists room to experiment. (Several correspondents commented that limits on reporting were more relaxed than in China.) Moreover, Chinese officials have been particularly emphatic about the need for Chinese media to pioneer a new news agenda in Africa. At a seminar on Chinese-African media cooperation in 2013, China's ambassador to Kenya—in a speech that may have been written by the former Reuters intern—called the monopoly of "the international media discourse" by a "small number of countries" an "ongoing conspiracy." He then went on to define a "Chinese perspective" in an unusually specific and direct way. He declared it was

> unacceptable to continue to portray Africa as a continent overtaken by poverty, war and turmoil. It is also unethical to force a bad image on China-Africa relations. Indeed, China and Africa should flatly refuse to be part of this insincere scheme. . . . [M]ore and more Chinese media groups are setting camp in Africa. They have gradually changed the rules of the game and created a regime, in which Africa is positively presented to the world. I call this "the Chinese perspective.". . . [O]ur media should report China-Africa friendship positively. . . . It is normal for others to both admire and be suspicious about the current China-Africa relations. But this must not be in the case among the Chinese and African media players.[11]

Central media editors and *lingdao* often mention this need for a different voice, one that could counterbalance Western media's emphasis on the ills of the continent, and offer a balanced view on the opportunities Africa offers. Most of them refer to positive reporting, a style of journalism that focuses on collective achievements rather than divisive issues or sensational news. Some claim the need for a new form of developmental journalism. Print and agency journalists sometimes mention examples of positive stories of Africa. *China Daily*'s Nairobi correspondent, for example, has written features on Rwanda's IT boom. A Xinhua correspondent recalled:

> I was in Kampala in 2011 to cover the AU [African Union] summit, which focused on health, together with the AP stringer, a Westerner. I filed twenty stories; he filed two. Our main story was how infant and childbirth mortality figures had improved, because this was the focus of the summit. We were also paying attention to the aftermath of the recent terror attacks in Kampala and to whether the AU was going to send troops to Somalia. But the AP correspondent didn't write about health at all; he said this was not newsworthy. This is a difference in attitude: if you compare infant mortality to the West, then it is not news, but if you compare it to the past, then it is.

Yet it is not clear to what extent such reporting can be said to have set new agendas or shifted journalism in a more "positive" direction. Content analyzes of CCTV's and Xinhua's English-language reporting on Africa provide little indication of this agenda having taken root. Indeed, they find that conflict-related news is either equally or more prominent in CCTV's report-ing than in that of its competitors.[12] In line with the ambassador's admoni-tion, it is in the coverage of China-Africa relations that a positive approach can be discerned.

Indeed, when asked for examples of positive reporting, several CCTV journalists mentioned the BBC documentary *The Chinese Are Coming* as a negative benchmark of reporting on China-Africa relations against which their own reporting stood out. The documentary, in their view, focused on conflicts between Chinese managers and local workers at Zambian copper mines, but failed to convey how Chinese investment gave these mines a new lease on life and returned former miners to their jobs after years of driving taxis. *The Chinese Are Coming*, they charged, depicted Chinese-owned mines as responsible for environmental damage and resource plundering without any mention of how non-Chinese-owned mines in the area scored on the same counts. Yet none of the journalists took the opportunity to rectify this perceived bias and exploit their advantages, including access to Chinese companies, to attempt to produce a more nuanced picture. Overall, then, one can conclude that institutional constraints override the opportunities to experiment with agenda-setting if it would require departing too far from existing practices. It is possible that, as one central media correspondent in Africa suggested in an e-mail, this was because of insufficient knowledge and experience of the continent. "Even if they want[ed] to be professional or take a side, the problem is they are unable to. Because their knowledge and understanding on this continent is superficial and shallow, which may easily lead to an extreme report[ing] influenced by either Western rhetoric or [the] central government's propaganda."

As a result, an overarching narrative that could rally African and Chi-nese journalists behind a common purpose seems to be lacking. Although uneasiness towards the ways in which some international media portray Africa is a shared feeling, and positive reporting has been advanced as a possible response, these have not coalesced towards a distinctive model of reporting that could offer a radical alternative. Chinese media in Africa seems to have accepted the rules of the game set by other players before their emboldened engagement with the continent and it is not clear yet, possibly to the journalists themselves, what the next move is going to be: either to-wards greater professionalism and specialization, leading audiences to tune on Chinese channels for information on economy and finance, for example, or towards a more radical view of the world.

DIFFERENCES IN REPORTING: THE CASE OF EGYPT

This does not mean that there are no differences in the ways media, and individual reporters, cover a major story. These differences are to a large extent defined by the central versus commercial media dichotomy, but individual perspectives are not inconsequential.

During the period of my research, the Arab Spring, especially in Egypt, has been a major world news story, including for Chinese media. As mass movements against authoritarian governments emerged in the Middle East with a broad middle class participation, they were at first the subject of a blanket gag order, as the Chinese government was afraid that they might inspire similar initiatives in China. (Indeed, calls for a "Jasmine Revolution" circulated on the Chinese Internet for a while, although they did not gain a large following and were swiftly snuffed out.) The terms "Arab Spring" and "Jasmine Revolution" remained banned, and the first stories on the movements were not published until several months had passed since the first demonstrations in Tunis. In the event, the outcome of the movements and the ambivalent Western interventions in their support was sufficiently dispiriting that reporting proving the official line—attempts to export "Western democracy" were irresponsible at best and a deliberate attack on a nation at worst—would be fairly easy to produce. Egypt had by then gone through mass rallies that overthrew long-time President Mubarak, democratic election that brought to power an Islamist government, a period of street violence, and a military coup that essentially restored the draconian rule of Mubarak's time.

All media with significant foreign news coverage either had correspondents on the ground throughout the events (Xinhua has a regional bureau in Cairo) or repeatedly dispatched reporters to Egypt as events unfolded. We have already seen at the beginning of this chapter how a reporter for a business media network generally regarded as liberal, without expressing a political preference, wanted to show his readers that the transition to democracy was fraught but meaningful. Two CCTV correspondents who reported from Cairo saw the events in a very different light. The first recalled:

> I reported from Tahrir Square on the second anniversary of Mubarak's ouster in February 2013. They used tear gas, so I was also coughing. Journalists from different countries would perceive what was happening differently. Shortly before

that there had been news that an American journalist was raped there. So Americans would have different expectations of what was happening there and what demonstrators would be saying.

I interviewed thirty people and ended up using five or six interviews. An American journalist would probably have chosen a different five or six. My conclusion was that social polarization was deepening. Differences in opinion were very big. Some supported [democratically elected Islamist President Mohammad] Morsi, some supported Mubarak, some opposed both. I was struck by how this country, which used to be the most powerful Arab country that even dared to go to war with a superpower like Israel, was on the brink of splitting [*fenlie*]. This made me think of my own country. It probably would not have made an American journalist think of that. I felt that probably only the army could prevent the country from splitting. Stabilizing the country, ensuring that this formerly great country was still there, would be a meaningful thing. So personally, when I heard that [General Abdel Fattah al-] Sisi [the leader of the coup that unseated Morsi] was running for president, I was glad. The same thing with Libya or Iraq. I am not saying that Gaddafi or Saddam were great, but right now it's chaos. I am not sure that mainstream US journalists are in a position to comment on Egypt, or Iraq, or Libya in such an objective way. Perhaps I saw different things from what an American saw, or perhaps it was a different part of those things that struck me.

For this correspondent, the Egypt story was not a fraught or failed transition to democracy but a collapse of a previously powerful country that only the army could prevent from disintegrating, a prospect that, for him, paralleled one China might face if those promoting *fenlie*, or "splittism" as the Communist Party calls separatism in Xinjiang and Tibet, have their way. Although the correspondent was reflexive about his own position, he nonetheless believed that such a parallel objectively existed, as posited by China's government rhetoric; and since it was, as implied in the same government discourse, supported by the same Western forces, Western journalists could not see it with the same objectivity. By the same token, he assumed that his perspective would be shared by other Chinese journalists who would sense the same parallels.

Yet this was by no means entirely so. Another CCTV correspondent reported from Tahrir Square when Morsi took office and again when he was forced out of office. She made an effort "to report objectively," but she was influenced by her Egyptian crew's opinions. When Morsi's Muslim Brotherhood came to power they had a lot of support, and they "genuinely wanted to improve Egypt." But later, people she talked to began doubting their choice. There was widespread lawlessness, mothers were afraid for their daughters returning from work, and there was infighting among the anti-Mubarak forces. "Many public intellectuals in China demand democracy, democracy, democracy. . . . But what did democracy do to Egypt? If you saw Egypt you had to realize that democracy was a good thing but it needed long preparation. . . . There is a long tradition in China of instruction via stories. We tell stories of foreign countries to call attention to certain things in China, or even to lead (*yindao*) public opinion. Egypt's failed experiment with democracy is an example."

In the end, this reporter, too, came to the conclusion that only the army could restore order, although she continued to report the opinions of various sides. For her, the story was ultimately about the functioning of the country, and she consciously and willingly supported the Chinese government's line of using the Arab Spring as a cautionary tale. Yet it would not be entirely correct to conclude that her point of view was identical to her colleague's. For her, democracy was at least part of the story, and her endorsement of the military was reluctant.

Although the two CCTV correspondents ended up defending the Chinese government's position, their views were clearly strongly felt. Indeed, with one of them, our conversation evolved into a rather personal debate in which, talking about a report on the BBC's website about a Chinese dissident, she first accused the broadcaster of bias and "brainwashing," then—without knowing who they were or what they had done—went on to attack the arrested dissidents and to defend the government crackdown, and then ended by asserting that Chinese and Westerners have different needs and can never follow the same model. Although she reproduced many of the familiar tropes of China's government-supported nationalist discourse, there was no doubt about the genuineness of the anger with which she denounced the dissidents or expressed her love for China.

TALKING TO THE *LINGDAO*

At what point does a journalist become a *lingdao*? In commercial media, only the executives and editorial board members of a paper or website are thought of as such, but in the central media, which follow more traditional hierarchies, a senior page editor or producer, or an older overseas bureau chief, may already be seen as one. Whatever it is that makes a *lingdao,* however, a person's standing as such is always visible in the way in which journalists pay attention to his or her opinions and wishes. Of course, *lingdao* display the same attitude towards their own higher-level *lingdao.* One bureau chief reportedly scheduled the visit of his senior *lingdao* for a Saturday and required that all staff, including freelancers, be present to welcome him. One of the reporters interpreted this as a demonstration both of commitment to the senior *lingdao* and of authority over his subordinates.

Many journalists I talked to stressed the importance of a *lingdao*'s personality for the atmosphere and productivity of the bureau or newsroom. Particularly, but not only, for correspondents with a somewhat liberal bend or an impatience with institutional constraints, getting support from a "progressive" *lingdao* was important. There were major differences between overseas bureaus of the same central media organization in terms of how disciplined or else relaxed staff life was or how seriously the chief took competition in output. A new *lingdao* could also mean that a bureau that used to be open to a researcher's inquiries and even permitted him to attend newsroom meetings was no longer so. Such differences in style did not, however, necessarily reflect political liberalism or conservatism. And although several liberal-leaning reporters assured me that senior *lingdao* of their organizations were of that persuasion too, in the end, it is doubtful how much difference this made for those organizations' output. While the presidents of CCTV and Xinhua—invariably men—have often been apparatchiks from the Propaganda Department or SARFT, the censorship bureau, the deputy head of Xinhua's foreign department, Han Song, is a prolific science fiction writer and very active on Weibo who has in the past often posted comments critical of the government on his microblog. CCTV's deputy editor-in-chief in charge of international news, Sun Yusheng, used to be an investigative reporter who launched the iconic 1990s investigative news shows, *Oriental Horizon* and *Focal Point*; his book on that work, entitled *Ten Years*, "used to be like a bible for journalists," as one reporter told me. The story goes that when a propaganda department official called to stop a report about a Beijing taxi company linked to children of high officials, Sun did not pick up until it was aired.

The top *lingdao* among CCTV's foreign news editors, however, is the director of the international news department, Pan Linhua. Pan has worked in the department for over twenty years, although she has never been posted abroad: by the time the network's overseas expansion took place after 2008, she had a young child, and going abroad would have been inconvenient. Pan graduated with a degree in international news from Shanghai Foreign Languages University in 1993 and later completed a master's in communication at Tsinghua University. In 2005–2006, she received a Chinese government scholarship to pursue a master's degree in international public policy at Johns Hopkins University; this included a two-week internship at CNN and one week at NPR. She was involved in organizing reporting from the Kosovo and Iraq wars and was producer of Shijie Zhoukan (Weekly World Bulletin), an in-depth news program edited by Lin Yu, a Leeds University master's graduate in communication.

Although these experiences left Pan with an appreciation of PBS and investigative reporting by the *New York Times* and the *Washington Post*, they did not necessarily increase her trust in Western media: one of her few microblog posts in 2014 was a repost of a March CCTV interview with a Ukrainian man who had taken part in the demonstrations demanding the resignation of pro-Russian President Viktor Yanukovich. The report identifies the man as a mercenary hired by the pro-Western opposition; he explains that he only did so for the money and considers the new government illegitimate. While CCTV's news also featured supporters of the new government, Pan chose to disseminate a feature that questions the Western version of the events in the Ukraine as a democratic revolution and, in line with the Chinese government's position, supports Russia's line without overtly approving its intervention.

"Even though CCTV is now present in many places, we don't necessarily understand them," Pan told me. "Chinese people's understanding of foreign countries remains superficial, like foreigners' understanding of China. We want to encourage journalists to analyze why events are taking place and reflect more on their background, even though television is not the best medium for this." I asked if she shared the indignation of Chinese reporters in Africa about the BBC's documentary *The Chinese Are Coming*. "Yes; when you know the situation is more complex and still choose to simplify it like this, it is immoral. BBC has good reporting, but what they report from China is basically just critical."

Pan's staff includes over one hundred editors who process the "packages"—footage, audio, and scripts—sent by the correspondents and forward them to the appropriate channels, mainly the main Channel 1 and Channel 13, the news channel. Most of the packages come from the three regional bureaus: Nairobi, Washington, and London (the latter with a lower status, as it does not have its own airtime). At the beginning of my research, all three were headed by women in their early forties with extensive experience as foreign correspondents; the head of the Nairobi bureau was subsequently promoted to head CCTV's French channel and was replaced by a man.

The Nairobi and Washington bureaus are located in nondescript but upmarket downtown office buildings. CCTV's immediate neighbor in Nairobi is USAID, the US government's development aid agency. At the reception, four big television screens show the BBC, CNN, CCTV and Al-Jazeera, with the BBC's sound dominating. The BBC is also running on another big screen in the office of the managing editor of the Chinese service.

The smaller London bureau, rented from AP, is in a hip converted factory building at the fashionably redeveloped Camden Lock. Russia's RT (Russia Today), the state-owned foreign-language news channel, and Brazil's O Globo television rent offices in the same building so they can make use of AP's satellite communication facilities. Unlike Xinhua, which prefers buildings of its own with strict security and the brass plates favored by Chinese government bodies, CCTV's facilities are relatively easy to access and devoid of visibly "Chinese" symbolism—although some journalists say this is because, since Xi Jinping has been in power, no *lingdao* has dared to make a decision to buy a building for fear of being investigated for corruption.

Some eighteen out of the forty Chinese staff in the Nairobi bureau (it also has around eighty locals), and over forty in Washington, work for the Chinese service, as do most of the roughly twenty staff in London. Here, too, there are meetings at which the stories of the past week are discussed and evaluated and stories for the coming week are planned and distributed in an informal way, depending on individual competencies and interests. After first securing Pan's approval for their proposed stories via an online system, reporters prepare their packages and submit them, also online. Usually, the packages need dubbing and captioning. The reason for captioning is historical: in the past, many correspondents did not speak standard Mandarin. Nowadays, more and more correspondents send finished packages that are aired directly.

The editors, in Beijing and Washington, work in shifts round the clock. Each shift is in charge of producing programming for a certain time slot, for example 1:00 p.m. to 5:00 p.m., but the shift is longer than the slot. Every shift has a pitch meeting (*xuantihui*) at which decisions are made about the stories to be aired. The main themes of the day are decided in the morning pitch meeting. The producer in charge of the shift, who keeps an eye on Xinhua, AP, Reuters, BBC, and CNN news running on screens in her office, is ultimately responsible for deciding which stories to air. He or she passes the program plan on to the editor in charge of the channel's news program, who then makes a final selection, balancing international news against that provided by other departments, such as domestic news. On average, the approval process takes about two hours. Before every shift change, the outgoing shift prepares the handover to the incoming one.

China-related angles are generally preferred. For example, in a story about the Ebola outbreak in West Africa, a correspondent found a doctor who had studied in China and spoke Chinese. Such a story would get Chinese viewers interested and give CCTV a unique advantage in access. Features and documentaries offer more room for in-depth reporting. CCTV has two separate documentary channels in Chinese and English, but documentarists are a separate group with its own travelling reporters. Foreign correspondents do, however, produce short, documentary-style features of eight to twelve minutes for programs such as Faces (Shijie Miankong), Global Watch (Huanqiu Shixian), and Oriental Horizon. One segment of Faces, contributed by a correspondent in Nairobi, profiled a boy who lives in a highland village in Kenya where athletes come to train; the boy had no shoes but hoped to learn to run fast so he could build a big house for his family. Pan mentioned this as an example of a story they proceeded to produce despite expecting moderate interest from viewers. Referring to the Chinese government's increased interest in overseas aid projects, sometimes unpopular with Chinese viewers who believe domestic poverty should be addressed first, she added: "We need to educate common people about the world so that they understand better the environment in which Chinese foreign policy operates. This is important because foreign policy increasingly has to take into account popular opinion. So the function to 'correctly guide public opinion' is important."

* * *

After my conversation with senior *People's Daily* bureau chief Zhao Juan, I spent some time trying to make sense of the way she responded to my questions about the relationship between the requirements for journalistic professionalism and Communist partisanship. Unlike most others, the energetic and plainspoken sexagenarian did not try either to reconcile or defend them, or to play them down. She simply sidestepped the questions. I wondered what Zhao's journalistic ideals really were. Did she have any? Was she a nationalist, a believer in the Party, a news professional, or a cynical marke-teer, to use a variation on existing typologies of Chinese journalists (Hassid 2011; Dai 2013)? Perhaps Zhao never reflected on such categories, or at least not in a way that was related to her work. She was used to the system, knew how to work it, and lived it, enjoying her job. It was not necessarily that the contradictions inherent to it were not visible to her, but she had long since taken on the habitus of a *lingdao* who did not question the edifice she was part of.

When I told a Chinese anthropologist teaching at an American college of the research I was engaged in, she responded: "I'd love to know how they manipulated the news." I told her that few if any of the correspondents I had talked to saw themselves as engaging in manipulation. "Oh? But they don't report on demonstrations by the Falungong, do they?" she countered, refer-ring to a religious organization banned in China. No, I had to admit; they did not. So how did manipulation occur? Perhaps, first, by not seeing certain events, including Falungong demonstrations, as news; second, by obeying explicit gag orders, such as on the Dalai Lama; third, by rationalizing the avoidance of certain stories as being outside their beat ("I am a business reporter") or in other ways ("It's unethical to report inside information from companies"); and fourth, by acknowledging that a story, for one reason or another, was unlikely to pass the editors.

Notwithstanding all that, most central media journalists saw themselves as patriotic professionals trying to do a good job in a media environment that was manipulated all around the world. John, the correspondent whom we encountered at the beginning of chapter 2, told me that the Chinese government saw international media as a competition of ideologies. "I thought this was bullshit and brainwashing" and that there could be a neu-tral, ethical standard, he continued. "But now I think it's true. All media have an agenda," whether it is national or corporate. "I am not saying West-ern media is not reporting the truth, and I am not here to convince you that what I write is the truth. It's complementary."

CHAPTER 4

Finding the "China Peg"

WHEN visitors enter the lobby of CRI's headquarters on Beijing's western outskirts, they find themselves facing a large slogan: "A Stand for China, An Eye for the World, A Concern for All Humanity" (*Zhongguo lichang, shijie yanguang, renlei guanhuai*). Developing a "Chinese stand" or a "Chinese voice" is a central motif in official statements about the ongoing international media expansion. Although such statements are driven by the broader agenda to strengthen China's "soft power" as defined by the work of Joseph Nye, what the Chinese government hopes to achieve, both internally and internationally, is the "symbolic power" that sociologist Pierre Bourdieu described as "the power to make people see and believe, to get them to know and recognize."[1]

Most correspondents for the central media I talked to considered it natural that when they reported on Chinese officials' overseas activities they would stick to statements distributed by officials in advance, often under the journalists' byline, a practice established after 1989. (Some did lament the fact that this took away their insider's advantage in reporting on China's role in important international events, such as the Iran nuclear talks in Geneva.)[2] They also accepted that when they covered international issues on which the Chinese government had a clearly identified stand—for example, the approach to North Korea—they would largely support China's position (whether and how to present opposing views depended on the organization and the individual). But in their daily reporting, a "Chinese stand" did not, for most correspondents, mean speaking for the government, or even correcting prejudiced views of China—although it did for some. As an Africa-based Xinhua reporter quipped with a pun, what the agency needed was not more "stand" (*lichang*) but more "market" (*shichang*). "You can only have an ideology if you can sell it," he commented wryly. Clearly, he did not see himself as a salesman.

This reporter was pragmatic about occasionally writing propaganda pieces and saw it as simply part of working for a state news agency. (Others used the terms "public" or "state-sponsored," as if drawing a closer parallel between Xinhua and public media in Europe.) His colleague saw working for China's strategic interests as an important part of her job but aspired to do this in a professional manner and "hated" writing propaganda. Echoing a sentiment widely held among central media journalists, she said that there were national agendas behind all media—including the BBC, which she had once dreamed of working for—but nonetheless admitted to being "confused" about her "dual identity" as "PR officer for the government" and professional journalist.

What a "Chinese perspective" did mean to most correspondents— regardless of political stance and type of media—was identifying a China-related "peg" to attract the interest of the Chinese audience, "as you would use something to attract a child's interest when you wanted to tell him something," in the words of a former correspondent for the liberal commercial paper *Southern Weekend*. For some, this state of affairs was regrettable. A reporter from *Southern Weekend*'s sister publication, *Southern People Weekly*, which specializes in in-depth interviews, recalled that when he travelled to Japan in 2010 with a colleague from *Southern Weekend*, the colleague kept asking all his interviewees about freedom of opinion, in order to contrast it with China. He, however, thought it was more important to find out what Japanese people themselves were concerned with. Another *Southern Weekend* correspondent commented that the idea of a "Chinese perspective," which assumes news stories were written from the perspective of a particular nation, was a limitation that Chinese journalists including himself have internalized, adding that he would like to break through it and look at relations between individuals instead of relations between nations.

A Xinhua reporter saw the requirement to report from a Chinese perspective as "another of those vague things. No one told us what that is." For example, on Syria, her assumption was that Western media would speak for the United States, unconditionally opposing the Syrian government and supporting the opposition, so the "Chinese angle" would be to provide a more balanced picture. But after she was posted abroad, she realized that Western reporting was more nuanced as, at press conferences, Western correspondents too raised questions about rights violations by the opposition. Therefore, "if a Chinese angle means being different from Western media, I don't think that's necessary."

In contrast, a number of correspondents saw the need for a "Chinese perspective" as an opportunity. A CCTV correspondent told me that the expansion of Chinese media networks meant that much more news reached Chinese audiences first hand, in a form that reflected their way of thinking, rather than in processed form via Western media. Now, Chinese journalists were in a position to "infuse their news reporting with Chinese people's way of thinking." Similarly, Eric Gui, the Xinhua editor who wrote a book to educate Chinese readers about Africa, explained that his intention was to give "explanations that belong to Chinese people" to questions about the continent because "Western explanations depart from a Western stance."[3]

A senior Xinhua correspondent in Europe, who was in charge of directing the reporting of local stringers across the continent, shared this view. He explained, for example, that Xinhua's stance on the refugee crisis that unfolded in 2015 was that it was a result of the Arab Spring, which in turn had been a product of Western intervention and the attempt to forcibly democratize the Middle East. As for how to solve the crisis—the conflict between humanitarian and security concerns that dominated European politics—the agency did not have a stance on that since Chinese diplomacy remained neutral on the issue. The reporter noted that younger colleagues tended to be naïve about the origins of the crisis, simply reporting what EU officials said without paying sufficient attention to United States and EU responsibility.

As we saw in chapter 3, some correspondents rejected the idea of a national perspective even if they did privilege stories with a Chinese component. "Journalists like me don't consider ourselves as writing from a Chinese perspective," the Europe correspondent for a commercial media organization told me. "I assume my readers are at least somewhat global-minded people." Yet most correspondents, whether for central or commercialized media, saw nothing wrong with the view that reporting on foreign countries should focus on policies and experiences—whether positive or negative—that were relevant for China's development, as senior *lingdao* in the central media have urged journalists to do. Back in 2004, He Chongyuan, founding editor-in-chief of *Global Times*, encouraged his staff to write about "how foreign countries solve employment problems, housing problems; how they plant trees and grass and protect the environment."⁴ Ten years later, the director of CCTV Europe, introducing a collection of articles by her correspondents, asked the question what, "as an Asian developing country, China can learn from Europe," both in practical terms like air quality monitoring, conservation of monuments, football culture or vocational education and in more abstract matters like postwar trust-building and unification.⁵ On the other side of the print media spectrum, *21st Century Business Herald*'s foreign desk editor summed up the paper's international reporting strategy in the catchphrase "China's road, global values" (*Zhongguo daolu, quanqiu jiazhi*), referring to the relevance of universal values for China's current development path. A foreign desk editor for Caixin described stories on the dismantling of censorship in Burma or the multiple candidates for the Vietnamese presidency as veiled criticism of stalled reforms in China. A *People's Daily* story about a shoe repair stall that has been run by the same old cobbler for the last forty years right next door to the New York Stock Exchange, without the latter feeling offended by its "poor neighbor," is an implicit comparison to Beijing, where unpopular city management officers (*chengguan*) chase small craftsmen out of upmarket locations. "Have you ever seen a cobbler in Wangfujing?" the correspondent asked me, referring to a shopping street in central Beijing. And we have seen how all correspondents reported on the events in Egypt with China in mind.

How correspondents go about finding a "China peg" depends on many factors: their organization's nature and way of operating, audience interest as perceived by editors and correspondents, and reporters' own interests and political position. A CCTV correspondent told me that even a feature series on the Arctic, broadcast during a Spring Festival holiday, had to begin with Chinese researchers at the Spitsbergen polar station. "We had to find a way to connect the topic to China, otherwise there is no interest." When a Europe-based correspondent for a central media organization went to Greece to cover the economic crisis there, her report focused on the inefficiency and nepotism in government institutions rather than on excessive welfare or a culture of indolence, themes popular in both Western and Chinese narratives of the crisis, or else a crisis of European-style liberal democracy in general, an interpretation favored by more anti-Western Chinese pundits.⁶ While some Greek commentators appealed to China to "rescue" Greece, this correspondent wanted to make the point that Greeks still lived better than people in China. "I hope that Chinese people will get more welfare and not work so hard," she said. In the context of her political preferences— she thinks that China is not a very tolerant society and should be more open, which locates her on the liberal side of the liberal-nationalist scale, one of the central ones in China's politics today—her critique of inefficient state institutions and endorsement of the welfare state as viable clearly has allusions to China.

In contrast, when an African country passed a law restricting media freedom that was widely criticized in the West—and sometimes linked to growing Chinese influence—a central media correspondent told me that although she reported it as a brief news item, she did not feel there was a connection to China, as the new regulations were directed against Western and, perhaps, local media. She, as a correspondent, did not feel either personally affected or solidary with these outlets. As for the local journalists in her organization, "they have been working for us for a long time and know what kind of media we are, so they didn't write anything. They know what we want—things like African reactions, positive quotes about Xi's visit—and they deliver it." Had a commercial media outlet written about the same affair, they may have drawn parallels to China.

Some of the "softer," "human interest" stories are explicitly framed as contrasting "Chinese" or "Oriental" (*dongfang de*) to "Western" (or "African") behavior or thinking, thus underlining the difference between "them" and "us"—even if, in the end, the tension is resolved and what is formerly alien is made to seem more understandable. For example, a London-based CCTV correspondent gave a story on the thirtieth anniversary of the Falklands War between Britain and Argentina the title "Reflecting on Reporting the 30th Anniversary of the Malvinas War: Defining Heroism in East and West."[7] The reporter describes her surprise at meeting a British "hero" of the war by stating that, "as a Chinese," she expected to meet someone who had committed a heroic act rather than someone who "in our culture" would merely be seen as "an old soldier."[8] This contrast leads to a discussion of differing cultures of commemoration—remembering those who sacrificed their lives in acts of bravery versus commemorating all who died—and the story ends in the reporters affirmation that, indeed, a man who suffered severe burns in the war but remained an optimist and sought out his former enemies to reconcile with them can be seen as a hero. This story makes the "European viewpoint" more understandable to the Chinese reader, but only after first emphasizing its cultural foreignness.

"WE DON'T DO CRITICAL"

While approaches to making a story relevant to China vary, the general expectation that they should somehow be relevant limits what reporters *see* as stories. Although many correspondents said they were personally interested in social and cultural issues, a common refrain was that Chinese audiences were not, so these were hard to report on. "Human interest" stories from abroad are therefore rarely reported by foreign correspondents and tend, instead, to be edited translations from foreign media by *Reference News* and *Global Times*, two popular newspapers that specialize in digesting the foreign press. Visual and online media are a partial exception. CCTV has a program called *Faces* (Shijie Miankong) to which foreign correspondents contribute, and occasionally, interviews with "ordinary people" make it into the main news programs. Reporting on the 2011 massacre in Norway, when a right-wing extremist killed seventy-seven people, was one such occasion.

Sina Finance, the financial portal of China's most popular content provider, has dozens of stringers around the world contributing to a page called "Overseas Wind" (Haiwai Lai Feng).[9] Globus, a Caixin venture focusing on foreign reporting, works with a similar arrangement. "We want to cover Europe from a more authentic viewpoint," said Sina Finance's Europe bureau chief. News from Europe tend to account for a very small fraction of foreign news in China; an analysis of *People's Daily* from the 1990s till the mid-2000s, for example, found that their share was no higher than 3 percent, focused largely on European integration and EU-China relations and generally treating the EU as a single entity.[10] When I asked a *People's Daily* correspondent in Europe what he found the most interesting aspect of life here, he said it was why EU institutions spent so much taxpayer money on pointless deliberations, travel, and the related infrastructure. After 2008, the recession, the European debt crisis, and later the refugee crisis became leading stories. A fourth major story was what Chinese media labeled the "Juncker Plan," a plan by the European Commission to increase investment in infrastructure.[11] In European media, this was not framed as a major story, but Chinese media linked it to the expansion of Chinese investment in Europe and the Chinese government's own plans to promote infrastructure investment abroad.

According to Sina's bureau chief, Chinese readers who followed the official media got the impression that "all Europeans live in misery" caused by their declining economies; but in fact, people continued to have fun.[12] It was the diverse ways of life in European countries that she wanted her stringers to cover, and these "stories of difference"—were popular with readers.[13] "Chinese people are amazed by Europeans: why [do] Dutch people ride bicycles, when in China only poor people do?" A former Paris-based stringer commented that the stories she reported were on issues that French people were interested in too. Similarly, a Boston-based stringer filed several stories exploring different aspects of the terrorist attack on the Boston Marathon in 2012 and the public role of women in the US election campaign the same year.

Although the "Overseas Wind" page carries financial stories, a large percentage of the stories are about society and even politics. Financial media has, at least in the past, had more latitude in reporting than other Chinese media because the government has an interest in reliable business information; in addition, top economic decision makers have tended to be more liberal than other high officials.[14] In the early 2000s, this resulted in financial papers pioneering investigative reporting on sensitive subjects such as SARS and environmental pollution. If stories are framed as being about economics, they are seen as not very sensitive and subjected to less rigorous self-censorship, and journalists who seek more freedom in their reporting sometimes specialize in finance for that reason.[15] Furthermore, online media has no page limitations and can afford to be less concerned about readers' interest in particular stories, a factor that greatly preoccupies both newspaper and audiovisual media editors and often fuels conservative attitudes that channel reporting towards the tried-and-true.

Nonetheless, there are also non-financial print news outlets that occasionally publish in-depth foreign reporting. These include Xinhua's *Globe* and *Oriental Outlook* magazines, *China Newsweek*, which belongs to China News Service, and *Southern People Weekly*, which has, among others, published an exclusive interview with Burmese opposition leader Aung San Suu Kyi. A number of books have also been published by foreign correspondents, although, in contrast to books by Western China correspondents such as Peter Hessler's *River Town*, none are widely known within the profession. For example, Xinhua's Liu Hong has published nine books based on his overseas postings in Kosovo, Afghanistan, Israel, and the United States. While some of those—like *The American "Conspiracy,"* discussed in chapter 2—are more polemics than reportage, others largely narrate personal experiences in and around battlefield situations (e.g., *Tears in Jerusalem*).[16]

Considering the focus on stories relevant to China, one would expect that challenges faced by Chinese companies abroad would be widely reported in Chinese media, at least in the more market-oriented ones. This is not the case. Foreign correspondents tend either to gloss over conflicts or to reproduce official rhetoric. "We never report Western criticism of China, only responses to it, just as you wouldn't talk in public about someone insulting your wife, even though you may discuss it with her," a Xinhua editor explained. In an e-mail, a Xinhua correspondent wrote: "On topics on China especially on criticism, it is expected for a government-funded and run news wire to take sides. You can't expect otherwise. And I think Xinhua scribb[l] ers expect and accept government-run news wire on these issues take sides. Like I expect and accept VOA [Voice of America] takes sides on US-related topics. BBC maybe trickier."

"I've tried to report mismanagement, corruption, and labor abuse," an Africa correspondent for a central newspaper explained:

> It's nothing to hide, because it's a bilateral issue: there are causes on both sides, for example corrupt officials that look through their fingers as local mine bosses take on illegal Chinese workers. But in the end, nothing came of it. Some companies told me they've learned their lesson: they talked to the BBC very frankly, talking about problems on both sides, but the results were very negative for them. So the Chinese media is trying hard to counterbalance these negative reports. If they do a story that presents both sides, they [editors and managers] worry about how it will be used. I would like to do something on labor abuse, but I cannot do without Chinese sources.

Accordingly, reports on opposition to Chinese investment in Africa have been extremely rare, largely limited to blog posts or articles by journalists from the liberal commercial or online media on short fact-finding trips paid by Western or Chinese foundations.[17] A CCTV correspondent prepared a story on a shooting that took place at a Chinese-owned mine in Africa, but the story was not aired. *21st Century Business Herald*'s Brussels and New York correspondents have reported on some of the difficulties surrounding acquisitions by Chinese companies in Europe and the United States, but their articles have, with a few exceptions, been phrased in oblique terms— for example, speaking of "political noise." Xinhua and *People's Daily* have privileged access to Chinese officials and state enterprises and therefore often know more than others about the background of such cases, but face a more or less explicit, though unwritten, policy that prohibits the reporting of criticism of China or Chinese companies abroad; exceptions to this are only made when an event has been widely reported in social media, and then only if the senior "leadership" authorizes it. Otherwise, such reporting can only take the form of *neican* written for government officials—and even these, as one Xinhua bureau chief put it, cannot be too negative, as journalists must consider the sensitivities of various officials. Some foreign correspondents consider such briefs the only way to influence policy making and write them often on their own initiative; others have no interest in producing them and only do so when pressured by their superiors.[18] Xinhua's overseas bureaus are also beginning to produce custom-made reports for Chinese companies abroad.

Other central media leave correspondents somewhat more room. For them, avoiding critical reporting is a combination of choice, conscious and more or less institutionalized self-censorship, business expediency, and an unconscious blindness to the topic or simple complacency and lack of interest. Pressing journalists on why their reporting appeared to omit critical elements resulted in a variety of answers that suggested a combination of all of these: why report the negative if biased Western media were doing it anyway (a CCTV reporter); it would be a waste of everyone's time since the editor would cut them out (a *People's Daily* correspondent and a Xinhua bureau chief); it would be unethical to reveal confidential information from corporate sources (a Xinhua correspondent); corporate pressure on the editor made such reporting difficult, and maintaining a good relationship with them was important both for the paper and for the individual correspondents who need sources (correspondent for a market-oriented paper); there was a lack of organizational support, not enough time, and limited reader interest (correspondents across the full range of media). In some cases, such as ivory smuggling from Africa, correspondents added concern for personal safety.

Interestingly, some journalists viewed reporting on such conflicts as investigative reporting, which very few foreign correspondents—bar those for Caixin and a few for CCTV—regarded as their job. "We don't do critical things," as a Xinhua bureau chief in Africa put it. Yet, in an apparent paradox—but consistent with other scholarship on Chinese journalists—investigative journalism and reportage as practiced in Anglo-American media remains a highly attractive model (albeit one to be admired in principle, rather than one that can be striven for in actual practice) for most journalists, not just those working for liberal media.[19] A CRI reporter unhappy about the global dominance of Western media regularly read the *New York Times'* Chinese website (which is blocked in China) and liked its way of "examin[ing] the large through the small." A correspondent for *People's Daily* mentioned the *Wall Street Journal*'s story on deposed Chinese official Bo Xilai's family wealth and a former *Financial Times* correspondent's book on the Chinese Communist Party as examples of the type of in-depth reporting Chinese journalists abroad should aspire to. A number of my interviewees mentioned former *New Yorker* China correspondent Peter Hessler's *River Town*, a book on a small town in Sichuan province, with admiration. While Tom was proud of his story on elephant poaching, his fellow Xinhua correspondent in another country filed a story about a Chinese ivory smuggler who was sentenced to a prison term. After she heard from a high-ranking Chinese diplomat that the ivory trade was an embarrassment for China, she thought it was important for people in China to realize that the ivory trade harmed China's image. Still, the editors killed the story. Then, later, after the Chinese government burned a stockpile of confiscated ivory, an editor called her, saying that she could now report on the topic.

The stories on poaching, as long as they did not publicly implicate China, were welcome because they corresponded both to government interests and to the sensibilities of the young urban middle class. In contrast, "If I write about arrests of opposition members but the Chinese readers or media are not interested, then it is useless," a Xinhua journalist in Africa explained. "A story that no one reads cannot be a good story. Only a story with a high pickup rate can be satisfying." Thus, foreign reporting may have the potential to become more investigative by latching on to issues whose discussion in China is both relatively free and lively while working their way around those that are considered sensitive.[20]

At the time of my research, some commercial media, particularly Caixin, clearly went farther and deeper in reporting on Chinese companies overseas engagements. Because of the limited correspondent network of these media, in-depth, investigative stories were limited to coverage of the United States and Europe. The English version of an article analyzing the failure a Chinese company's road construction project in Poland in Caixin's *New Century* magazine was the runner-up to one of the British Foreign Press Association's 2011 awards. Another article in *New Century*, in 2013, reported in depth on an US court ruling that indicted several Chinese exporters of vitamin C for price fixing. The article reported on the contradictions in a Chinese official's court testimony and concluded that the price fixing occurred on advice from a Chinese government body. This was clearly a subject touching on "national interest" that central media could not report on.

21st Century Business Herald also published some stories that mentioned criticism of Chinese companies, for example a Senate hearing on the acquisition of Smithfield, a US meatpacking company, by a Chinese investor, and allegations of discrimination against Asian Americans at East Asia Bank after it was purchased by the state-owned Industrial and Commercial Bank of China, although the latter has been removed from the paper's online archive. In its reporting on the trade dispute between the European Union and China on the prices of Chinese-made solar panels, the paper included the opinions of those arguing for punitive tariffs. But the paper steered clear of cases that involved criticism of the Chinese government, for example the controversy around the telecommunications company Huawei's bids to build network infrastructure in the United States, which was scuttled for reasons of "national security." As described in chapter 1, the room for reporting in commercial media has become progressively tighter. Thus, a star reporter for a commercial paper was surprised to see that his editor, whom he described as "relatively audacious" in challenging the limits of what is permitted, cut his interview with Burmese opposition leader Aung San Suu Kyi and removed her criticism of the Chinese government and Chinese companies, leaving only one mild sentence about how Chinese companies should consider local livelihoods.

There are limits even to the degree of criticism internal briefs (*neican*) can contain, even though these are often written to inform *lingdao* about issues deemed too sensitive to report openly, and have in fact historically been used as a form of intelligence on officials in China. These limits are defined not only by political taboos but also, as a correspondent explained, by the interests of powerful political or business groups in China, which may retaliate against journalists. "Nowadays you cannot be too negative. Some 50 percent 'China is strong and powerful' and 50 percent negative is OK, because the officials who read them have their own sensitivities." Moreover, *neican*, too, are often superficial as correspondents lack the time or willingness to investigate. The author of a *neican* on a court case filed against a Chinese state enterprise accused of corruption in obtaining an Africa railway construction contract concluded it was the work of the company's foreign competitors, but her conclusion was based on her interpretation of articles in the local press.

DEALING WITH CENSORSHIP

In Western analyses of Chinese media, the focus on censorship tends to overwhelm all other concerns, and Chinese journalists anticipate such a focus when meeting a researcher from Europe. Mindful of this, I did not make the question of censorship central to my conversations with journalists; in any case, I was interested in understanding the factors shaping their work on their own terms. Although quite a few mentioned constraints on reporting in abstract terms, when asked whether they have personally been unable to report on a story they wished to, very few admitted to it. To an extent, this was undoubtedly due to the wariness of central media reporters about being quoted on the censorship system in foreign media, something that can lead to dismissal or even arrest. But in many cases, journalists have internalized the limits on reporting to such a degree that selecting stories that fit within those limits stops being a conscious act of selection or self-censorship and becomes an automatism. And even instances where they misjudged those limits tended to register not as traumatic offences against journalists' freedom but as nuances of the system that they had yet to master.

It was in this spirit that a central media correspondent told me that after a terrorist attack occurred in the African country in which she was posted, the Chinese ambassador declined to be interviewed on the safety of Chinese citizens. Surprised by this refusal, she finally realized that this was because China did not want to discourage Chinese tourists from visiting the country. The country's president had criticized the United States and the UK for issuing negative travel advisories, and China wanted to score a point by not following their example. "In fact, Africans are friendlier to whites than to Chinese," the reporter told me matter-of-factly,

> which is understandable because they have a longer relationship with them
> and know what to expect. The Chinese are often discriminated against or
> singled out for extortion at the airport. And it is also true that some of this is
> caused by the behavior of some Chinese. Then again, many of these behaviors
> are the same as in China. The BBC's *The Chinese are Coming* reported on the
> lack of protective clothing for African workers; but the same workers in China

have no protective clothing either. Of course, none of this is reported because it is not in the national interest. And what would it change if we reported it?

"We report that both sides are very good to each other," she ended with a laugh. This correspondent was in a position of producing nuanced reporting on Chinese engagement in Africa that could serve the purpose of providing credible alternative coverage to that of the Western media, which she believed was biased, and she had expressed her desire to do so. Nonetheless, she took her inability to do so as a matter of course.

Unlike those based in China, foreign correspondents rarely receive explicit gag orders. When they do, the orders are usually temporary, until the propaganda organs decide how to cover a particular important event. Thus, when anti-Chinese violence broke out in Vietnam in May 2014, news in central media was embargoed until the following day, and online news platforms were instructed not to report on the events. The morning of the following day, *Global Times* published a story that reported on the attacks and the Vietnamese government's arrests of alleged perpetrators. Other media did not break the story until the evening, and when they did they closely followed the Ministry of Foreign Affairs' press release rather than dispatching their own correspondents. None of the official media's reports linked the attacks to China's positioning of an oil rig in disputed waters, which had caused this particular wave of anti-Chinese protests. It "was as though the violence in Vietnam had come out of nowhere, rather than being the culmination of several days of maritime clashes and anti-China demonstrations."[21]

Even in newsroom pitch meetings dealing with foreign news, it is rare to hear a more specific comment than that a particular topic is "sensitive." Common sense and experience shape decisions on how to report, or how not to report, particular subjects. It is clear to everyone that coverage of Chinese dissidents or Tibetan and Uighur exiles is off limits. One central media correspondent accredited at the 2009 Frankfurt Book Fair, where China was the guest of honor, attended the presentation of a dissident writer but wrote nothing about it, or indeed about the political controversy that surrounded the clash between the official Chinese writers' delegation and writers invited directly by the organizers, although that story dominated German media.

There were dozens of media there, but no one was allowed to report the opposition. The Propaganda Department rented a "war room" at the book fair and

organized dinner every day as a casual team meeting to keep an overview of
the whole reporting. . . . At this kind of event, the chief of every media will distribute and coordinate tasks. I am sure that they got instruction from the propaganda department. For normal journalists, taking me as example, besides
the normal reports, I got the task to take part in a small conference hosted by
oppositional Chinese writers, but only listen and note if anything important.

Another correspondent said that remarks by Chinese scholars who were
critical of the government, for example the economist Xu Xiaonian, a critic
of state enterprises, or He Weifang, a law professor who spoke out in support
of jailed dissident Liu Xiaobo, would be cut from reports on public events,
but she believed that such speeches by personalities well known in China
had news value, she would report some of their comments anyway. When
Lung Ying-tai, a public intellectual well-known in China who was then
Taiwan's minister of culture, gave a talk in London, a central media correspondent said it was acceptable to report what she said about cultural exchange between China and Taiwan, but not what she said about China being
undemocratic.

Another topic most correspondents avoided was religion. While there
was no direct ban on coverage of religion, editors and *lingdao* are highly
sensitive of offending religious, particularly Islamic, feelings. A CCTV reporter proposed what she felt was a positive story on Moroccan women in
which she wanted to stress their emancipation, displayed in such things as
the large number of women who do not wear head covering. This story was
at first approved, but then killed by a higher *lingdao* who felt it may offend
Muslims. He was probably mindful of the strict guidelines on reporting on
ethnic and religious issues inside China rather than any possible international repercussions.[22]

Except in the case of Japan, central media journalists generally avoid
direct criticism of foreign governments, unless precedent or editorial guidance suggests that such criticism is acceptable or even desirable in a particular case. Thus, Chinese media did not report criticism of the Kenyan
government for its handling of the 2013 terrorist attack on Nairobi's Westgate shopping mall. "We just wrote down the facts and you could see that
the Kenyan government was trying to hide something," a correspondent told
me. Nor did Chinese media criticize the Ghanaian government for its mass
arrests of Chinese gold miners in the same year. But they forcefully blamed
Malaysia for its apparent incompetence in investigating the disappearance

of an airplane with mostly Chinese passengers in 2014—after the Chinese government has done so. Although an experienced and committed reporter, this correspondent too has on occasion misjudged the limits of critical reporting: a story she wrote about a slum was killed by editors who said it was too negative and harmful to the image of the African country, which, after all, was China's friend.

Conversely, a liberal journalist, commenting online, wrote ironically that "you can never go wrong cursing American imperialism and blaming foreign enemy forces. Even if the cursing is misplaced, the main thing is you can show the *lingdao* how loyal you are, how you will never sell out on the national interest, how you are a strong beam that supports China as it marches with a raised head and a bulging chest at the head of the world."[23]

But while blaming "foreign enemy forces" may be "politically correct" and common, correspondents in the United States are not expected to criticize the US government on their own initiative. As a CRI *lingdao* told me, in reporting on the United States, "there are two guiding principles: one, 'China and America are in the same boat' and two, 'fights between spouses are a normal thing.'"[24] "The US and China have too much distrust and misunderstanding towards each other," she continued. "China is big but awkward on the international stage, and too reserved: we tell you nothing, we don't want to show you our statistics. Every day there are China stories in the *Washington Post* and the *Wall Street Journal*, and basically all negative. China also misunderstands the US and interprets everything the US does as attempts at containment. China doesn't yet have enough self-confidence. My goal is to reduce the misunderstandings."

The requirement to report in a "balanced" fashion is often invoked by both correspondents and editors. No less an authority than Party General Secretary Hu Jintao called for "truthful, accurate, complete, and objective" reporting at the 2009 World Media Summit, and I have often heard variations on this sequence from journalists.[25] "There is no point in going into the story with a preconceived opinion. A journalist may have his own view, but it should not be part of the story. For example, he is inclined to support climate change theory, but that does not mean he should not give equal space to skeptics in his articles," a *21st Century Business Herald* correspondent explained.

But what "balance" means is, of course, open to institutional and individual interpretation. As a *Global Times* correspondent said, the editors want balanced views, but they do not care which local papers she quotes or what their political stand is in local politics. In other words, "balance," in this case, is determined by the editors' ideas on a subject rather than the spectrum of opinions in the country from which the reporting is done. As a CRI editor commented, "You have to report both sides, but of course it's a matter of who comes first and who comes later." For example, reporting on a US congressional hearing at which China was accused of manipulating its currency, she first quoted these voices and then those in favor of China. Another US correspondent said that a Chinese perspective sometimes meant balancing American reporting if it tilted to one side, and at other times it meant amplifying an event. As an example, he mentioned the coverage of the shooting of Michael Brown, a young black man, by a white police officer in Ferguson, Missouri, in August 2014. Until December, Washington-based correspondents for Chinese media made a near-constant beeline for Ferguson, "for reasons you can understand," the correspondent said with a half-smile. Did this attention not go against the idea of positive reporting? "If we wanted to report positively, we shouldn't have gone there at all," he replied. Ferguson allowed correspondents to make a point not only about continuing racial tensions and gun proliferation, but also about rural poverty in the United States, all without appearing ideological or biased.

Some subjects are intuitively sensed to be sensitive although there have been no instructions about them. A CRI correspondent said that in such cases, "when you aren't clear about the [government's] stance, you follow Xinhua," for example on the Russian invasion of Crimea. A correspondent said he did not report on the controversial Gibe Dam, one of the largest dams in Africa that is being built in Ethiopia by a Chinese company, because the project has triggered a conflict about water use between Ethiopia and neighboring Kenya, and reporting would be "intervening in the conflict." On other subjects unrelated to China, correspondents described their reporting as impartial, sometimes pointing out that their stance may not always be identical with that of the Chinese government. For example, a correspondent in Zimbabwe mentioned that a Chinese diplomat contacted him and complained that his report on the seizures of white-owned farms by black army veterans was not sufficiently supportive of President Mugabe's government. In the correspondent's mind, the story was impartial as it mentioned both support for and opposition to the occupations.

A Jerusalem-based central media correspondent commented that, in a few stories, she had portrayed Israel as too much of a victim (*tai can*) and Palestinians too much as villains (*tai huai*), and the editors would not let that pass. "This is just common sense. This is what 'representing China's stance' means. Doesn't the Foreign Ministry always say it opposes settlements and wants a peaceful solution? So surely the Arab world is [seen as] a bit better than Israel." When new in Israel, she once interviewed two experts at Bar Ilan University, but did not realize that they were both "rather pro-Israel." These experts were quite good at using media (*liyong meiti*). Her report was rejected; those interviews could not be used. Later she learned that she had to interview "neutral experts," or if she interviewed one "pro-Israeli" expert she also had to interview one who was "pro-Palestinian." (Interestingly, this correspondent did not consider the fact that an Israeli expert might not actually be pro-Israeli, but may in fact be critical of the Israeli government, which would be a sensitive issue for Chinese listeners in itself.)

But, as we have seen, the principle of balanced reporting is set aside in central media when the Chinese government or Chinese economic interests are involved. "When there are strong conflicts, as with Japan, you cannot give the two sides equal coverage, but you must still use local voices as much as possible," a CRI editor said. Reports on the activities and speeches of Chinese officials abroad follow official handouts verbatim, as do stories about foreign governments' China-related communiqués or visits. Foreign visits of Chinese government leaders, in particular, are covered according to a well-established routine, in which correspondents must first file "warm-up" stories, then cover the visit itself, and finally report on positive local reactions to it. "There are no written instructions about this—nobody will say you are not allowed to write about this on your own—but it is an established custom, and the journalists and the editors won't risk deviating from it," a Xinhua reporter said. So when Xinhua reported on a Chinese ambassador "defend[ing] China-Africa relations against baseless Western criticism," no context or explanation was provided about what the criticism was or why relations needed to be defended, and no distinction was made between the ambassador's words and those of the article.[26] When I pointed this out to the author, he explained that although the story was "not very good" and the speech was hardly newsworthy—"same thing being said so many times"—he had to file it because the country's national news agency reported on the speech, and his editors would have reprimanded him for failing to do so. And, as the report concerned an official speech, he was in any case expected to "take sides."

An issue that vexed many correspondents was the removal of parts of their interviews. It often cost them considerable effort to secure an interview with a well-known "expert" or a politician. They saw these interviews as achievements both in themselves and because they hoped to be able to contact these interviewees again if events so required. It was therefore important for them that the interviewees be satisfied with the outcome. Yet academics and politicians, particularly in the West, tended to make both positive and critical statements about China, and the critical part would routinely be cut. The result would likely draw displeasure from the interviewee who would feel that his or her statements were distorted and manipulated, and might result in a refusal of further interviews. The correspondent, unable to apologize and blame the outcome on censorship, would take personal blame. Although reporters may have expected the cuts, in these cases, they were reluctant to pre-censor the text as they realized that their further access to the source depended on a more or less integral or representative text of the interview being published.

Such situations were particularly frequent when correspondents were asked to report on worldwide reactions to an important official event in China, such as a Party congress. At such times, they were pressed to supply "expert" comments right after the event. But, as a *People's Daily* correspondent complained:

> Editors' thinking has not changed. They wanted us to report good things [i.e., positive reactions] to the CCP plenum for the next day. This could work in Africa or Pakistan, because they are friendly towards China, but I had no way of doing this. People [local commentators] were very disappointed with the communiqué; even if I could get comments [the editors] might not have liked them. In the end, I got reactions from some Chinese people here. There is no point reporting negative comments; the editor will cut them out, so reporting them is just a waste of everyone's time, mine and theirs.

In general, journalists for central media have little room to express their point of view on world events in their reporting. If at all, they do so on social media, although those with liberal views tend to be more cautious in doing so than those with nationalistic or "realist" approaches to international affairs. For example, a senior Xinhua foreign desk editor wrote on his microblog that the conflict between the West and Russia over Ukraine is good for China, which should not commit to either side but instead take advantage of the fact that the focus of Western containment efforts may shift away from China. Another Xinhua reporter explained in a podcast by the

Sina news portal why he would vote for the incumbent French president, the conservative Nicolas Sarkozy, instead of the challenger, the socialist François Hollande, who eventually won the election. Of course, it would not be acceptable for any of these views to be associated with Xinhua as an organization.

"AREN'T YOUR WESTERN MEDIA BRAINWASHED TOO?"

"You Westerners think we Chinese journalists are brainwashed. But aren't your Western media brainwashed too?" This comment from a CCTV correspondent, while unusually direct, represents a view many Chinese journalists, especially those working for central media, agree with: that the global media landscape is rigged against China and that this requires forceful correction. Some are strengthened in this conviction when they discover the extent to which local media in places like Africa appear to replicate what from their perspective are Western clichés. "Many Africans complain that CNN and BBC are not objective, but still follow them," an Africa-based reporter remarked. Why, a London-based central media correspondent asked, was it that British reporting on China is so similar and so negative?

Another correspondent echoed her, telling me that a video of BBC journalists being prevented from entering a Chinese dissident's house on the company's Facebook page made her very angry. Although neither BBC radio or television reported on the failed attempt to interview the dissident, from whose house the reporters were turned away by thugs, this was, for her, unprofessional behavior and an example of BBC's pursuit of negative coverage. "And yet BBC is seen as a credible medium! Not for me, not since yesterday."

This reporter's anger, which after my rejoinders became more emotional and developed into a vocal endorsement of the arrest itself, was the more noteworthy because of her background. Unusually for a journalist of her generation at a central media organization, she has a three-year vocational higher education (zhuanke) degree in English. She worked as a secretary before obtaining a job with Beijing's local television station in 1997 and then moved to central media two years later. "No relations, no background, just chance," she replied to my query whether she may have had connections that helped the transfer. On her first day on the new job, she saw an incontinent boy and his grandmother who, she assumed, must have been petitioners from the countryside trying to get redress for a medical error. This

experience left a deep impression on her: she resolved to make documentaries to let people know about situations like this. But without connections,
she had no chance to move to documentary making, and as her department
increasingly shifted towards entertainment journalism she was so "fed up"
with her job that when Greenpeace advertised a videographer's position, she
applied, unsuccessfully. It was her organization's second internal round of
recruitment for overseas postings, in 2010, that propelled her into news reporting and foreign correspondence in Africa and Europe; over ten years
after joining she is still single, and still interested in reporting on "ordinary
people." Yet for all her sensitivity to social injustice and a profile that sets
her sharply apart from the middle-aged men in the apparatus, she turned
into a passionate defender of the Chinese government when it was attacked
by Western media.

Another central media correspondent, perhaps the most critical of the
Chinese government I have talked to, said he approved of Western media's
criticism of China's human rights record, but did not understand why Western media did not criticize India's caste system. He remarked that Chinese
media were full of enthusiastic reports of the wedding of Prince William of
England, but Western media reports on the sixtieth anniversary of the PRC
were overwhelmingly negative.

While the view that Western media are biased against China is rather
widely shared, only some correspondents believe that conveying a "Chinese
perspective" to their audiences should be part of their work. "My job is to
cast some light on the positive side," a CCTV correspondent in Africa said,
as "every Western story is twisted and discriminating." When I asked why
this was necessary, considering that many Chinese viewers already assume
that Western media is biased against China, she replied that many Chinese
still believe foreign media.

But even those who do not see such "correction work" as their job are
influenced by a vision of competition between China and the West for global
dominance as a defining, though implicit, frame that informs their interpretation of events around them. As a result, among correspondents for
central media, occasional personal interactions with foreign journalists are
tinged by suspicions of their motives and do not develop into a sense of col-
legiality. Indeed, some of these interactions confirm or strengthen those
suspicions, although others soften or shake them. A central media correspondent, who once hoped to work for the BBC, came to the conclusion that
BBC journalists, too, "write for their country's agenda" after she was posted

to Africa. "The election coverage was a perfect example." She found that the BBC's coverage was skewed in favor of the candidate supported by Western powers. A correspondent for *21st Century Business Herald* concluded that US media was being censored too, as he believed anchor Christiane Amanpour was cut off during an interview with a pro-Russian activist in Ukraine. A *China Daily* correspondent told me that he "used to be a constructivist, but now I am a realist," meaning that he now believed national interest objectively existed rather than being merely a discourse created by power holders. "Western media choose to tell things that suit their agendas. In Syria, no one paid attention to the Christians and the other groups who supported Assad." These journalists are deeply skeptical about the idea that any reporting can be independent of the reporter's position, and are therefore suspicious of those Chinese journalists or bloggers whom they see as aligning themselves with a Western "perspective."

Cosmopolitan Professionals in the Service of the Nation

A NTHROPOLOGISTS like telling stories of complexity, especially in settings where complexity is routinely overlooked. When I began talking to Chinese correspondents, I was sure that, beneath the "soft power" story of the overseas expansion of China's propaganda apparatus, there was a diversity of individual ambitions and life choices, just as the stories of repression, collaboration, and resistance in domestic Chinese media conceal a multiplicity of individual journalistic strategies.[1] In the years that followed, my conversations supplied ample evidence of that variety, even within the "central media," which is more directly aligned with state agendas. The correspondents I have interviewed are in many ways a diverse bunch and do not fit easy stereotypes. Yet, this anthropological study is itself almost a stereotype. This book documents complexity, but it is also, as the journalist who accused me of "looking for the things I want to hear" sensed, the product of an anthropological focus on complexity, which, here, wishes to uncover human agency beneath the seeming uniformity of institutions dominated by a strong, authoritarian state that has set clear goals.

The scholarly quest can be value-free, but more often—and this is the case here—it is not. Contrary to their predecessors a hundred years ago, contemporary anthropologists mostly like, even celebrate, the ability of human beings to cope with, circumvent, and manipulate institutional constraints imposed by the group, the nation, the church, or capital. They delight in pointing out the fallacies of seeing culture as a set of immutable, binding rules that can predict behavior. Anthropologists tend to be chroniclers of human creativity and contradictoriness, tirelessly unraveling discourses of national interest, security, heritage, authority, hostility and compassion, showing how they are constructed and how people's actual behavior is never what these discourses claim it should be. In this sense, they work in ways opposite to, for example, international relations scholars of the realist school, who take these concepts for granted and assume that states, and other groups, are driven by collective interests.

Yet anthropologists have also grown suspicious of terms such as "resistance" or "freedom," precisely because these, too, simplify complex processes, over-romanticize individual action at the expense of context, and create binary oppositions that often do not correspond to the experiences and beliefs of those they are applied to. Moreover, historically, the advocacy of freedom and individual choice has been associated with late imperialism and more recently with global capitalism and neoliberalism, which many anthropologists see as a continuing hegemonic force. For these reasons, while much anthropological literature arguably deals with issues of freedom versus conformity, it typically shies away from tackling them and is reluctant to claim that certain behaviors, arrangements or situations have "liberating potential" or entail more freedom than others, or that more freedom is ethically preferable to less—with the somewhat ironic exception, perhaps, of situations that are understood as struggles against the global neoliberal hegemony.[2]

Most of the time, the tensions implicit in such a posture remain unaddressed.[3] Anthropology's recent interest in morality and hope offers a way to reflect on it, since hope is often related to change compared to the present situation.[4] Jarrett Zigon, for example, distinguishes "preserving hope" (an unreflective being-in-the-world that is directed at things not getting worse) and "active hope" that is related to "intentional and ethical action."[5] The relationship between hope for change and the desire to be free from the constraints of the present, and conversely, the relationship between conformity and hopelessness, is not a simple one. Here, however, suffice it to note that the identification of hope as a positive and universal aspect of human life in itself represents a step away from the anthropological agnosticism that is suspicious of all value judgment.

Arjun Appadurai takes a clearer step in this direction when he, building on the work of economist Amartya Sen as well as his own earlier interest in the anthropological significance of imagination, identifies individuals' "capacity to aspire" as inherently positive and argues that this capacity has been expanding.[6] In other words, people have been increasingly able to imagine different ways of living than those they were born into and, in some cases, to take action to attain them. The catch in this argument is that it may overestimate the liberating potential of the individual imagination, paying insufficient attention to the forces that shape it (for example, the mediated imagery of consumption under global capitalism), which may prove as hegemonic as the disciplinary or moral regime an individual aspires to break away from. Such a view is most consistently articulated, though not in this particular debate, by Richard Shweder: he argues that longer life and better health are not universal aspirations (it may be, for example, more important to an individual to go to heaven or to be reborn in a more desirable form), and any other indicator of "human development," including freedom and choice, is necessarily much less so.[7]

Appadurai attempts to forestall such criticism by emphasizing that he sees the capacity to aspire in collective rather than individual terms. But this leads us back the question of who gets to define the boundaries of the collective and articulate visions of the good life, and how then we are to deal conformity with and dissent from those visions.

Anthropologists' wariness of the uncomplicated celebration of dissidents or "freedom fighters" who articulate liberal ideals and act in their name is justified, since it often obscures the more complex meanings that actions acquire in the context of different societies and reinforces the cartoonish, black-and-white image of "Western democracies" as the unproblematic norm. And yet the attention to individual meaning-making, when combined with a refusal to engage with the conventional vocabulary of freedom, authoritarianism, fear, conformity, dissimulation and so on risks ignoring the forest of troubling global trends for the trees of human agency. True enough, few if any Chinese journalists are brainwashed pawns of state propaganda, but their willingness to accommodate and often internalize dominant nationalistic interpretations of the world must nonetheless be seen in conjunction with the growth of repression in China, the spread of authoritarian, nationalist state ideologies, and the weakening of plural societies around the world.

THE VIEWS OF OTHERS

Many central media correspondents agree with the idea of "positive reporting" and bristle at being seen as brainwashed puppets, but still chafe at the constraints they face. They see themselves as cosmopolitan persons in the sense that they want to be open to the views of others, but they remain committed nationalists in their work and their thinking. There are also those who are hostile or uninterested in the views of non-Chinese, and some of them are among the most highly reputed reporters within their organizations. Such correspondents sometimes talk about how they find it impossible to talk to Western journalists because their approach to events is so different.

But even personal friendships with Western colleagues sometimes co-exist with blanket resentment of the presumed agenda of "Western media" or of the West's past aggression towards China. A CCTV correspondent jokingly reports how being "stood up" by a French interviewee who did not show up for their appointment made her so furious as to want to "settle all scores beginning from 1860," a reference to the Opium War that, though joking, nonetheless reveals how, for many, Europe is still closely associated with China's past humiliations.[8] Conversely, loyalty to the state's agenda does not always stand in the way of human concern towards those on the other side. A CCTV journalist, for instance, helped an anti-Gaddafi rebel in Libya obtain medical treatment in China despite supporting the Chinese government's view that Gaddafi's overthrow was illegal. Although her actions may well have served China's and CCTV's interests by garnering some credit with the rebel forces, which resented China's position, it was nonetheless an initiative she took as an individual. The views of such journalists, as well as the views of colleagues who disagree with them but struggle to translate their more critical views into reporting, show that the government's line on the nation's rightful fight against a Western conspiracy is not simply a top-down affair. It also corresponds to grassroots sentiment, and reporters are caught in between.

This is true, too, for correspondents for the commercialized media. Only a handful of journalists identify with the mission described by former *Southern Weekend* senior foreign reporter Qin Xuan in this way: "In the past decade, information exchange between ordinary Chinese people and international society at the personal level has become a common occurrence, but in people's minds, there still is a solid and thick wall that reporting must constantly work at removing."[9] One of these few, Chen Yan, is one of China's best-known foreign affairs reporters. Chen is just half a decade older than most journalists interviewed for this book, but is one of very few foreign-affairs journalists of his generation in the commercial media who are still active; those a few years younger sometimes respectfully call him "Teacher Chen."

Chen, who has written for many commercial papers but has never been posted abroad, has not studied in the West, and his conversational English is not good. He has none of the worldly air of some of the younger correspondents and dresses in an understated, slightly old-fashioned way that could identify an engineer as well as a small businessman. During his studies, he spent some time in the Middle East, and that region, as well as Asia, remains his chief interest. It is mostly these countries that he has covered, traveling extensively on short assignments that produced some risqué stories such as a telephone interview with the wife of a detained Lao human rights activist.

Although his reporting trips were mostly limited to two a year, the timeframe was generous—once he spent fifty days in the Middle East—and Chen had the privilege of doing only features, two or three a month, with no further obligations, an arrangement almost unparalleled in Chinese media. By 2014, however, as the room for journalism outside the official line diminished, Chen, an outspoken liberal, clashed with his management with increasing frequency. His travel budget was also slashed. Finally, he moved to a smaller publication.

Most of Chen's reporting is intended as implicit criticism of China, whether about Vietnam's decision to allow private ownership of land or about the overthrow of the Mubarak regime. With the story about the Lao activist, Chen says, he wanted to help him but also to show his readers that social activism was something normal, not a subversive activity to be afraid of. In 2012, when he wrote about Indian economic reform, he focused on the checks and balances in India's federal political system that slowed down the setting up of special economic zones, a government plan inspired by China's experience. While central media largely interpreted this as a matter of inefficiency, Chen was interested in the ability of local governments to oppose central plans. When he visited Burma after the end of military rule, he was interested in civil society organizations that tried to facilitate reconciliation between the central government and the ethnic insurgencies in the country's north. Could there be a role for such groups in Tibet or Xinjiang? None of these parallels were spelled out in the articles, but they would have been obvious for readers.

Chen sees advocating liberal values as part of his mission. Until the recent media crackdown, the group he wrote for was known for this advocacy, although not all journalists and editors were equally invested in this project. While some journalists at other commercial media criticized its style as overly emotional and occasionally long-winded (*shui*, literally "watery"), for Chen, his former organization did not go far enough. During our first conversation, Chen said: "I don't approve of the way [it] fights. We are opposition, but at the same time, we have to consider the Party," for example, the balance of power between hardliners and reformers. "Actually, everyone should express their opinion" instead of trying to tiptoe around the Party's sensitivities while smuggling messages in between the lines. "But I don't want to be Mandela." Another prominent Chinese foreign affairs journalist asked, in an article published in the United States, whether "the linguistic tricks Chinese journalists use to express their opinions" were "just another form of self-censorship."[10] With the proliferation of instant online media, as there was less and less need for journalists to focus on the "three Ws" (what, where, when), Chen believed they should concentrate even more strongly on advocacy and opinion in order to help readers make sense of the news.

Soon, it became clear that being more outspoken was not an option, and even the previous "linguistic tricks" were no longer tolerated. Because of his outspoken criticism of government harassment of journalists after the 2013 events at *Southern Daily* (see chapter 1), Chen believed he might himself be on the state security organs' target list. At the time of his most recent change of jobs, Chen was seriously considering leaving both journalism and China, as he felt print media were longer able to set the political agenda and were increasingly stifled by censorship. Chen once commented that if he had a child, he would want to "run away" from China so the child would not have to grow up there. On another occasion, he remarked that he and his wife did not own an apartment, a rarity for a professional couple their age these days and almost certainly an indication of disdain for a family man's social obligation to strive for financial security and accumulation. Ironically, the birth of Chen's child may in the end have played a role in his decision to stay in the profession and in the country for the relative existential security it provided.

When asked about the angle they took in reporting a particular story, most journalists justified it by referring to criteria of professionalism or objectivity, unless it was on a subject that they viewed as requiring defending the "Chinese stance." Very few reporters, even if they believed that the cards in global media were stacked against China and needed to be reshuffled, were prepared to renounce completely the seemingly universalistic values of journalistic professionalism. Those who diverged from this were at the two extremes of the political spectrum of Chinese media: journalists at

People's Daily or Xinhua who believed that media always had to work for the national interest and those of the old guard of the Southern group who, like Chen, believed that reporters should focus on enlightenment advocacy rather than on the "three Ws."

One of Chen's younger allies and admirers is Xiang Ling, a foreign desk editor at highly regarded commercialized newsmagazine, about a decade his junior. In 2009, after graduation from a university in central China—"my teacher was liberal-leaning," she explains—she joined Xinhua in the expectation that she would be sent abroad. Her first assignment was at *International Herald Leader,* an offshoot of *Reference News.* But a year at the organization made her change her mind. Disappointed by foreign correspondents' stories about their daily routine and hurdles on reporting and distraught when a *lingdao* commented that a story she wrote on a scandal around food safety "should not be so balanced," she quit and moved to the commercial magazine. Xiang struggles daily with her doubts whether her work, with all its limitations, is meaningful, but has no interest in moving to public relations, the other easily available option. She tells herself that her magazine still runs stories no one else does. For instance, one of their stories questioned the accepted view that Japanese refused to face their war past while Germans had done so successfully. "This is very un-PC." But by 2014, the magazine was having unprecedented difficulties getting its cover stories—on issues the editors considered safe—through censors and repeatedly faced the threat of being pulled off newsstands. In most cases, a compromise was eventually worked out, but one whose cover story was on a senior Chinese imam was banned from open sale (subscribers still received it).

Xiang's magazine does not cover hard news and distinguishes itself from other news media by having less of a focus on the United States. "We are more interested in ideology and politics, particularly in countries that are comparable to China, and these tend to be developing countries." They often write about North Korea—because journalists are freer to write about this than other subjects—and Vietnam, but also Japan. They published a story on Vietnam's "de-Sinicization": the program that mandates discontinuing the use of Chinese software in government departments and other contracts that are perceived to expose the country to Chinese influence. The angle Xiang instructed journalists to use is that this campaign, like other Vietnamese government actions, copies China's own programs to purge the government of depending on the United States. This is a sort of reflexivity that goes against the grain of usual reporting in China.

Xiang goes on some reporting assignments of her own. She has, for example, covered the national elections in India and the Valdai Forum, Russia's answer to Davos. Here, she was primarily interested in Russian attitudes to China, and found that contrary to what some Chinese commentators have said, Russian politicians did not see China as an ally.

Echoing Chen, Xiang says if she had a child she would not want it to go to school in China and have its views shaped the way her own had been. Pointing to a book about Germans under Nazism she was reading when I first met her, Milton Mayer's *They Thought They Were Free,* she suggested people in China lived with a similar illusion. Beyond such bold but private criticism of Chinese society, Xiang has taken the risky step of helping political prisoners: on WeChat, she called on her friends to donate money to the wife of Ilham Tohti, an Uyghur academic sentenced to life in prison on separatism-related charges.

Chen Yan says he had at one point in his college years been attracted to the nationalistic ideas espoused by journalism professor Li Xiguang, the author of *Behind the Demonization of China.* Another prominent liberal foreign affairs journalist for a commercial magazine said he read a similar book, *China Can Say No,* in secondary school and "found it great," until, together with a group of friends, he started listening to Voice of America and Radio Free Asia, another US station broadcasting in Chinese, "because we thought it was cool." Xiang, however, recalls Zhang Yihe's 2004 book *The Past Is Not Another Country* (Wangshi bing bu ru yan), which someone had brought back from Hong Kong, as having a decisive influence on her thinking while at secondary school. Zhang's book, published but then banned in mainland China, was about the 1957 Anti-Rightist Campaign, a crackdown on intellectuals who had criticized the Party; it whetted Xiang's appetite for more literature critical of communist totalitarianism, including *1984.* So by the time she enrolled for her master's degree with the liberal professor, her views had been more or less formed. She points out that a classmate who studied with the same professor was and has remained a Maoist.

Chen's and Xiang's openly political stances are atypical of foreign correspondents. In some cases, their reticence to embrace a normative mission had undoubtedly to do with political constraints, existential insecurities, and perceived audience expectations. But, as we have seen, it was also related to understandings of journalistic professionalism. Even so, many correspondents do say that they want their readers to know the world better.

When I told a Xinhua editor about a correspondent's wish to change what she felt was a negative perception of Israel in China, he responded: "If you want to change the balance for its own sake, you're not a journalist. It has to be for the sake of truth." A correspondent for a central newspaper similarly commented that journalists who wanted their readers to think one way or another were "not outstanding journalists."

Many of these journalists interpreted the requirement to be professional and objective within a framework of "patriotic professionalism."[11] As we have already seen in chapter 4, the line between situations that required objectivity and those that required the defense of "China's interests" was blurred and often unclear to the reporters themselves, as evidenced by the fact that they would often shift from the former kind of explanation to the latter as they explained why they chose a particular approach to a story. That reporting had to be "balanced" was a requirement frequently mentioned by editors and reporters, and yet, at least in central media, it was also understood that "balance" meant different things depending on whether or not the Chinese government had an explicit point of view or specific instructions on the subject. For a foreign desk editor at CRI, an example of objective reporting was that reports on former British prime minister Margaret Thatcher's death, when mentioning the Falklands War between Britain and Argentina, did not talk about an Argentine "invasion" of the islands but about a "dispute," and referred to the islands using both their English and Spanish names. Yet the editor considered this framing "objective" not because it was a factually unbiased account of the conflict but because the Chinese government had been neutral in it. In some situations, she added, one had to "cooperate" (peihe) with the government. But other correspondents' active and even effusive identification with what they perceived to be the nation's agenda suggested something more than simply the internalization of the necessity to obey authorities' instructions.

Furthermore, unlike, for example, schoolteachers, most (though certainly not all) state media correspondents, despite many complaints, feel that their working conditions are, on the whole, improving and that their organizations are becoming more professional.[12] While they appreciate the broadening of the room for technical innovation—for example, with the formatting of programs—they show little concern with the tightening of the room available for critical views, perhaps because that room has been tight throughout their professional careers, and whatever shifts are taking place matter little for their daily work. In 2016, an unusual blanket ban was issued on reporting any news related to the Panama Papers—the biggest corporate data leak in history, which caused the resignation of Iceland's premier and named politicians in scores of countries involved in offshore tax haven schemes—because the papers also implicated Xi Jinping's brother-in-law and two Politburo members. But a CCTV correspondent just shrugged: "So we don't report. What can we do?" (*Global Times* ignored the ban and published an editorial declaring the Panama leak a tool of American propaganda against Russia and China. The editorial was later deleted.)

Humans are rarely consistent in their beliefs and actions, and it is not surprising that young Chinese correspondents, under conflicting pressures, often express contradictory opinions about their work. John, the correspondent who questioned the validity of my research in such a poignant fashion, dismissed political constraints as an excuse for poor journalism, then in the same breath called Xinhua a "defender of policy" rather than a real news agency. He stressed his wish to "tell stories with African voices" and yet called himself a realist who knew that all media, first and foremost, served their own agenda. Just as a cosmopolitan habitus coexists, for some, with nationalistic views, so the universalistic discourse of journalistic professionalism overlaps, to a large extent, with the belief that media is part of politics.

By the end of 2013, the balance between professionalism and representing national interests seemed to be shifting in favor of the latter. In October 2014, the shift culminated in the "Forum on Literature and the Arts," the first since Mao's time, at which Xi Jinping, emulating Mao, recalled that literature and the arts must serve the purposes of the Party, and urged writers to take patriotism as the central theme of their work and "guide the people to establish and uphold the correct views of history, the people and the country," naming the nationalist blogger Zhou Xiaoping as a positive example (see chapter 1).[13] In parallel, campaigns unfolded against social scientists and university professors who "eat the Party's rice and smash the Party's pots," a formulation reportedly used by Xi himself, or otherwise challenge or neglect ideological correctness.[14] "So-called 'experts' and 'scholars' with Western backgrounds who have infested/infiltrated (*hunru*) some government organs, some cadres who are in bed with the Party but have different dreams have not only not been criticized but been promoted and given important assignments," a report warned ominously.[15] The spread of such Cultural Revolution-style attacks suggested that the government was now openly backing the view that China was suffering under a cabal of liberal public intellectuals, a mantra that had been staple for *Global Times*— which attacked "some Chinese media" for borrowing American media's terms in reporting on the Gulf War and inadvertently "serving as their weapon" over ten years earlier—but had rarely surfaced in official communications.[16] This was undoubtedly related to the warning in the internal Party Document No. 9 that notions of media independence and "universal values" threatened the Party's survival.[17]

The new language amounted to upending the status quo that had allowed public intellectuals and prominent journalists to occupy positions both "inside the system," where they would refrain from making openly oppositional statements, and in international professional networks, where they sometimes would not. A minor purge ensued in media and academia. While few foreign desk journalists were directly affected, Qiao Mu, a journalism professor and director of the Centre for International Communications Studies at Beijing Foreign Studies University, was demoted, reportedly for supporting multiparty elections despite his nationalist credentials.[18] (Qiao had been a student and protégé of the prominent nationalist scholar Yan Xuetong, but had made critical comments about the Propaganda Department.) Accordingly, central media leaders such as CCTV President Hu Zhanfan warned journalists that seeing themselves primarily as professionals was a mistake (see chapter 3). It was around this time that CCTV correspondents were instructed to ask US officials more assertive questions. By 2016, remaining liberal media leaders felt pressed to the wall. In February, Caixin's English website made public the deletion of an article by a "government censorship organ."[19] For an organization that had always depended on its connections to parts of China's top leadership for its small freedoms, breaking the taboo on disclosing censorship must have been an act of desperation.

The announcement came in the wake of a highly publicized visit by Xi Jinping to Xinhua, CCTV, and *People's Daily*, where he emphasized that media should work for the Party—even as he admonished staff at CCTV America, via a video connection, to report "objectively and truthfully." Interpreting this as a new policy, a reporter for the *New York Times* suggested that it makes it "harder for foreign governments to determine which Chinese journalists operating in their countries are legitimate news gatherers and which ones are agents serving propaganda, intelligence or other official interests."[20] In reality, Xi's speech hardly marked a new era: it merely underscored a set of longstanding policies that have been, in the past years, gradually tightened. Separating news gathering from propaganda has never been possible for most Chinese reporters abroad. On the contrary, as a Xinhua correspondent commented, Xi's reminder that Chinese media were and remained government departments made it only more urgent that they develop a standing as bona fide international news media in order to better serve the Party's interests. Indeed, a *People's Daily* reporter pointed out that a new regulation was issued in 2015 that prohibits Chinese journalists from publishing in foreign media—but simultaneously, another regulation says that Chinese journalists are encouraged to publish in foreign media in order to "make our voice" heard. Whether such a publication deserves praise or punishment depends, then, on how it is judged by the *lingdao*.

COSMOPOLITAN LIFESTYLES, NATION-CENTERED WRITING

The days when Xinhua correspondents lived in embassy compounds and were the only Chinese journalists in town are largely over. The majority of Chinese correspondents now live in rented housing that is scattered all over town rather than being concentrated in the same building. Yet, on the whole, central media correspondents—unlike those for commercial media—remain relatively sequestered from local society: most of them rarely socialize with non-Chinese, and their daily routines are structured more by their bureau chiefs, colleagues, and editors back in China than by the world around them. Very often, like other expats, they are comfortable and familiar with the international scene of downtown cafes but are not very familiar with how locals live; some use local Chinese media as sources on what is happening locally. This is so even at those Xinhua and CCTV bureaus where significant numbers of local staff have been hired to boost foreign-language services. Restrictions on private interaction with foreigners have not been completely lifted: *People's Daily* reporters are prohibited from having amorous/sexual relations with them, while *People's Daily*, Xinhua, and CCTV staff are technically required to obtain authorization from the organization before talking to them about their work, a requirement not everyone complies with strictly.

It does not help that most correspondents, whether for central or commercial media, live on a shoestring, and the costs of meals and entertainment aimed at networking cannot be reimbursed. A CCTV reporter in Europe described how she waited in vain for an interviewee to show up because, to save on roaming fees, she had turned off her cellphone and had therefore failed to receive his message cancelling the appointment.[21] A further obstacle is that, compared to the past when correspondents trained in so-called "minor languages" (*xiao yuzhong*, anything other than English and Russian) were often posted to regions of their linguistic competence, young reporters tend to speak English but rarely anything else. Most bureaus in Jerusalem had no Hebrew or Arabic speaker during the period of my research, and among five journalists at *People's Daily*'s Brussels bureau there was not a single speaker of French. It does not come as a surprise that feeling lonely is a recurrent theme in accounts of being a foreign correspondent.

Few journalists are sufficiently familiar with the society they report on to be able to pick up on the deeper implications of a story; surprisingly often, in "soft" news, they report unverified hearsay or make simple factual mistakes, such as calling the conservative British tabloid *Daily Mail* a left-wing newspaper (a *Global Times* correspondent) or placing the Falkland Islands in the Pacific Ocean instead of the Atlantic (a CCTV reporter). In some stories with a more personal touch, annoyance with Europe's slowness and "culture of appointments" or African corruption is mixed with appreciation of people's good manners or ability to "enjoy life": a perfectly reasonable reaction from a casual visitor, but perhaps a little anodyne for a foreign correspondent.[22] Some Chinese correspondents, when asked about their general impressions of the country they are stationed in—and this included both those in Africa and Europe—find strikingly little to say that is positive.

Even so, the personal habitus of Chinese correspondents is increasingly cosmopolitan. Not only is their range of interactions with local society broadening—a significant change compared to ten years ago is that correspondents for Xinhua, *People's Daily*, and other media are now allowed to take families with them, resulting in children being enrolled in local or international schools—so is their ability and desire to transcend a national framework when reflecting on their own or others' lives. A number of journalists choose to have children while abroad—not only in Europe but also in Africa and Southeast Asia—because they consider the environment less polluted and the lifestyle more relaxed. Some commercial media correspondents are in relationships with or married to non-Chinese. Some want, and do, tell their readers about foreign lifestyles. And a few actively embrace "compassionate cosmopolitanism:" a young Xinhua correspondent in Africa does volunteer work every weekend in a slum and wanted to write about it so Chinese readers may be moved to help—and so Chinese companies might become better at their "social responsibility" work. Many acknowledge how being abroad has changed their thinking and values, often in complex ways. One CCTV correspondent in Europe said, for example, that she first reacted with an overwhelming enthusiasm for how things are done there: "Everything in Europe was good and everything in China was bad." Later, she developed what she describes as a more differentiated view, acknowledging positive and negative sides both here and there and refraining from criticism of more nationalistic or conservative views in China.

Yet, as we have seen, none of this necessarily translates into reporting that transcends national concerns. The cosmopolitan persona projected by many correspondents sometimes appears hard to square with stories that reproduce official speeches, sometimes full of anti-Western invective—even if such stories now account for only a small proportion of their writing. Some journalists are comfortable with the role of "speaking for China," others insist that they have no business influencing their audiences and rationalize reproducing official propaganda as an unavoidable part of working for state media, sometimes drawing parallels to Voice of America or the French news agency AFP. A few wish they could report stories about the world for its own sake, without regard to a Chinese perspective, but this is not what their editors, senior management, or indeed readers want. In other words, it appears that systemic constraints, some of which are more internalized than others, are the main reason for the rather narrowly national perspective that prevails in the stories. In any case, on the whole, journalists unsurprisingly tend to choose and frame stories in a way that conforms to expectations dictated from home.

The in-depth financial reporting of *21st Century Business Herald*, the "soft" social stories of Sina Finance, the critical analysis of Caixin, but also the extended scope of reporting by CRI, CCTV, Xinhua, and even *People's Daily* certainly present Chinese readers with much more information on the world, and arguably more diverse and nuanced information, than what was accessible to them just ten years ago. Overall, this is a less black-and-white, more complex world, which is exactly what many correspondents say they aspire to picture. Even *Global Times*, whose heavily redacted foreign reporting—typically put together by editors from material supplied by *People's Daily* correspondents and stringers—is often tendentious and sometimes sloppy, and whose op-eds generally propagate a view in which America, China, and Japan are locked in a merciless struggle for dominance, presents a more multifaceted world than the sterile official version of its parent paper did in the past. And while important foreign news sources such as the Chinese version of the *New York Times* remain blocked, China's lively social media offers instantaneous (though selective) translations of most important stories published abroad, along with commentary to suit all tastes from the ultranationalist to the liberal.

It is therefore safe to say that Chinese readers are, or can be if they so choose, better informed about the world than they were only a short time ago. For many correspondents, a better-informed Chinese public—or better-informed political and economic elites—is what they see as the goal of their work. Others formulate farther-reaching aims of improving Chinese society, which generally means making it more humane, more civil, and better governed—although *People's Daily* and *Southern Weekend* journalists are likely to disagree on how to achieve this. But although many believe, and some lament, that the Chinese public's curiosity about world affairs is limited by an optic that is focused on how China is refracted through them, very few see making the Chinese public more open to the world or changing China's relationship to it as a professional goal. Because of this, despite all the distance that Chinese media have covered in their foreign reporting in the last decade or two and their internal diversity, correspondents can still be said to be working, consciously or unconsciously, on changing the world rather than China. They do so by representing it in terms that are palatable to Chinese audiences and as a foil to Chinese endeavors rather than as an end in itself—even if the audiences and endeavors in question differ across media. Where journalists are concerned, the Chinese, it seems, does not so much encounter as subsume the foreign.[23]

*　*　*

It has been pointed out by several authors that the concern with the "foreign" (by default understood as the "Western") has persistently been driven by desires to validate China's achievements or alternatively, to decry its failures through its reflection in foreign eyes.[24] Today, both the Chinese government and many intellectuals are actively working to "move China out of a position of being fixed, of being defined and understood on someone else's terms" and into a position where *its* definitions of others are seen as credible and widely accepted.[25] For those engaged in this effort, like for those working in the tradition they oppose, the foreign remains largely a foil. Foreign correspondents for both central and commercial media, regardless of their political persuasion, remain steeped in the former intellectual tradition and therefore either willingly contribute to or, at any rate, do not actively counteract the latter trend. While state officials no longer have a monopoly on defining the terms that describe China's others, they continue to play a central role in guiding and coopting those who define those terms. It is here that *Global Times*, which deliberately serves as a bridge between popular online discussions and the authoritative voice of officials and "experts," plays a central role. (Its editor-in-chief regularly claims to represent mainstream public opinion.)

In the 1990s, the *New York Times* shifted to a foreign reporting less focused on political news and more "environmental issues, histories of ethnic friction and economic developments that might no longer be confined to the financial section of the paper." "We are interested in what makes societies different," wrote the paper's foreign desk editor at the time.[26] This sort of reporting stood a chance to make "audiences feel more realistically at home in the world.[27]" Twenty years later, in his comment bemoaning the decimation of American foreign correspondents, his successor (and later the paper's executive editor), Bill Keller, wrote that the *New York Times* or the BBC still maintain their networks because "our identity (our brand, to use the obnoxious term of the art) promises the world."[28]

Despite the growth of Chinese foreign correspondent networks, no Chinese media has as yet made that promise. Commenting on the reporting about the Malaysian Airlines flight's disappearance, *21st Century Business Herald*'s Zuo Zhixian reportedly exclaimed: "China has no real international news."[29] And as a Caixin correspondent said, uncannily echoing Keller: "There is no medium in China that has a mission to cover the world." Later on, after having quit the paper, he e-mailed a more damning comment:

> State-owned [media are] too biased and incapable; non-state-owned too constrained with budget, hence no good journalists. When I arrived here [on his last reporting trip] and saw international news organizations with teams working on a project and active interactions between reporters and editors, I kept feeling ashamed as a journalist from China: no wonder there is no the *New York Times* and BBC. China is not in a position to blame the West [for] see[ing] us in a distorted way, because we don't even bother to closely look at them.

A *People's Daily* correspondent agreed with him. "We are very lucky not to lack money. But we cannot do proper news reporting that is truthful and objective, because we don't respect the rules of news reporting. How can we then have credibility? We have 1.3 billion people and no good news media. This is very sad."

While limiting foreign news stories to those that can be linked to the readers' own nations is hardly unique to Chinese journalists—in fact, it is such common practice that media scholars have even introduced a special term for it, "domestication"—the absence of more "cosmopolitan" media in a news market with the size, diversity, and global engagement of China is nonetheless striking.[30] Journalists working for Chinese media abroad are aware they can rely on resources that other international media outlets lack or are losing, and that they can enjoy greater freedom than their colleagues in Beijing or at more sensitive foreign posts, and yet they seem unable to seize this opportunity. So far, the emergence of a global network of Chinese correspondents does not appear to have had a major impact on how Chinese people see the world and China's place in it, any more than having a tangible effect on how people elsewhere see China. If such shifts are taking place, or are to take place in the near future, the impetus is likely to come from other corners, notably the personal experiences narrated by young Chinese outside China via the channels of social media. Indeed, such stories are often circulated far more widely and read by more people than those by professional reporters. China Goes Global (Zhongnan Duihua), a website launched by a Chinese journalism graduate from Columbia University with contributors in Africa and South America, is an example of a more professionalized attempt at "citizen journalism" abroad. It takes a critical view of mainstream Chinese reporting and Chinese migrants' attitudes to local societies. The site has published investigative reporting, including a story on the role of Chinese in the illegal ivory trade that has been widely reposted on the Chinese Internet. More generally, as technological and political limits on free expression in China mount even as Chinese-language media around the world grow ever more interconnected, many talented young journalists, professional and part-time, choose to operate transnationally, living outside China and contributing to a variety of established and startup media both in China and outside it.

As Chinese media and audience expectations evolve and as more educated, mobile Chinese engage with the world in different capacities—for example as part of a growing global corps of expatriate managers—the emergence of such transnational journalism, centered on individuals and networks rather than conventional organizations, will be a crucial new trend to watch in China's foreign reporting. So will be the impact of more casual user-generated stories. At the same time, as the world appears to be heading for a period of more conflict, with the premium on "being there" rising again but with Western networks having fewer resources, there is a chance that Chinese correspondents will have the opportunity and the ambition to hone their skills. Yet overall, foreign correspondents, from anywhere but particularly from China, work in a world where both the resources of professional journalism and the room for critical journalism are likely to continue shrinking. This will limit their potential to make audiences feel at home in, or at ease with, the world.

Notes

INTRODUCTION

1   Among many others, this is the central concern in Joshua Kurlantzick's *Charm Offensive* (2008), Martin Jacques' *When China Rules the World* (2009), William Callahan and Elena Barabantseva's *China Orders the World* (2012), and David Shambaugh's *China Goes Global* (2013).

2   Three recent books that discuss the way Chinese businesses proliferate in the world are Howard French's *China's Second Continent* (2015), Juan Pablo Cardenal and Heriberto Araújo's *China's Silent Army* (2014), and Fokke Obbema's *China and the West* (2015). The first two of these stress the ways in which the process furthers the Chinese government's aims.

3   Nyíri and Zhang 2010.

4   Shirk 2011b, 227.

5   Ibid., 228–29.

6   See Schütz 1946 on the emergence of the "well-informed citizen" in the United States.

7   Hannerz 2004, 20–21.

8   On "compassionate cosmopolitanism," see Ibid. 27, cf. Boltanski 1999.

9   Hannerz 2004; Polumbaum 2008.

10 Pan 2000, 272.

11 Ibid., 272–273.

12 See, for example, Boyer 2013.

13 See also Zhang 2011, 101.

14 Crapanzano 2004, 2.

15 See, for example, Calhoun 2002.

16 Rapport 2012, 2.

17 Hannerz 2004, 20–21.

18 Glick Schiller et al. 2011.

19 Hoffman 2010; Hansen 2014.

20   Driessen 2015.
21   Hannerz 2004, 36–37.
22   Hannerz 2003.
23   Boyer 2013; Bishara 2012.

CHAPTER 1

1   Zuo 2011, 64.
2   This figure is also cited by Anne-Marie Brady (2015, 54). Various sources have re-
     ported the total funding to be around $2 billion to $9 billion (e.g., Shambaugh
     2013, 227). As with other data related to government spending, no figure is particu-
     larly reliable, in part because there is no clear bookkeeping to show what part of
     the funding central media organizations have received was intended for over-
     seas expansion. Many of the transfers will have been ad hoc rather than part of a
     planned budget. It appears that the funding is only available to central media or-
     ganizations, but it is hard to tell whether other, smaller ones have also benefited
     from it. No information is made public about the distribution of the funding,
     but there is an element of competitiveness, as news organizations more successful
     at "making China's voice heard" are supposed to be allocated more funding in the
     future.
3   Men 2016.
4   General Administration of News and Publications 2012.
5   See Nelson 2013 and Gagliardone 2013 for two recent, opposing analyses. Other
     contributions to this debate include, among others, Sun 2010, Lye 2010, Wu 2012,
     and Brady 2015.
6   Shambaugh 2013, 222–23.
7   *Global Times* 2010; for an earlier instance of similar criticism at *Global Times*, see
     He Chongyuan 2004, 282.
8   Yang 2003.
9   Davies 2013. On Xi's criticism of officialese and the importance he attributes to
     lively and forceful political speeches, see Zheng Zhizu 2014.
10 See also Xin 2009; Nelson 2013; Gagliardone 2013.
11 Zhang 2011; Xin 2012.
12 Yuan Bingzhong 2006.
13 Zhao 1998; Esarey 2005; Qian and Bandurski 2011; Stockmann 2012, 50–76; Zhu
     2012, 28–53.
14 Shirk 2011a, 11–29; Bandurski 2012.
15 Qian and Bandurski 2011.
16 Brady 2009.
17 Nathan 2003.
18 Shirk 2011a, 32.
19 Tong 2012; Repnikova 2014; Dombernowsky 2014.
20 Yang Xiao 2014.
21 See Repnikova 2014.

22   See also Repnikova 2014.
23   *Cankao Xiaoxi* 2014.
24   Peter, Carrasco et al. 2016.
25   Hu Yong 2014.
26   Polumbaum 2008; Tong 2012.
27   De Burgh 2003.
28   See Bai 2014.
29   See also Hassid 2011.
30   Zheng 2013.
31   Dombernowsky 2014, 58.

CHAPTER 2

1   Hannerz 2004.
2   See, for example, De Burgh 2003; Tong 2012.
3   See also Xu 2009, 359–65.
4   *Southern People Weekly* 2011.
5   Lu Yan 2013, 28.
6   Ibid., 33.
7   On the editorial line of *Global Times*, see Hu Xijin 2011, *Southern People Weekly* 2011, and Lu Yan 2013.
8   Hassid 2011; Kuang et al., n.d.
9   *Southern People Weekly* 2011.
10   Hu Xijin 2011, v.
11   Mi Bohua 2011, i.
12   Ibid.
13   *Southern People Weekly* 2011.
14   Lu Yan 2013, 24.
15   Qin Xuan 2014b.
16   Yang Xiao 2014.
17   http://finance.sina.com.cn/column/international/.
18   http://finance.sina.com.cn/column/international/zhuangqiaoyi.
19   Nelson 2013.
20   For a critique of such a view of Soviet society, see Yurchak 2005.
21   Qin Xuan 2014a.
22   Huang Hongxiang 2014.
23   Zheng 2004, 258.
24   Sopsun 2014; Ma Shaohua 2014.
25   Qin Xuan 2014a.
26   See, for example, Luo Changping 2014; Desimeng 2014.
27   He Xiaoshou 2014; Ma Shaohua 2014.
28   Yangge 2014.
29   Lu Yan 2013, 26.
30   *Southern People Weekly* 2011.

31　Ibid.

32　Sun Wei et al. 2013.

33　"Yuenan yaoshi xiang chongchang lishi jiaoshun ta jiang you dedao chengquan na yi tian" (If Vietnam wants to learn history's lesson again, the day will come). http://mil.huanqiu.com/observation/2014-05/4994670.html.

34　This tendency can also be seen in two collections of editorials (*Global Times* 2011, 2013).

35　*Southern People Weekly* 2011.

36　Lu Yan 2013, 27.

37　See, for example, Guo 2003.

38　Lu Yan 2013, 25; See also He Chongyuan 2004.

39　Lu Yan 2013, 31.

40　*Southern People Weekly* 2011.

41　Lu Yan 2013, 31.

42　Ibid.

43　*Southern People Weekly* 2011.

44　Yuan Bingzhong 2006, 8.

45　Ibid., 10.

46　Quoted in Zhao 1997, 735.

47　Musyoka 2013.

48　Liu Hong 2011, 3.

49　Ibid.

50　For a review of the coverage of the Arab Spring, see Zhang Shixin 2013.

CHAPTER 3

1　Gui 2012, 9. The title of the book, *Shifeizhou,* is a pun that can be roughly translated as "The truths and untruths (*shifei*, true/false) about Africa (*feizhou*)."

2　On the "hero narrative" in Chinese journalism in Africa, see Zhang and Matingwina 2016.

3　*Jiji xuanchuan wo dang he zhengfu de zhengce zhuzhang, youli pibo xifang meiti bu shi yanlun, zengqiang zai guoji shang de huayuquan.*

4　*Jianchi dangxing yuanze shi laolao zhangwo yulun gongzuo zhudongquan de shouyao qianti.*

5　*Dangxing yuanze dou bu neng diu, bu neng wang, jue bu neng you sihao hanhu, pianli he dongyao.* Li 2013.

6　Jacobs 2012.

7　Liu 2004, 2.

8　Liao 2013.

9　For a discussion of the psychological benefits of state-enterprise paternalism, see Cliff 2015.

10　Cliff 2015.

11　Liu 2013.

12　Zhang Xiaoling 2013; Marsh 2014; Madrid-Morales 2016.

CHAPTER 4

1   Bourdieu 1991, 221.
2   See, for example, Liu 2015.
3   Gui 2012, 9.
4   He Chongyuan 2004, 283.
5   Shen 2015, 3.
6   For an analysis of mainstream Chinese media narratives of Europe in the mid-2010s, see Men 2016.
7   Yang 2015, 147. Malvinas is the Argentine name for the Falkland Islands, preferred by the Chinese government and media.
8   Ibid., 150.
9   http://finance.sina.com.cn/column/international.
10   Zhang 2011.
11   Men 2016.
12   Indian journalist Manu Joseph (2013) has made a similar comment on the discrepancy between the mainstay of Indian media's view of Europe and visitors' experiences.
13   I borrow the term "stories of difference" from Hannerz 2004.
14   Hu Shuli 2011.
15   Stockmann 2012; cf. Dombernowsky 2014, 66.
16   Liu 2005.
17   See, for example, Li and Rønning 2013.
18   Because *neican* are not published, their claims cannot be challenged, and the quality of the reporting is unknown. In one example, a *neican* produced by a Xinhua correspondent about the controversy in an African country surrounding a railway being constructed by a major Chinese state enterprise concluded that it was being stoked by the company's competitors. This conclusion was supposedly based on contacts with the authors of the articles in the local press. The correspondent did not actually investigate the behavior of the competitors or obtain evidence.
19   De Burgh 2003; Tong 2012; Zhu 2013; Dombernowsky 2014.
20   See also Li and Rønning 2013.
21   Chubb 2014.
22   See Brady 2012.
23   Piaoguo de yun, 16 March 2014. www.wenxuecity.com/news/2014/03/16/3099989_print.html.
24   See also Stockmann 2012.
25   Ibid., 134.
26   Xinhua, "Envoy to Zimbabwe defends China-Africa relations," *China Daily*, 23 October 2013. www.chinadaily.com.cn/xinhua/2013-10-23/content_10394738.html.

EPILOGUE

1   See, for example, Hassid 2011.
2   See Laidlaw 2002.

3   A recent debate between the anthropologists Nigel Rapport and Ronald Stade (2014) goes some way to make these matters explicit. The subject of the debate is irony, and Rapport suggests that irony can be a form of public engagement on the side of freedom and against the categories of cultural essentialism. Stade questions the legitimacy of such an anthropological engagement.

4   See, for example, Crapanzano's 2003, 2004; Zigon 2009.

5   Zigon 2009, 253.

6   Appadurai 2004, 2007. Appadurai's "capacity to aspire" is related to Crapanzano's (2004) "imaginative horizons."

7   Shweder 2000.

8   Guo 2015, 129.

9   Qin Xuan 2014.

10 Yang Xiao 2014.

11 Hoffman 2010.

12 On pessimism among schoolteachers, see Hansen 2014.

13 Lam 2015.

14 Buckley and Jacobs 2015.

15 *Zhongguo shehui kexue bao* 2014.

16 He Chongyuan 2004, 282.

17 Buckley and Jacobs 2015.

18 Ibid.

19 Forsythe 2016.

20 Wong 2016.

21 Guo 2015, 128.

22 See, for example, Yang 2015.

23 I owe this formulation to Mikkel Bunkenborg.

24 See, for example, Chen 1995.

25 Schmidt 2013.

26 Hannerz 2004, 26.

27 Ibid.

28 Keller 2012.

29 Qin Xuan 2014.

30 On "domestication," see Berglez 2013; Olausson 2013.

Glossary of Chinese Terms

baodaoyuan　报道员　reporter; a job title ranking under *jizhe* and used for locally
　　hired staff at some bureaus outside China

biannei　编内　employees of a state institution; nomenklatura

bianwai　编外　employees of the market arm of a state institution; non-nomenklatura

bianyi　编译　"translating and editing"; producing news stories based on other media

canbianbu　参编部　reference department; the department handling internal
　　reference reports at Xinhua News Agency

cehuabu　策划部　programming department

chunqiu bifa　春秋笔法　language tricks to convey hidden criticism

da cabianqiu　打擦边球　"playing with the edge," or skirting the limits of what
　　is morally or legally permissible.

daibanren　带班人　shift supervisor

danwei　单位　work unit; place of work, especially a state institution or state
　　enterprise

dangxing　党性　partisanship; ideological and disciplinary commitment to the
　　Communist Party

dushibao　都市报　"metropolitan newspaper" (tabloid)

fagaoren　发稿人　"releaser"; a senior editor at Xinhua with the right to sign off
　　on a story

fenlie　分裂　split; a term used to describe territorial separatism, especially in China

fuqidian　夫妻店　"mom-and-pop shop"; a bureau manned by a married couple

gongyi　公益　"public interest"; philanthropy; charity

haogao 好稿 a "good article," an internal award at several media

heshi 核实 verify

huayuquan 话语权 discursive power, voice

jiankanre 监看人 reviewer (at CCTV)

jinqu 禁区 forbidden topic; taboo

jizhe 记者 journalist, reporter, correspondent

kaohe 考核 performance evaluation

laobaixing 老百姓 ordinary people, man-in-the-street

lichang 立场 stance

lingdao 领导 "leaders"; senior officials or managers

Makesizhuyi xinwenguan 马克思主义新闻观 "Marxist news perspective" that Chinese journalists are required to follow

peihe 配合 cooperate, usually with a state institution or official

peihe baodao 配合報道 a report created with contributions by correspondents at multiple locations

Qiaoban 侨办 Overseas Chinese Affairs Bureau of the State Council

qipin 企聘 employee with a company contract; see *bianwai*

san ge tiejin 三个贴近 "three getting-closers": getting closer to reality, the masses, and life; a news doctrine formulated by Chairman Hu Jintao in 2003

shewei 社委 editorial committee member of a media group; senior official in charge of supervising individual media organizations

shichang 市场 market

shichanghua 市场化 commercialized

shiping 时评 commentary

shiye 事业 vocation

shoushilü, shoutinglü 收视率, 收聽率 audience ratings

Tebie Baodaozu 特别报道组 Special Reports Group

tizhi 体制 political system; in China, the Party-state apparatus

tizhinei　体制内　"within-the-system"; individuals or institutions within
the Party-state apparatus

tuozhan xunlian　拓展训练　"development training" for new staff

xiao yuzhong　小语种　"minor languages"

xuantihui　选题会　pitch meeting

you chang wu wen　有偿无闻　"compensation for no news"; withholding
compromising news in exchange for payment

yulun daoxiang　舆论导向　guiding public opinion

yulun jiandu　舆论监督　supervision by public opinion

zhan　站　station; name of overseas bureaus in some media organizations

zhiqingquan　知情权　right to know

zhuanyezhuyi　專業主義　professionalism

Zhongguo lichang, shijie yanguang, renlei gunhuai　中国立场，世界眼光，
人类胸怀　A Chinese Stand, a Global Perspective, a Concern for All
Humanity (a CRI slogan)

zongjian　总监　director of channel; intendant

zuhequan　组合拳　"clenched fist"; report contributed by correspondents
at multiple locations

MEDIA NAMES

21st Century Business Herald　21世纪经济导报　21 Shiji Jingji Daobao
Liberal business daily under the Southern Media Group

Caijing　财经
Liberal financial monthly published by Wang Boming

Caixin　财新
Liberal financial media group led by Hu Shuli

China Newsweek　中国新闻周刊　Zhongguo Xinwen Zhoukan
Newsweekly under China News Service

China-South Dialogue　中南对话　Zhongnan Duihua
Website run by young Chinese "citizen journalists" in Africa

China Radio International (CRI)　中国国际电台　Zhongguo Guoji Diantai

Faces　世界面孔　Shijie Miankong
CCTV show profiling individuals from around the world

First Financial Daily 第一财经日报 Di-yi Caijing Ribao
    Financial daily under Shanghai Media Group

Focal Point 焦点访谈 Jiaodian Fangtan
    Investigative news program on CCTV, famous in the 1990s

Foreign Affairs Weekly 纵横周刊 Zongheng Zhoukan
    Independent foreign news analysis website run by Michael Anti (2006–10)

Global Times 环球时报 Huanqiu Shibao
    Nationalistic commercial daily focused on international affairs under *People's Daily*, led by Hu Xijin

Globe 环球 Huanqiu
    Foreign affairs newsweekly under Xinhua News Agency

Guangming Daily 光明日报 Guangming Ribao
    Daily under the Central Committee of the Chinese Communist Party specializing in ideology, culture, and education

Huanqiu Qiguan 环球奇观
    Global Curiosities, CRI's online TV channel

Huanqiu Wencui 环球文萃
    Former name of *Global Times*

International Herald Leader 国际先驱导报 Guoji Xianqu Daobao
    Foreign affairs daily affiliated with *Reference News*

NewsRadio FM 90.5 环球资讯广播 Huanqiu Zixun Guangbo
    CRI's Chinese-language international news channel, aimed at audiences in China

Oriental Horizon 东方时空 Dongfang Shikong
    Investigative news programme on CCTV, famous in the 1990s

Oriental Morning Post 东方早报 Dongfang Zaobao
    Commercial daily under Shanghai Press Group

Oriental Outlook 瞭望东方周刊 Liaowang Dongfang Zhoukan
    Shanghai-based weekly magazine under Xinhua News Agency

The Paper 澎湃 Pengpai
    News and analysis website under Shanghai Media Group

People's Daily 人民日报 Renmin Ribao
    The Chinese Communist Party's central daily

Phoenix TV 凤凰卫视 Fenghuang Weishi
    Hong Kong-based Mandarin-language satellite channel

Phoenix Weekly 凤凰周刊 Fenghuang Zhoukan
    Phoenix TV's newsweekly

Reference News 参考消息 Cankao Xiaoxi
>   Daily digest of foreign-media owned by Xinhua News Agency

Southern Metropolitan Daily 南方都市报 Nanfang Dushibao
>   Liberal Canton-based commercial tabloid under the Southern Group

Southern People Weekly 南方人物周刊 Nanfang Renwu Zhoukan
>   Liberal Canton-based weekly under the Southern Group

Southern Weekend 南方周末 Nanfang Zhoumo
>   Formerly liberal Canton-based weekly under the Southern Group

References

Chinese characters are provided when they are essential for finding a reference.

Appadurai, Arjun. 2004. "The Capacity to Aspire: Culture and the Terms of Recognition." In *Culture and Public Action*, edited by Vijayendra Rao and Michael Walton, 59–84. Stanford: Stanford University Press.

———. 2007. "Hope and Democracy." *Public Culture* 19(1): 29–34.

Bai, Hongyi. 2014. "Between Advocacy and Objectivity: New Role Models among Investigative Journalists." In *Chinese Investigative Journalists' Dreams*, edited by Marina Svensson, Elin Sæther, and Zhi'an Zhang, 91–112. Lanham, MD: Rowman & Littlefield.

Bandurski, David. 2012. "Jousting with Monsters: Journalists in a Rapidly Changing China." In *China In and Beyond the Headlines*, edited by Timothy B. Weston and Lionel M. Jensen, 29–49. Lanham, MD: Rowman & Littlefield.

Berglez, Peter, ed. 2013. *Global Journalism: Theory and Practice*. New York: Peter Lang.

Bishara, Amahl A. 2012. *Back Stories: U.S. News Production and Palestinian Politics*. Stanford: Stanford University Press.

Boltanski, Luc. 1999. *Distant Suffering: Morality, Media and Politics*. Cambridge: Cambridge University Press.

Bourdieu, Pierre. 1991. *Language & Symbolic Power*. London: Polity.

Boyer, Dominic. 2013. *The Life Informatic: Newsmaking in the Digital Era*. Ithaca, NY: Cornell University Press.

Boyer, Dominic, and Ulf Hannerz. 2006. "Introduction: Worlds of Journalism." *Ethnography* 7(1): 5–17.

Brady, Anne-Marie. 2009. *Marketing Dictatorship: Propaganda and Thought Work in Contemporary China*. Lanham, MD: Rowman & Littlefield.

———. 2012. "'We Are All Part of the Same Family': China's Ethnic Propaganda." *Journal of Current Chinese Affairs* 41(4): 159–81.

———. 2015. "China's Foreign Propaganda Machine." *Journal of Democracy* 26(4): 51–59.

Buckley, Chris, and Andrew Jacobs. 2015. "Maoists in China, Given New Life, Attack Dissent." *New York Times*, 4 January. www.nytimes.com/2015/01/05/world/chinas-maoists-are-revived-as-thought-police.html?_r=1 (accessed 27 October 2015).

Calhoun, Craig J. 2002. "The Class Consciousness of Frequent Travelers: Toward a Critique of Actually Existing Cosmopolitanism." *The South Atlantic Quarterly* 101: 869–97.

Callahan, William A., and Elena Barabantseva, eds. 2012. *China Orders the World: Normative Soft Power and Foreign Policy.* Baltimore: Johns Hopkins University Press.

Cankao Xiaoxi (Reference News). 2014. "Waimei: Xi Jinping cheng Zhongguo jiang jianzhi qiangda xin meiti jituan" (Foreign media: Xi Jinping says China will build strong new media groups), 20 August.

Chen, Xiaomei. 1995. *Occidentalism. A Theory of Counter-Discourse in Post-Mao China.* Oxford: Oxford University Press.

Cardenal, Juan Pablo, and Heriberto Araújo. 2014. *China's Silent Army: The Pioneers, Traders, Fixers and Workers Who Are Remaking the World in Beijing's Image.* New York: Broadway Books.

Chong, Cindy Cheung-Kwan. 2015. "Politics of Homeland: Hegemonic Discourses of the Intervening Homeland in Chinese Diasporic Newspapers in the Netherlands." In *Media and Communication in the Chinese Diaspora. Rethinking Transnationalism*, edited by Wanning Sun and John Sinclair, 109–29. Abingdon, UK: Routledge.

Chubb, Andrew. 2014. "China's Information Management in the Sino-Vietnamese Confrontation: Caution and Sophistication in the Internet Era." *China Brief* 14 (11). www.jamestown.org/programs/chinabrief/single/?tx_ttnews[tt_news]=42471&tx_ttnews[backPid]=25&cHash=453b536d62561783e824d35af8020a43#.VfLEjH2-fIV (accessed 11 September 2015).

Cliff, Tom. 2015. "Post-Socialist Aspirations in a Neo-*Danwei*." *The China Journal* 73: 132–58.

Crapanzano, Vincent. 2003. "Reflections on Hope as a Category of Social and Psychological Analysis." *Cultural Anthropology* 18(1): 3–32.

———. 2004. *Imaginative Horizons; an Essay in Literary-Philosophical Anthropology.* Chicago & London: The University of Chicago Press.

Dai, Wenming. 2013. "Hybrid Journalists—Chinese Journalists in an Era of Reform: Their Values and Challenges." Working paper, Reuters Institute for the Study of Journalism, University of Oxford. https://reutersinstitute.politics.ox.ac.uk/sites/default/files/Hybrid%20Journalists-Chinese%20Journalists%20in%20an%20era%20 of%20reform%20-%20their%20values%20and%20challenges.pdf (accessed 17 August 2015).

Davies, Gloria. 2013. "Fitting Words." In *China Story Yearbook 2013: Civilising China*, edited by Geremie R. Barmé and Jeremy Goldkorn, 384–409. Canberra: Australian Centre on China in the World.

De Burgh, Hugo. 2003. "Kings without Crowns? The Re-emergence of Investigative Journalism in China." *Media, Culture & Society* 25: 801–20.

Desimeng. 2014. "Tanxun Mahang feiji shilian shijian zhenxiang, Zhongguo meiti weihe buru xifang meiti" (Why Chinese media are doing worse than Western media in the search for truth in the missing Malaysian Airlines plane case), Guancha.cn, 16 March. www.guancha.cn/desimeng/2014_03_16_214258.shtml (accessed 21 March 2014. The post has been deleted but is archived at http://blog.of21.com /archives/12139).

Dombernowsky, Laura. 2014. "Chinese Journalism Students: Balancing Competing Values." In *Chinese Investigative Journalists' Dreams*, edited by Marina Svensson, Elin Sæther, and Zhi'an Zhang, 53–73. Lanham, MD: Rowman & Littlefield.

Duara, Prasenjit. 1995. *Rescuing History from the Nation: Questioning Narratives of Modern China.* Chicago: University of Chicago Press.

Driessen, Miriam. 2015. "Migrating for the Bank: Housing and Chinese Labour Migration to Ethiopia." *The China Quarterly* 221: 143–60.

Esarey, Ashley. 2005. "Cornering the Market: State Strategies for Controlling China's Commercial Media." *Asian Perspective* 29(4): 37–83.

French, Howard W. 2014. *China's Second Continent: How a Million Migrants are Building a New Empire in Africa.* New York: Alfred A. Knopf.

Gagliardone, Iginio. 2013. "China as a Persuader: CCTV Africa's First Steps in the African Mediasphere." *Ecquid Novi: African Journalism Studies* 34 (3): 25–40.

General Administration of News and Publications (Xinwen Chuban Zongshu). 2012. *Guanyu jiakuai wo guo xinwen chuban ye zouchuqu de ruogan yijian* (Opinions on accelerating the international expansion of our country's news and publishing industry), 10 January. www.chinaxwcb.com/2012-01/10/content_236045.htm (accessed 11 April 2014).

Glick Schiller, Nina, Tsypylma Darieva, and Sandra Gruner-Domic. 2011. "Defining Cosmopolitan Sociability in a Transnational Age: An Introduction." *Ethnic and Racial Studies* 34 (3): 399–418.

Global Times (Huanqiu Shibao). 2010. "Shandai meiti, peiyu guoji dabao" (Treat the media well, create major international papers), 12 January, 1.

———. 2011. *Jiang zhenhua de Zhongguo* (A truth-speaking China). Beijing: Kexue Chubanshe.

————. 2013. *Zhenhua Zhongguo* (A truth-speaking China). Beijing: *People's Daily* Press.

Gui Tao 桂涛. 2012. *Shifeizhou* 是非洲 (Africa: Truths and falsehoods). Beijing: Zhongguo Dabaikequanshu Chubanshe.

Guo Xining 郭西宁. 2015. "Shenshi fengdu ji dianyou yu yaoji jiu zhi guanxi" (Gentleman's manners and the relationship between e-mail and medicine-grade liquor). In *Yangshi jizhe touguo jing kan Ouzhou* (CCTV journalists look at Europe through the looking-glass), edited by Yang Shanshan 杨姗姗, 127–29. Beijing: China Economic Publishing House.

Guo, Yingjie. 2003. *Cultural Nationalism in Contemporary China: The Search for National Identity Under Reform.* London: RoutledgeCurzon.

Hannerz, Ulf. 2003. "Being There . . . and There . . . and There! Reflections on Multi-Site Ethnography." *Ethnography* 4 (2): 201–16.

————. 2004. *Foreign News.* Chicago: University of Chicago Press.

Hassid, Jonathan. 2011. "Four Models of the Fourth Estate: A Typology of Contemporary Chinese Journalists." *The China Quarterly* 208: 813–32.

Hansen, Mette Halskov. 2014. *Educating the Chinese Individual: Life in a Rural Boarding School.* Seattle: University of Washington Press.

He Chongyuan 何崇元. 2004. "Guoji xinwen bianji de 'si ge yishi'" (The "four awarenesses" of international news editors). In *Zenyang zuo guoji xinwen bianji* (How to be an international news editor), edited by Liu Hongchao 刘洪潮, 281–88. Beijing: Zhongguo Chuanmei Daxue Chubanshe.

He Xiaoshou. 2014. "Mahang shilian shijian zhong de Zhongguo meiti" (China's media through the MH 370 disappearance case), *Xinmin Wanbao*, 18 March. http://star .news.sohu.com/20140318/n396780031.shtml (accessed 5 April 2014).

Hoffman, Lisa. 2010. *Patriotic Professionalism in Urban China: Fostering Talent.* Philadelphia: Temple University Press.

Hu Shuli. 2011. "The Rise of the Business Media in China." In *Changing Media, Changing China,* edited by Susan L. Shirk, 77–90. Oxford: Oxford University Press.

Hu Xijin. 2011. "*Huanqiu Shibao* sheping shi zenme xiechulai de" (How *Global Times* editorials are written), iii–vi. In *A Truth-Speaking China*, edited by *Global Times*. Beijing: Kexue Chubanshe.

Hu Yong. 2014. "Under Pressure. China's Market-Oriented Media Face a Precarious Future." *Nieman Reports*, Winter: 30.

Huang Hongxiang. 2014. " 'Zhongguo zouchuqu' yu Zhongguo NGO de zouchuqu" ("China going out" and Chinese NGOs going out), 8 April. www.chinagoingout.org /archives/973 (accessed 27 November 2014).

Jacobs, Andrew. 2012. "Pursuing Soft Power, China Puts Stamp on Africa's News." *New*

York Times, 16 August. www.nytimes.com/2012/08/17/world/africa/chinas-news-media-make-inroads-in-africa.html?pagewanted=2&_r=0 (accessed 26 July 2015).

Jacques, Martin. 2008. *When China Rules the World.* London: Penguin.

Joseph, Manu. 2013. "Transplanting Europe's Joy and India's." *International New York Times*, 5 December, 2.

Keller, Bill. 2012. "Being There." *New York Times,* 2 December.

Kuang, Xianwen, Erik Albæk, and Claes H. de Vreese. N.d. "Self-Caging or Playing with the Edge?: News Selection Autonomy of News Media in Authoritarian China." Paper presented at the Annual ICA Conference.

Kurlantzick, Joshua. 2008. *Charm Offensive: How China's Soft Power is Transforming the World.* New Haven: Yale University Press.

Laidlaw, James. 2002. "For an Anthropology of Ethics and Freedom." *Journal of the Royal Anthropological Institute* 8: 311–22.

Lam, Willy. 2015. "Xi Jinping Consolidates Power While Presiding Over Tilt Towards Ultra-Conservative Ideals." *China Brief* 15: 21.

Langkilde, Desmond. 2013. "Why China is Making a Big Play to Control Africa's Media." *Tourism Tattler* (Lusaka), 19 October. http://www.tourismtattler.co.za/why-china-is-making-a-big-play-to-control-africas-media/#sthash.IAnsw9pV.dpuf (accessed 14 December 2013).

Li Congjun. 2013. "Laolao zhangwo yulun gongzuo zhudongquan" (Firmly grasp the initiative in discourse work), *People's Daily*, 4 September. http://media.people.com.cn/n/2013/0904/c40606-22798147.html (accessed 14 November 2013).

Li, Shubo, and Helge Rønning. 2013. "Half-Orchestrated, Half Freestyle: Soft Power and Reporting Africa in China." *Ecquid Novi: African Journalism Studies* 34 (3): 102–24.

Liao Yi (2013) "Makesizhuyi xinwenguan jiaoyu huodong baogaohui zai Beijing juban" (Conference reporting on Marxist news perspective education activities held in Beijing), Xinhua, 31 October. http://news.xinhuanet.com/newmedia/2013-10/31/c_125626825.htm (accessed 27 July 2015).

Liu Guangyuan. 2013. "Deepen China-Africa Media Cooperation and Enrich the China-Africa Community of Shared Destinies." Speech at the seminar on China-Africa Media Cooperation, Nairobi, 18 November. http://www.fmprc.gov.cn/eng/wjb/zwjg/zwbd/t1100583.shtml)#sthash.VlDzRku8.dpuf (accessed 14 December 2013).

Liu Hong 刘洪. 2005. *Tears in Jerusalem. He Shalong zuo lingju* (Being neighbours with Sharon). Beijing: Zhongguo Wenlian Chubanshe.

———. 2011. *Meiguo "yinmou"* (The American "conspiracy"). Beijing: Zhongguo Hua-qiao Chubanshe.

Liu Hongchao 劉洪潮, ed. 2004. *Zenyang zuo guoji xinwen bianji* (How to be an inter-national news editor). Beijing: Zhongguo Chuanmei Daxue Chubanshe.

Liu Xin 劉欣 (2015) "Yi he wenti jieduanxing xieyi chutai baodao jishi" (How the step-wise agreement on Iran's nuclear question was signed), 165–84. In *Yangshi jizhe tou-guo jing kan Ouzhou* (CCTV journalists look at Europe through the looking-glass), edited by Yang Shanshan 楊姍姍. Beijing: China Economic Publishing House.

Lu Yan. 2013. "*Huanqiu Shibao* shi zenme liancheng de" (How *Global Times* was tem-pered), *Phoenix Weekly* (Fenghuang Zhoukan), 25 September, 23–33.

Luo Changping. 2014. "Mahang shilian baodao deshi" (Reporting on lost Malaysian plane: gains and losses), Jizhezhan.net, 5 April. www.jizhezhan.net/article. php?id=490 (accessed 6 April 2014).

Lye Liang Fook. 2010. "China's Media Initiatives and Its International Image Building." *International Journal of China Studies* 1(2): 545–68.

Ma Shaohua 马少华 (2014). "Mahang shilian: Zhongguo meiti luohou zai nali" (MH dis-appearance: Why are Chinese media behind?) WeChat post on Qianyan wanyu 仟言万语 group account, 19 March. http://mp.weixin.qq.com/s?__biz=MjM5OTAxNTE 0OA==&mid=200088886&idx=1&sn=7f45ad3c25edfde2f45826b382fb065a&scene= 2&from=timeline&isappinstalled=0&uin=MjA3NDUzNjIwMA%3D%3D (accessed 5 April 2014).

Madrid-Morales, Dani. 2016. "Why Are Chinese Media in Africa? Evidence from Three Decades of Xinhua's News Coverage of Africa." In *China's Media and Soft Power in Africa: Promotion and Perceptions*, edited by Xiaoling Zhang, Herman Wasserman, and Winston Mano, 79–92. Basingstoke, UK: Palgrave Macmillan.

Marsh, Vivien. 2014. "Chinese State Television's 'Going Out' Strategy—a True Global News Contraflow? A Comparison of News on CCTV's Africa Live and BBC World News TV's Focus on Africa." Paper presented at the conference "China's Soft Power in Africa: Emerging Media and Cultural Relations between China and Africa," Not-tingham Ningbo University, Ningbo, 5 September.

Men, Jing. 2016. "Chinese Media in Brussels and EU-China Relations." *International Communication Gazette* 78 (1–2): 9–25.

Mi Bohua 米博华 2011. "Ju zhongren zhihui, cheng yi jia zhi yan" (Unite the wisdom of the masses and turn them into a single voice). In *A Truth-Speaking China*, edited by *Global Times*. Beijing: Kexue Chubanshe, i–ii.

Musyoka, David. 2013. "Interview: Expert Sees Opportunities for China-Africa Media to Expand Global Influence." *The Africa Daily*, 19 November. www.theafricadaily.com /15/post/2013/11/interview-expert-sees-opportunities-for-china-africa-media-to -expand-global-influence.html#sthash.yrWeywk6.dpuf (accessed 7 March 2015).

Nathan, Andrew J. 2003. "Authoritarian Resilience." *Journal of Democracy* 14 (1): 6–17.

Nelson, Anne. 2013. *CCTV's International Expansion: China's Grand Strategy for Me-dia?* Washington, DC: Center for International Media Assistance.

Nyíri, Pál. 2005. "Global Modernizers or Local Subalterns? Parallel Perceptions of Chinese Transnationals in Hungary." *Journal of Ethnic and Migration Studies* 31(4): 659–74.

———. 2006. "The Yellow Man's Burden: Chinese Migrants on a Civilizing Mission." *The China Journal* 56: 83–106.

———. 2013. "Chinese Investors, Labour Discipline and Developmental Cosmopolitanism." *Development and Change* 44 (6): 1387–1405.

Nyíri, Pál, Juan Zhang, and Merriden Varrall. 2010. "China's Cosmopolitan Nationalists: 'Heroes' and 'Traitors' of the 2008 Olympics." *The China Journal* 63:25–55.

Obbema, Fokke. 2015. *China and the West: Hope and Fear in the Age of Asia.* London and New York: I. B. Tauris.

Olausson, Ulrika. 2013. "Theorizing Global Media as Global Discourse." *International Journal of Communication* 7: 1281–97.

Pan Zhongdang. 2000. "Spatial Configuration in Institutional Change: A Case of China's Journalism Reforms." *Journalism* 1(3): 253–81.

Peter, Alain, Silvia Carrasco, and Chen Mengshu. 2016. "Power Interplay and Newspaper Digitization: The Pengpai Case." Paper presented at the conference "China and the Changing Geopolitics of Global Communication," University of Westminster, London, 9 April.

Polumbaum, Judy. 2008. *China Ink: The Changing Face of Chinese Journalism.* Lanham, MD: Rowman & Littlefield.

Qian, Gang and David Bandurski. 2011. "China's Emerging Public Sphere: The Impact of Media Commercialization, Professionalism, and the Internet in an Era of Transition." In *Changing Media, Changing China,* edited by Susan L. Shirk, 38–76. Oxford: Oxford University Press.

Qin Xuan. 2014a. "Guandian: Mahang shijian baolu Zhongguo meiti de 'ruanlei ying shang'" (Opinion: Malaysian Airlines incident reveals "hard wound" to Chinese media's "soft spot"), BBC Chinese Service, 21 March. www.bbc.co.uk/zhongwen /simp/china/2014/03/140321_ana_chinamediaonmissingplane.shtml (accessed 27 March 2014).

———. 2014b. "Liehen hen nan mihe: Lun dangxia guoji xinwen jiazhiguan de weiji" (A rift that's hard to heal: On the current value crisis in international news reporting), unpublished article courtesy of author.

Rapport, Nigel. 2012. *Anyone.* New York and Oxford: Berghahn.

Rapport, Nigel, and Ronald Stade. 2014. "Debating Irony and the Ironic as a Social Phenomenon and a Human Capacity." *Social Anthropology* 22 (4): 443–78.

Schmidt, Heather. 2013. "China's Confucius Institutes and the 'Necessary White Body.'" *Canadian Journal of Sociology* 38 (4): 647–66.

Schütz, Alfred. 1946. "The Well-Informed Citizen. An Essay on the Social Distribution of Knowledge." *Social Research* 13(4): 463–78.

Shambaugh, David. 2013. *China Goes Global: The Partial Power.* Oxford: Oxford University Press.

Shen Jianing 申家寧. 2015. "Xuyan" (Preface). In *Yangshi jizhe touguo jing kan Ouzhou* (CCTV journalists look at Europe through the looking glass), edited by Yang Shanshan 楊姍姍, 1–4. Beijing: China Economic Publishing House.

Shirk, Susan L. 2011a. "Changing Media, Changing China." In *Changing Media, Changing China,* edited by Susan L. Shirk, 1–37. Oxford: Oxford University Press.

———. 2011b. "Changing Media, Changing Foreign Policy." In *Changing Media, Changing China,* edited by Susan L. Shirk, 225–52. Oxford: Oxford University Press.

Shweder, Richard A. 2000. "Moral Maps, 'First World' Conceits, and the New Evangelists." In *Culture Matters: How Values Shape Human Progress,* edited by Lawrence E. Harrison and Samuel P. Huntington, 158–76. New York: Basic Books.

sopsun. 2014. "Mahang shilian di-shi tian: Zhongguo meiti weihe zaoyu 911?" (MH disappearance, day 10: Why did Chinese media meet with a 9/11?), *Dongfang Luntan* (*Oriental Morning* online forum), 18 March. http://bbs.eastday.forum.php?mod=viewthread&action=printable&tid=1886216 (accessed 27 March 2014).

Southern People Weekly (Nanfang Renwu Zhoukan). 2011. "*Huanqiu Shibao* bu gaoxing" (*Global Times* is not happy), 24 June.

Stockmann, Daniela. 2012. *Media Commercialization and Authoritarian Rule in China.* Cambridge: Cambridge University Press.

Sun, Wanning. 2010. "Mission Impossible? Soft Power, Communication Capacity, and the Globalization of Chinese Media." *International Journal of Communication* 4: 54–72.

Sun Wei 孙微 et al. 2013. "Yingguo yong 'gangtie fangxian' song tieniangzi" (Britain sees off Iron Lady with an iron cordon), *Global Times* (Huanqiu shibao), 18 April, 16.

Tong, Jingrong. 2012. *Investigative Journalism in China.* London: Bloomsbury.

Wong, Edward. 2016. "Xi Jinping's News Alert: Chinese Media Must Serve the Party," *New York Times,* 22 February.

Wu, Yu-shan. 2012. "The Rise of China's State-Led Media Dynasty in Africa." SAIIA Occasional Paper No. 117. Johannesburg: South African Institute of International Affairs.

Xin, Xin. 2009. "Xinhua News Agency in Africa." *Journal of African Media Studies* 1(3): 363–77.

———. 2012. *How the Market is Changing China's News: The Case of Xinhua News Agency.* Lanham, MD: Lexington Books.

Xu, Xiaoge. 2009. "Development Journalism." In *The Handbook of Journalism Studies,* edited by Karin Wahl-Jorgensen and Thomas Hanitzsch, 357–70. New York and London: Routledge.

Yangge 阳歌 (Doug Young). 2014. "Qian Lutou She jizhe: Zhongguo meiti shu zai na?" (Ex-Reuters correspondent: Where do Chinese media lose out?) *Shanghai Observer* (Shanghai Guancha), 21 March.

Yang Qi 楊起. 2003. "Zhu wai jiu wen" (Nine questions on being a foreign correspondent). In *Zenyang dang zhu wai jizhe* (How to be a foreign correspondent), edited by Yan Weimin 顏為民 43–50. Beijing: Shijie Zhishi Chubanshe.

Yang Shanshan 楊姗姗, ed. 2015. *Yangshi jizhe touguo jing kan Ouzhou* (CCTV journalists look at Europe through the looking-glass). Beijing: China Economic Publishing House.

Yang Xiao. 2014. "Moral Hazard," *Nieman Reports*, 31 January. http://niemanreports.org /articles/moral-hazard/ (accessed 8 December 2014).

Yuan Bingzhong 袁炳忠. 2006. *Wo zai Baigong dang jizhe* (I was a White House correspondent). Chongqing: Chongqing Chubanshe.

Yurchak, Alexei. 2005. *Everything Was Forever Until It Was No More: The Last Soviet Generation.* Princeton: Princeton University Press.

Zhang, Li. 2011. *News Media and EU-China Relations.* New York: Palgrave Macmillan.

Zhang, Shixin Ivy. 2013. "The New Breed of Chinese War Correspondents: Their Motivations and Roles, and the Impact of Digital Technology." *Media, War & Conflict* 6 (3): 311–25.

Zhang, Xiaoling. 2013. "How Ready is China for a China-Style World Order? China's State Media Discourse under Construction." *Ecquid Novi: African Journalism Studies* 34 (3): 79–101.

Zhang Yanqiu and Simon Matingwina. 2016. "Constructive Journalism: A New Journalistic Paradigm for Chinese Media in Africa." In *China's Media and Soft Power in Africa: Promotion and Perceptions,* edited by Xiaoling Zhang, Herman Wasserman, and Winston Mano, 94–105. Basingstoke, UK: Palgrave Macmillan.

Zhao, Suisheng. 1997. "Chinese Intellectuals' Quest for National Greatness and Nationalistic Writing in the 1990s." *China Quarterly* 152: 725–49.

Zhao, Yuezhi. 1998. *Media, Market, and Democracy in China: Between the Party Line and the Bottom Line.* Urbana, IL: University of Illinois Press.

Zheng Yi. 2013. *Contemporary Chinese Print Media: Cultivating Middle Class Taste.* Abingdon, UK: Routledge.

Zheng Yuanyuan 鄭圓圓. 2004. "Wo zai Faguo zuo zhu wai jizhe de tihui" (My experience as a foreign correspondent in France). In *Zenyang zuo guoji xinwen bianji* (How to be an international news editor), edited by Liu Hongchao 劉洪潮, 251–56. Beijing: Zhongguo Chuanmei Daxue Chubanshe.

Zheng Zhizu 郑志祖 (pseudonym). 2014. "Xi Jinping zenme duanzao quan xin guanhua tixi" (How Xi Jinping shaped a whole new official language), *The Paper*, 12 November.

Zhongguo Shehui Kexue Bao. 2014. "Jue bu yunxu za Gongchandang de guo" (Absolutely not allowed to break the Communist Party's pot), 5 November. http://i.ifeng.com /news/sharenews.f?aid=91555580&frm=timeline&isappinstalled=0 (accessed 22 October 2015).

Zhu, Ying. 2013. *Two Billion Eyes.* New York: The New Press.

Zigon, Jarrett. 2009. "Hope Dies Last: Two Aspects of Hope in Contemporary Moscow." *Anthropological Theory* 9 (3): 253–71.

Zuo Zhixian 左志坚. 2011. "Zhongguo daolu, quanqiu jiazhi: guojibu caozuo linian ji qi fangfa" (Chinese road, global values: the international desk's operating principles and methods). In *Chuang shiji: Yi zhang caijing baozhi he ta de shiji mengxiang* (Creating a century: A financial paper and her dream for the century), edited by *21st Century Business Herald* (21 shiji jingji daobao), 64–66. Canton: Nanfang Daily Press.

Index

9/11, 58
Abe, Shinzō, 67
Abramoff, Jack, 105
advertising, 29, 30, 35, 39, 40, 54, 89
Afghanistan, 26, 64
AFP (Agence France-Presse), 55, 65, 120, 167
Africa: business reporting, 112; Chinese advice to, on journalism, 64; Chinese correspondents in, 9–10, 52, 53, 98, 105–7, 140, 142, 152–53; Chinese investment in, 140, 144; Chinese media presence in, 10, 21; Chinese mining in, 124, 140, 146; Chinese tourism in, 118, 144; and "development journalism," 45; local staff in, 107–8, 117–18; media freedom in, 137; mobile apps for, 38, 98; national politics, 111–12; as pilot for international media products, 21; poaching and ivory smuggling, 111, 141, 142; relations with China, 74, 123, 124; reporting on, 99–100, 108, 111–12, 122–24, 144–46, 148, 149, 163; strategic importance of, 98; terrorist incident in, 144; treatment of Chinese in, 144; volunteer work in, 166; Western media in, 151; Xinhua bureaus in, 20, 95, 105–9, 111; Xinhua regional bureau chief, 25–26, 63, 119, 120. See also Nairobi; Zimbabwe
African Union, 123
AIESEC, 3
Al-Jazeera, 130
Alibaba, 30
AllAfrica.com, 119
Amanpour, Christiane, 153
anchors, 80, 103, 113, 153

Annenberg School for Communication, 84
"Annie" (correspondent in Africa), 98–100, 106, 108
anonymity, 12
anthropology of journalism, 17, 154–55
Anti, Michael (Zhao Jing), 50
anticolonial movements, 45
Anti-Rightist Campaign (1957), 161
anxiety. See existential insecurity
AP: correspondents in Africa, 108; desk editors, 72; election coverage, 99; mentioned, 55, 63, 65, 77, 119, 130, 131
Appadurai, Arjun, "capacity to aspire," 155–56, 178n6
April Fool's Day, 100
Arab Spring, 69, 75, 85–86, 121, 125–27, 135, 176n50
Arctic, 136
armchair reporting, 96, 97
Asia TV, 37
assistants: to foreign journalists, 51, 77, 80, 93, 103; local, 86, 107–8, 117, 165
audience interest: and China-centered reporting, 26, 66–67, 92, 134, 136–37, 138, 142, 168, 170; and the Malaysia Airlines incident, 18; online media and, 139; and stories about Africa, 98, 131, 137; "stories of difference" (Hannerz), 139
audience ratings (shoutinglü), 66
Aung San Suu Kyi, 77, 139, 143

Bai Qiang, 100–103
balanced reporting, 91, 99, 123, 146–49, 162

BBC: *Africa* magazine, 119; Alistair Cooke's *Letter from America*, 85–86; bias of, 140, 151, 152–53; documentary *The Chinese Are Coming*, 124, 129, 144; mentioned, 84, 109, 121, 130, 131, 134, 169; Newshour, 67; reporting from China, 129; reporting on Africa, 108

Belgrade: Chinese embassy bombing, 58, 64; postings in, 62

benefits, 115. *See also* bonuses

biannei and *bianwai* employees, 115

bianyi (translation and editing), 106

Big Three, 55. *See also* AFP; AP; Reuters

bird flu, 71

bloggers, 35, 44; Han Han, 93–94; Zhou Xiaoping, 35, 163

blogs, 10, 11, 31, 35, 37. *See also* microblogs

Bloomberg News, 39, 77

Bo Xilai, 142

bonuses, 27, 31, 32, 33, 41, 91, 98

Bosnian war, 62

Boston Marathon terrorist attack, 139

Bourdieu, Pierre, 133

Brown, Michael, 148

Brussels, Chinese correspondents in, 20, 25, 26, 75, 88

bureau chiefs: CCTV, 25, 113; *People's Daily*, 96–97; Xinhua, 25–26, 63, 93, 95–96, 119, 120

Burma, 75, 77, 121, 136, 139, 143, 158

bus strike (Singapore), 4

Bush, George W., 104

business reporting, 98, 112. *See also* financial media; *21st Ce-ntury Business Herald*

Caijing magazine, 19, 34, 51, 81

Caixin Media: advertising revenue, 39; censorship at, 33; China peg in stories, 136; correspondents for, 7, 19, 52, 53, 56, 65, 79, 80, 81, 169; critical analysis of, 167; disclosure of censorship, 164; filing and approval of stories, 75; and investigative journalism, 112, 141; multimedia offerings, 37; political risk-taking by, 30; reporting on Chinese companies abroad, 142–43; salaries and workloads, 42, 75; use of social media, 36, 37, 38. *See also* Globus; Hu Shuli; *New Century*; Xu Xiao

Cankao Xiaoxi (Reference News), 6, 46, 65, 138, 160

"capacity to aspire" (Appadurai), 155–56, 178n6

captioning, 130

Carter, Jimmy, 89

CBS, 21

CCTV: advertising revenue, 54; Africa reporting by, 21, 123–24; *biannei* and *bianwai* employees, 115; and blogging, 37; boot camps, 113; CCTV America, 21, 103–5, 117, 164; CCTV Europe, 80, 136; CCTV-4, 22; CCTV International, 22; cooperative reports, 72–73; correspondents for, 9, 68, 72, 74, 78, 79, 146, 157, 163, 167; documentaries, 131; editors, 74, 130–31; employment conditions, 31, 80, 116; expansion of foreign network, 20, 25, 51;extended scope of reporting, 141, 167; Faces, 131, 138; filing of "packages," 116; *Focal Point*, 41; foreign-language services, 27; *lingdao* of, 80, 128–29; living compounds, 98; local staff, 108, 165; London bureau, 130, 137; monitoring of, 121; Nairobi bureau, 129–30; overseas bureau floor plan, 117; overseas postings, 26; pitch meetings (*xuantihui*), 130–31; "positive reporting" strategy, 53; regional bureau chiefs, 25, 113; regional bureaus, 129–30; reporting from Cairo, 125–27; reporting on the Shen Hao affair, 30, 40; socialization of correspondents, 113; Special Reports Group, 116; and state control, 29; visit by Xi Jinping, 164; Washington bureau, 101–2, 129–30. *See also* Hu Zhanfan

Censored (Nieman report), 50

censorship: and Africa reporting, 122; of commercial media, 76–77; disclosed by Caixin website, 164; and discourse of objectivity, 41; of interviews, 149–50; journalists' views on, 144; of Middle East reporting, 85; by the Party's Propaganda Department, 31, 32, 34, 35; planting of articles, 34, 35; pushing the boundaries of, 45; removal from newsstands, 160; and reporting quality, 56; self-censorship, 31, 32, 33–34, 49, 144, 159; and technology, 32; tools and policies of, 31–35; tricks

censorship (*continued*)
for dealing with, 49, 159; in the United States, 65

central media: versus commercial media, 40–41, 52–53, 125; correspondents and reporters for, 43–44, 50–51, 54–55, 89, 90; demographics of correspondents, 51; editors, 51, 59–60, 66–67, 68, 71–72, 96; employment conditions, 31, 52; financial reporting, 89; foreign network expansion, 19–20, 25, 41, 174n2; freedom to report, 68; job security in, 78, 81; living arrangements, 98, 165; multiplicity of strategies within, 154; in ranking of media organizations, 114–15; relationships among foreign correspondents, 54; relationship with Chinese embassy, 53–54, 86, 99; reporting on Chinese government and Chinese economic interests, 149; salaries of correspondents, 23, 25, 27; socialization of correspondents, 113; US reporting, 65; use of foreign news as a foil for China, 66–67; vetting of topics, 70–71; welfare privileges, 115; and Western agendas, 44–45. *See also* CCTV; *China Daily*; China Radio International; *Guangming Daily*; *People's Daily*; Xinhua News Agency

Central Propaganda Department. *See* Propaganda Department

Chen Yan, 157–59, 161

children of journalists, 26, 101, 106, 107, 166

China as a global power, 4, 173n1

China Can Say No, 161

China-centered coverage, 26, 66–67, 86–87, 90, 92, 134, 136–37, 138, 142, 168, 170

China Central Television. *See* CCTV

China Daily, 20, 25, 53, 54, 123, 153

China Goes Global (Zhongnan Duihua), 170

China News Service (CNS): compared with Xinhua, 54, 91, 109; European correspondents, 53, 90–92; foreign bureaus, 91; journalists for, 48, 51; mission of, 54, 91; Washington reporter, 65; workloads and salaries, 91. See also *China Newsweek*

China Newsweek, 91, 139

China Radio International (CRI): Africa bureau, 21, 113; audience of, 67; correspondents for, 7, 48, 54, 68; editors for, 66, 67, 68, 149, 162; expansion of foreign network, 20; foreign-language services, 27–28; increased scope of reporting, 167; independence of, 29, 54, 66–67, 68; mobile TV app, 38; news programming, 66–68; online and video content, 38; overseas postings, 26; performance evaluation system, 27, 115; programming department, 68; reporting in the United States, 147, 148; slogan at Beijing headquarters, 133

China University of Communications (CUC), 113–14

China-Vietnam war, 61

China Will Not Be Bullied (Zhongguo Bu Ke Qi), 64

China's others, 168–69

The Chinese Are Coming (BBC documentary), 124, 129, 144

Chinese Communist Party: media as "throat and tongue" of, 16, 66, 84, 91, 109; membership, 53; Party Document No. 9, 31, 164; reporting on, 142; third plenary session, 74;. *See also* Propaganda Department

Chinese companies: acquisitions by, 140, 143; engagement with the world, 4, 173n2; reporting on, 140–41, 142–44, 177n18

Chinese dissidents, 127, 145–46, 151

"Chinese dream," 73

Chinese embassy: Belgrade, 58, 64; and central media reporters, 53–54, 99; Washington, 86

Chinese migrants, 5

"Chinese perspective," 134–35, 152, 167. *See also* China-centered coverage

"Chinese stance," 133–34, 159

choice, 16

chunqiu bifa (language tricks to convey hidden criticism), 49, 159

citizen journalism, 170

"clash of civilizations," 45, 65

climate change, 147

Clinton, Bill, 46, 63

CNC World, 21

CNN, 21, 119, 121, 129, 130, 131, 151

CNS. *See* China News Service

commentaries (*shiping*), 24

commercial media: career paths and job security at, 79–80; censorship of, 76–

77; central media view of, 52; corporate control of, 29–30, 76; demographics of correspondents, 26, 51; editors, 75–76; excluded from embassy activities, 54; falling advertising revenues and digitalization, 20; first overseas correspondents of, 19; parts of the world covered by, 75; political risk-taking by, 30; in ranking of media organizations, 114–15; relationship between editors and correspondents, 74–75, 76; resignations from, 48–49, 80; shrinking of, 39–41, 42; tightening of control over content, 143; viewed as more professional, 79; workloads and salaries, 27, 41, 52, 75, 80, 88

"commercial nationalism," 58

commercialization, 29-31

"compassionate cosmopolitanism" (Hannerz), 6, 166, 173n8

complexity, 154–55; "complicated China" principle, 60

conglomeration. *See* media groups

constitutional reform, 33

constructive journalism, 100. *See also* "positive reporting"

Cooke, Alistair, *Letter from America*, 85–86

corporate social responsibility, 53

corruption: in Africa, 100, 143–44; attacked in social media, 36; reporting on, 117, 140; Xi Jinping's war on, 50, 130

cosmopolitanism: and anthropology, 15–16; of Chinese correspondents, 6, 28, 46, 78, 156–57, 163, 166–67; and Chinese media, 6, 17, 170; compassionate (Hannerz), 6, 166, 173n8

COVEC company, 75

Crapanzano, Vincent, "imaginative horizons," 178n6

credibility, 23–25, 28, 32, 36, 120, 168, 169

credit crunch, 33

CRI. *See* China Radio International

critical reporting, 48–49, 140–43, 158, 162

cross-border philanthropy, 6

Cultural Revolution, 96

Daily Mail (UK), 37, 60, 72, 166

Daily Telegraph (UK), 112

Dalai Lama, 34, 92, 104, 132

"dancing in chains," 16

danwei system, 81, 117

democracy: in Africa, 100; in Egypt, 85, 125–27; export of, 125, 135; in the Ukraine, 129; in the United States, 86, 104; Western, 87, 136, 156

Deng Fei, 36

development aid, 6

"development journalism," 45, 63–64, 90, 99, 123. *See also* "positive reporting"

Diana, Princess, 58

Diaoyu Islands, reporting on, 102–3

digital media, 26–27, 37–40. *See also* social media

Ding Gang, 87

Directive on Accelerating the Expansion of Chinese Media Abroad (2012), 21, 91

"discursive power" (*huayuquan*), 32

dissidents, 127, 145–46, 151, 156

Document No. 9, 31, 164

documentaries, 131, 152

domestic reporting, 27, 67, 71, 80, 91, 104, 131

domestication, 170. *See also* audience interest

Doucet, Lyse, 86

DPA (German news agency), 77

Earnest, Josh, 105

East Asia Bank, 143

Ebola, 131

editorials, 34, 47–48, 61, 102, 163, 176n34

editors: censorship role of, 71, 74, 132, 141, 142, 143, 148–49; central media, 51, 59–60, 66–67, 68, 71–72, 96; commercial media, 74–76, 79–80; financial media, 90; framing and spinning of articles, 92, 112–13; interviews with, 12, 51, 79–80; levels of, 10, 72; meetings, 9; page editors, 47, 59, 60; role in publication process, 55, 56–57, 58–59; shifts of, 130–31; view of objective reporting, 162

Egypt: nationalism in, 14; reporting on, 75, 76, 85, 125–27, 136

election coverage, 38, 86, 99, 103, 139

enlightenment advocacy, 159, 160

"enthusiasts," 59

environmental journalism, 36, 105, 111, 139

Ethiopia, 148

EU. *See* European Union
Europe: Chinese correspondents in, 9–10, 84,
    101, 167; debt crisis, 87, 92; reporting on,
    70, 87, 138–39. *See also* European Union
European Union: refugee crisis, 13, 50, 135,
    138; reporting on, 87, 138; trade disputes
    with China, 75, 143. *See also* Europe
existential insecurity, 8, 16, 33, 42, 78–81, 161
extortion, 30, 40–41

Faces (Shijie Miankong), 131, 138
Falkland Islands, 137, 162, 166, 177n7
Falungong, 132
Federal Reserve, 90
fenlie (splittism), 126
Ferguson (Missouri), 148
financial media: editors, 90; investigative
    reporting by, 139; overseas correspondents
    for, 22, 88–90; specialized websites, 37;
    and state control, 29
financial security, 79, 159. *See also* existential
    insecurity
Financial Times, 39, 142
"firefighters," 12
First Financial Daily, 19
Focal Point (CCTV), 41, 128
Forbes, 39
Foreign Affairs Weekly (Zongheng Zhoukan),
    50
foreign correspondents: autonomy of, 52,
    54, 57; career paths of, 16, 25, 26, 80; chil-
    dren of, 101, 106, 107, 166; choices of, 16;
    code of personal conduct for, 96; commit-
    ment of, 89; compared with other Chinese
    migrants, 5; compared with other journal-
    ists writing about foreign countries, 11;
    demographic change in, 25, 26, 77–78; goals
    of, 168; intermarriage of, 100, 106–7; inter-
    views and conversations with, 7–12; lack
    of specialization, 102; lives of, in Europe
    versus Africa, 9–10; living arrangements
    of, 83–84, 88, 95, 96, 98, 100; mobility of,
    12, 51; networks of, 169, 170; potential to
    challenge nationalist views, 6; reasons
    for quitting, 100; salaries of, 22–23, 27,
    87, 101; social lives of, 89, 90–91, 98, 100;
    and the state, 16, 50; in the 2000s, 25;
    workloads, 26–27

foreign language proficiency, 26, 94, 120, 166
Foreign Press Association, 75
foreign press clubs, 100
foreign news sources, 3, 41, 77, 121, 167–68
foreign websites, blocking of, 32, 35, 49, 142,
    167
Forum on Literature and the Arts, 163
Fox, 21, 65
France, reporting on, 38, 74
France 24, 119
Frankfurt Book Fair (2009), 145–46
freedom, 62, 65, 107, 155–56, 178n3; Internet,
    84; of opinion, 31, 134; of the press, 13, 22,
    34, 41, 50–51, 63, 103, 137; of reporting, 70,
    71, 75, 96, 122, 139, 144. *See also* censor-
    ship; gag orders
freelancers, 11, 12
frontline journalism, 26, 62, 64, 94, 106

Gaddafi, Muammar, 85, 157
gag orders, 33, 34, 36, 125, 132, 145
General Administration of Press and Publi-
    cations (GAPP), 85
Geneva, correspondents in, 26, 63
Genting gambling resort (Malaysia), 3–4
Germany, 20, 73, 160
Ghana, 146
Gibe Dam (Ethiopia), 148
global capitalism, 155, 156
Global Times: accused of distortion, 48;
    attacks on liberal media, 163–64; auton-
    omy of correspondents, 57; circulation
    of, 6, 57, 58; compared with *People's Daily*,
    47, 96; contributors to, 35, 102; correspon-
    dents for, 51, 147; coverage of anti-Chinese
    violence in Vietnam, 145; coverage of Chi-
    nese embassy bombing, 58; on credibility
    of Chinese media, 23–24; and develop-
    ment journalism, 45; editorial policies, 60,
    68; editorials and opinion pieces, 11, 12,
    34, 46, 47–48, 61, 102, 163, 176n34; editors-
    in-chief, 45, 46–47, 59, 60, 61–62; English
    edition, 58; "firefighters" for, 12; interna-
    tional coverage, 35, 46, 70, 135–36, 167;
    launching of, 58; "Media Should Be Watch-
    dog of National Interest," 45; mentioned,
    8, 109; pseudonymous articles by govern-
    ment, 47; reporting on Japan, 48, 57–58;

reporting on taboo topics, 46–47; selection and putting together of stories, 58–61; stance of, 12, 47–48, 56, 58, 60, 61, 103, 169; "To China with Pressure," 46; translations from foreign media, 138; use of *People's Daily* correspondents, 57–58, 59; use of plain language, 24, 45, 61; views of, 46, 48; WeChat opinion feed, 38; "Will Western Countries Go Bankrupt One After the Other?" 61. *See also* He Chongyuan; Hu Xijin

Global Watch (Huanqiu Shixian), 131

Globe magazine, 12, 24, 64, 65, 139

Globus (Caixin Shijieshuo), 50, 138

Gong Li, 58

gongyi (public interest), 100

Google: blocking of, 32, 49; reliance on, for news, 112

government media. *See* central media

Graham, Phil, 5

Great Firewall, 5, 49

Greece, reporting on, 136–37

Greenpeace, 152

Guangming Daily, 20, 26, 107–8

Gui, Eric: on Chinese perspective, 135; *Shifeizhou*, 99–100, 176n1

Gulf War, 164

hacking, 77

"hacks" and "rebels" dichotomy, 43–44, 45–46

Hagel, Chuck, 102

Han Han, 93–94

Han Song, 36, 128

Hannerz, Ulf, 121; *Foreign News*, 6–7

Hao, Angela, 36

He Chongyuan, 61, 135–36

hero narrative, 100

Hessler, Peter, 94; *River Town*, 139, 142

He Weifang, 146

He Xiaoshou, 55

Hollande, François, 151

Hong Kong, 11; protests of 2014, 47, 51; retrocession to China, 67. *See also* Phoenix Television; *Phoenix Weekly*

hope, 155

horizons, construction of, 15

Hu Jintao, 21, 23, 24, 147

Hu Shuli, 34, 37, 62, 112

Hu Xijin: as editor-in-chief of *Global Times*, 45, 46–48, 61, 103; education and background of, 61–62; as reporter for *People's Daily*, 62; selection of stories for *Global Times*, 59, 60

Hu Yong, 41

Hu Zhanfan, 110, 164

Huang Can, 34, 35

Huanqiu Qiguan (Global Curiosities), 38

Huanqiu Wencui (Global Digest), 58, 61. See also *Global Times*

Huawei, 143

human interest stories, 137, 138. *See also* soft news

human rights, 31, 38, 50, 61, 107, 111, 152, 158

Hungary, 13–14

Huntington, Samuel, 45

Hurricane Katrina, 104

Iceland, 162

"imaginative horizons," 15, 178n6

in-depth reporting, 49–50, 89, 92, 102, 111–12, 116, 121, 131; financial, 167

Independent Social Research Fellowship, 9

independent websites, 43–44, 50, 52, 170

India: foreign correspondents in, 58; media in, 177n12; reporting on, 70, 152, 158, 161

Industrial and Commercial Bank of China, 143

infant mortality, 123

infrastructure investment, 138

International Federation of Journalists, 13

International Herald Leader (Guoji Xianqu Daobao), 38, 65, 160

International Monetary Fund annual meeting, 22

International New York Times, 119

International Online (Guoji Zai Xian), 67, 68

international relations, 6, 28, 101, 155

Internet activists, 84

internships, 64, 74, 77, 84–85, 89, 93, 114, 129

interviews, censorship of, 149–50

investigative journalism, 32–33, 36, 39, 41, 44, 75, 112, 139, 141–42, 170

Iran, 133

Iraq war, 62

irony, 178n3

Islam, 13, 70, 126, 146

isolationism, 14

Israel, 69–70, 148–49, 161, 166

Israeli-Palestinian conflict, 17–18, 64, 69, 148–49

ivory, 141, 142, 170

Japan: editorials and opinion pieces on, 61; in *Global Times*, 47, 48, 57–58; reporting on, 67–68, 77, 134, 146, 149, 160

"Jasmine Revolution," 125

Jerusalem, postings in, 69, 166

Jeune Afrique, 119

job security, 26, 31, 42, 79, 80, 115, 159

"John," 43, 46, 49, 54, 78, 132, 163

Jones, Paula, 63

Joseph, Manu, 177n12

journalism: conferences, 84, 146; as the first draft of history, 5, 19; programs, 20–21, 23, 88, 93, 96, 98, 113–14, 129; shrinking of, 39–41; standards for, 16–17, 41–42; tensions in, 28–29. *See also* investigative journalism; "positive reporting"; professionalism; propaganda function of journalism

journalists: age gap, 51–52; career paths of, 39–40, 80; commercial and central, 19–20, 52–55; foreign citizens, 33; frustrations of, 42, 74, 79; imprisoned, 44; interviews with, 8, 11–12; liberal, 8, 12, 30, 33, 43–44, 51, 164; licensing of, 85; output of, 10–11; salaries and lifestyles of, 42; as spies, 100–101; types of, 132; Western agendas and stereotypes, 43–45. *See also* central media; commercial media; foreign correspondents

Juncker Plan, 138

Keller, Bill, 169

Kenya. *See* Africa; Nairobi

Kerry, John, 34

labor abuse, 140

Laos, 158

Latin America, Xinhua bureaus in, 20

Leading Small Group on Deepening Reform, "Guiding opinion on advancing the integrated development of traditional and new media," 40

Li Congjun, 24, 109–11

Li Lin, 11

Li Xiguang: *Behind the Demonization of China*, 64, 65, 161; exponent of "development journalism," 63–64; internship at *Washington Post*, 64

liberal journalists, 8, 12, 30, 33, 43–44, 48–49, 51, 164. *See also* Chen Yan; Qin Xuan; Xiang Ling

liberal-nationalist scale, 137

Libya, 59, 75, 85, 157

Lin Yu, 129

lingdao (leaders): as career path, 80; in central media, 127–29; Chinese embassy, 53; in commercial media, 75, 127; personalities and styles, 128; senior editors and managers as, 10; stereotype of, 96; vetting of articles, 55, 69, 70. *See also* bureau chiefs

"linguistic tricks," 49, 159

Liren, crackdown on, 34

Liu Hong, 64, 139–40; *The American "Conspiracy"* (Meiguo "yinmou"), 24, 64–65, 139

Liu Hongchao, *How to Be an International News Editor*, 110

Liu Xiaobo, 46, 146

Liu Ying, 93, 93–94, 94–95, 99, 108–9

lobbying, 105

local staff, 107–8, 117, 165

London: CCTV bureau in, 129–30; correspondents in, 53, 55, 70–71, 72, 84–85; Xinhua regional hub in, 20

looted art, 92

Lu Zhenhua, 36

Lung Ying-tai, 146

Luo Xiaojun, 23

"Lynne," 88–90, 112

Ma Shaohua, 55

Malaysia Airlines incident (2014): Chinese response to, 4, 18; criticism of Malaysia's investigation, 18, 146–47; Internet and, 35; reporting on, 18, 19, 55–56, 169

manipulation, 132

Mao Zedong, 163

Maputo, news bureau, 10

"mass line," 24

Mayer, Milton, *They Thought They Were Free*, 161

meat adulteration scandal (2013), 92

media groups, 29, 30–31, 40, 77; Shanghai, 30

media marketization, 8. *See also* commercial media

media rankings, 114–15

metropolitan newspapers (*dushibao*), 29

Mi Bohua, 47

microblogs, 10–11, 35–37, 150. *See also* Weibo

Middle East reporting, 85–86

Miller, Lee, 77

mines, 124, 140, 146

Ministry of Education, 20–21

Mladić, Ratko, 62

mobile apps, 38, 98, 112, 118

moonlighting, 32

Morsi, Mohammad, 126–27

Mubarak, Hosni, 85, 125–26, 158

Mugabe, Robert, 148

Muslims, 13, 70, 146

Nairobi: CCTV bureau in, 129–30; Chinese-African media conference in 2013, 64; Chinese correspondents in, 10; reporting website based in, 52; terrorist attack on Westgate shopping mall, 146; TV in, 22; Xinhua regional hub, 20, 98–99, 112

Nanjing massacre, 57

"national character," 73

nationalism: and censorship, 31; and China's global engagement, 4, 5–6; and Chinese embassy bombing, 64; "commercial," 58; in Egypt, 14; of *Global Times*, 12, 58, 60, 61; in Hungary, 13, 14; journalists' views on, 28, 64, 90; manifestos, 64–65; and professionalism, 163; and reporting on the world, 7, 156–57. *See also* China-centered coverage; "development journalism"

nativism, 45, 64

NATO bombing of Chinese embassy, 58, 64

NBC, 21

"negative reporting," 52, 99. *See also* "positive reporting"

neican (internal circulation only) reports, 72, 73, 99, 100, 141, 143–44, 177n18

neoliberalism, 155

NetEase, 40

networking, 113–14, 165

New Beijing News (Xinjingbao), 34

New Century (Xin Shiji), 37, 39, 142–43

New York, 23, 88

New York Times: admiration for, 86, 87; assistantships and internships at, 77, 80; Chinese edition, 39, 167; Chinese-language website, 8, 142; compared with *People's Daily*, 102; followed by *People's Daily*, 23; international version, 119; investigative reporting by, 129; profile of Han Han, 94; purported misinformation campaign against China, 64; reporting on Africa, 108, 111–12; on separating news gathering from propaganda, 164; shift in foreign reporting, 169; as target of Chinese leadership sanctions, 8

New Yorker, 86, 94. *See also* Hessler, Peter; Osnos, Evan

news agendas, 23, 37, 44, 89, 99, 121–24

news blackouts, 33, 35–36. *See also* gag orders

News Bureau (State Council), 61

news radio, 66–67, 129, 151. *See also* China Radio International

news stories: award-winning, 75; followed by correspondents, 121; ideas for, 56; killed by editors, 71; "not for release in China," 71; pickup rates, 27, 107, 111, 119, 142; publication process, 55–57, 58–59

Newshour (BBC), 67

newspaper circulation, 6, 38, 46, 57, 58

NewsRadio FM 90.5, 66–67

Nieman Foundation report, 50

North Korea, 121, 133, 160

Norway, 138

NPR, 66, 129

Nye, Joseph, 133

Nyíri, Pál: opinion pieces for *Global Times*, 12; talk at Xinhua African bureau compound, 117–18

O Globo television (Brazil), 130

Obama, Barack, 94

objective reporting: attacks on, 110; in the financial media, 90; and partisanship, 97, 162; and professionalism, 41–42, 159, 162; relativity of, 63, 126; views on, 57, 68, 122, 151

official media. *See* central media
officialese, 24, 179n9
Olympics (2008), 5, 38, 46
one-sided reporting, 102–3
online news portals, 40, 49, 102, 145. *See also* microblogs; Sina
opinion writers, 11, 61, 87. *See also Global Times*
Opium War, 157
Orbán, Viktor, 13
Organization of Security and Cooperation in Europe, 13
Oriental Horizon (CCTV), 128, 131
Oriental Morning Post, 12, 40, 55
Oriental Outlook magazine, 12, 64, 65, 139
Osnos, Evan, 94
overseas aid, 131
Overseas Chinese Affairs Bureau of the State Council (Qiaoban), 91
overseas Chinese media, 91
Overseas Wind (Haiwai Lai Feng), 49, 138–39
Oxford graduates, 54, 84, 86

page editors, 47, 59, 60
Pakistan, 74, 150
Pan Linhua, 116, 128–29, 130
Panama Papers, 162–63
The Paper (Pengpai), 40
Paris: correspondents in, 53, 74; *People's Daily* bureau in, 25
partisanship, 42, 50, 97, 110, 119–20, 131, 162
Party Document No. 9, 31, 164
PBS, 129
Peking University, 93
Peng Liyuan, 38
Pengpai (The Paper), 40
People's Daily: article on Xinhua by Li Congjun, 109–10; Brussels bureau, 166; bureau chiefs, 96–97; China peg in stories, 136; "Chinese dream" series, 73; compared with *Global Times*, 6, 47; correspondent demographics, 25; correspondents for, 50, 52, 57–58, 78, 94, 101–2, 150, 164, 165, 169; credibility of, 23; editorials and opinion writing, 87, 102; editors, 96; expansion of foreign network, 20, 23, 24–25; extended scope of reporting, 167; interviews with

reporters for, 7, 8–9; local staff, 107, 165; news from Europe, 70, 138; online content, 38, 97, 102; Paris bureau, 25, 53; as party organ, 29, 94, 102–3; performance reviews and promotions, 97, 116; ranking and privileges of, 60–61, 114–15; reporting for *Global Times*, 57–58, 59, 60–61; "Reporting Live" column, 102; reporting on Chinese companies abroad, 140–41; reporting on "national character," 73; reporting on the Shen Hao affair, 40; "round robin" reports, 72–73; salaries and workloads, 27, 97; vetting of topics and stories, 70, 72; views on professionalism and the national interest, 160; visit by Xi Jinping, 164; Washington bureau, 25; work environment and living arrangements , 81, 96, 98. *See also* Bai Qiang; Mi Bohua; Zhao Juan
performance assessment, 26–27, 57, 97, 107, 115–16
"Peter," 84–90
"Philip," 81
Phoenix Television, 11, 28, 121
Phoenix Weekly, 36, 48, 51, 52, 79, 80. *See also* Qin Xuan
pickup rates, 27, 107, 111, 119, 142
pitch meetings (*xuantihui*), 59, 130–31
points-based system, 26–27, 107, 115–16
Poland, 20, 75, 142
polishers, 120
political prisoners, 161. *See also* dissidents
Polumbaum, Judy, 7
"positive reporting," 45, 53, 63, 96, 98, 99–100, 123–24, 148, 156
poverty: in Africa, 100, 123; domestic, 131; in the United States, 86, 148
press licensing, 33
price fixing, 143
professionalism: belief in, 68, 89, 90, 99, 159–60, 161–62; discourse of, 41–42; and inclusion of background, 112; and national interest, 163, 164; and partisanship, 28, 42, 131; "patriotic," 162; and propagandistic journalism, 32, 44–45, 46, 110, 134
professionalization, 24, 28, 32. *See also* professionalism
"progressive" journalism, 104, 113, 128

Propaganda Department: and central media
lingdao, 128; and master's programs in
global journalism, 20–21, 98; and media
censorship, 28–29, 31, 32, 34, 35, 76–77;
and selection of story topics, 70–71; provincial, 34
propaganda function of journalism, 28, 44,
46, 110, 114, 134, 164–65. *See also* soft
power
property tax, 67
Psaki, Jen, 105
public interest journalism, 90, 100
"public lies" versus "private truths," 51
public opinion, 18, 23, 28, 47, 68, 169; guidance of, 21, 28, 32, 40, 127, 131
public relations, 27, 39, 160
publication process, 55–57, 58–59
Putin, Vladimir, 46

Qiangguo Luntan (Strong Country Forum),
102
Qiao Mu, 164
Qiaoban (Overseas Chinese Affairs Bureau
of the State Council), 91
Qin Xuan, 48, 49, 157
qipin (staff on corporate contracts), 115, 117
QR codes, 97

Radio Free Asia, 104, 161
Rapport, Nigel, 178n3
"rational criticism" principle, 60
Red Cross, 70
Reference News (Cankao Xiaoxi), 6, 46, 65,
138, 160
refugees, 13, 50, 135, 138
releasers (*fagaoren*), 72, 118–19
religious topics, 69, 111, 146
Reuters: Africa reporting, 108, 119; compared
with Xinhua, 55, 72; election coverage, 99;
mentioned, 56, 65, 77
"right to know" (*zhiqingquan*), 32
Roubini, Nouriel, 89
"round robin" reports, 72–73
Russia, 14, 62, 161
Russia Today, 14, 130
Russia-Ukraine conflict, 37, 46, 148, 150,
153
Rwanda, 123

san ge tiejin (three getting closers), 24
SARFT (State Administration of Radio, Film,
and Television), 85, 128
Sarkozy, Nicolas, 38, 151
SARS, 139
Science and Technology Daily, 26
Scotland, independence referendum, 70–71
self-censorship, 31, 32, 33–34, 49, 144, 159
Sen, Amartya, 155
separatism, 126, 161
Shanghai, 40
Shanghai Media Group, 30; *First Financial
Daily*, 19; *The Paper*, 40
Shen Hao, 30, 40
shift supervisors (*daibanren*), 72, 118, 121
Shijie Zhoukan (Weekly World Bulletin),
129
Shweder, Richard, 156
Sina Finance, 36, 50, 89, 167; "Overseas
Wind," 49, 138–39
Sina news portal, 40, 49–50, 86, 151
Sina Weibo, 35, 36
Singapore, 4, 11, 77
Sisi, General Abdel Fattah al-, 126
Smithfield, 143
social media: impact of, 35, 170; policies
regarding, 36; as source of stories from
abroad, 168; used to engage with readers,
24, 38, 77, 150. *See also* blogs; microblogs;
WeChat
"socialization," 15, 98, 106, 113
soft news, 33, 38, 104, 137, 166, 167
soft power, 10, 22, 23, 25, 133, 154
solar panels, 75
South America, Xinhua bureaus in, 95
South China Morning Post, 77, 93
South China Sea, 18, 77
Southeast Asia, 45
Southern Daily, 40, 159
Southern Media Group, 30, 34, 40, 41, 51, 160.
See also *Southern Weekend*; *21st Century
Business Herald*
Southern Metropolitan Daily, 41, 55
Southern People Weekly: censorship of,
35, 49; in-depth reporting by, 139; inter-
views with correspondents for, 12, 33, 134;
interview with Hu Xijin, 62. *See also* Yang
Xiao

Southern Weekend: censorship at, 34–35; in-depth reporting by, 116; "firefighters" for, 12; opinion writers, 11; and "progressive" journalism, 104; reporters for, 7, 48, 52, 53, 134, 157; *Southern Weekend* Incident (2013), 34, 37; use of microblogs at, 37

"speak human language" campaign, 24, 179n9

Spring Festival, 73–74

Stade, Ronald, 178n3

State Administration of Radio, Film, and Television (SARFT), 85, 128

state enterprise paternalism, 117

State Grid, 29

state subsidies, 28–29, 58, 114

"stories of difference" (Hannerz), 139

strikes and sit-ins, 3–4

Strong Country Forum (Qiangguo Luntan), 102

study abroad, 3, 22, 39, 48, 66, 78, 84, 129

The Sun (UK), 72

Sun Yusheng, 128; *Ten Years*, 128

Syria, 59, 75, 134, 153

Taiwan, 11, 34, 37, 146

tax reform, 90

Tencent, 40, 86

terrorism, 123, 139, 144, 146

Thailand, 14

Thatcher, Margaret, 59, 60, 66–67, 162

"three getting closers" (*san ge tiejin*), 24

Tibet, 32, 34, 36, 38, 120, 126, 145, 158

tizhinei media. *See* central media

TMT Post, 39

Tohti, Ilham, 161

"Tom," 105–13

tourism, 3, 78, 118, 144

transnational journalism, 170

Tsinghua University School of Journalism, 21, 63, 77

Turkey, 14, 50

turnover, 80

21st Century Business Herald: censorship at, 30, 34; correspondents for, 7, 19, 33, 74–75, 147, 153; coverage of powerful companies, 29–30, 140, 143; in-depth financial reporting, 167; filing and approval of stories, 75; financial websites and social media, 36,

37–38; international reporting strategy, 136; salaries of correspondents, 27; and the Shen Hao affair, 30, 40, 76; short-term assignments, 75; and State Grid, 29. *See also* Luo Xiaojun; Zuo Zhixian

Ukraine, 129; Russia-Ukraine conflict, 37, 46, 148, 150, 153

United Kingdom, 14, 59, 60, 66–67, 92, 162. *See also* London

United Nations, 13, 26

United States: Chinese views of, 104–5; criticism of, 147, 148; culture and values, 105; editorials and opinion pieces on, 61; election coverage, 86, 103, 139; foreign correspondents in, 100–101; isolationism in, 14; poverty in, 86; reporting on, 64–66, 66, 86–87, 92, 104, 147; Washington correspondents, 20, 23, 53, 65, 101; White House correspondents, 25–26, 63, 65

University of Pennsylvania, Annenberg School for Communication, 84

urban planning, 90

USAID, 130

US State Department, 104

Valdai Forum, 161

Vietnam, 121, 136, 158; anti-Chinese riots in, 61, 145; de-Sinicization of, 160

virtual private networks, 32, 49

Voice of America, 64, 104, 140, 161, 167

volunteer work, 3, 166

Wall Street Journal, 39, 80, 142, 147

Wang Chaowen, 24, 119–20

Wang Chen, 23

Wang Jisi, 48

Wang Shanshan, 66–68

Washington correspondents, 20, 23, 53, 65, 101; White House correspondents, 25–26, 63, 65

Washington Post, 5, 13, 64, 129, 147

WeChat, 9, 10–11, 12, 32, 35, 38–39, 41, 161

Weibo, 7, 11, 36–37, 38, 62. *See also* Sina Weibo

welfare privileges, 115

welfare state, 137

"well-informed citizen" (Schütz), 6, 173n6

Western media: agenda of, 157; bias of, 54–55, 63, 122, 132; censorship of, 65, 153; Chinese criticism of, 63–65, 99, 105, 109, 120, 129, 151–53; competition with, 99, 152; criticism of China, 140; criticism of Chinese media, 54; reporting on Africa, 123, 124; reporting on China, 151–52; reporting on Egypt, 126

Western values, 31, 46, 105

White House correspondents, 25–26, 63, 65

wildlife protection, 111

William, Prince, wedding of, 59, 152

work units, 81, 117

world coverage, 75, 169–71. *See also* China-centered coverage

World Economic Forum (Davos), 89

World Health Organization, 71

World Media Summit (2009), 147

World Talk, 50

World Trade Organization, 22, 23

WTOP radio (United States), 66

Wu Fei, 106

www.morningwhistle.com, 37–38

Xi Jinping: brother-in-law of, 137, 163; "Chinese dream," 73; criticism of officialese, 24, 174n9; cult of personality, 51; at the Forum on Literature and the Arts, 163; on need for new media, 40; overseas visits, 38; praise for blogger Zhou Xiaoping, 35; repressive cultural politics of, 31, 33, 110, 163–64; visit to central media, 164–65; war on corruption, 50, 130

Xiang Ling, 160–61

Xiao Song (pseudonym), 68–69

Xinhua Europe, 24

Xinhua Finance, 36, 89

Xinhua News Agency: African bureaus, 20, 95, 105–9, 111, 117–19; Beijing headquarters, 120–21; buildings and compounds, 98, 100, 130, 165; bureau chiefs, 25–26, 63, 119, 93, 95–96; business reporting, 112; Cairo regional bureau, 125; changes in, 3, 25, 167; China Features department, 36; classification of bureaus, 95; commentaries, 24; commercial media view of, 52; compared with China News Service, 91; competition with Western agencies, 55; corre-spondents for, 48, 50, 51, 52–53, 54, 68, 69, 70, 74, 93, 135, 140, 150–51, 160; corre-spondents' views of, 109; "discourse work" of, 109–10; editors, 51, 63, 71, 72, 95; English-language teams, 118–19; European bureaus, 24, 90, 95, 119–20; flat of a female corre-spondent, 83–84; foreign correspondent demographics, 25; foreign correspon-dent network, 20, 23, 25; foreign-language newswriting exam, 94; foreign-language services, 21, 27; as government mouth-piece, 29, 84, 91, 99, 109, 160, 163; inter-marriage of correspondents, 106–7; inter-views with correspondents, 7; liberal jour-nalists for, 49, 51; *lingdao* of, 128; local staff, 117–18, 120, 122, 165; mobile apps, 38, 98, 118; monitored by other media, 131, 148; *neican* reports, 73, 99, 100; online content, 36, 38; overseas postings, 26, 94; Paris bureau, 38; performance assessment and promotions, 26–27, 107; "positive reporting" strategy, 53; press releases, 33; professionalism of, 24; ranking and privi-leges of, 114–15; regional bureaus, 117–19; reporting on Africa, 111, 123, 149; report-ing on Chinese companies abroad, 141, 177n18; salaries and bonuses, 27, 98; satel-lite television channel, 38; "socialization" at, 106; stereotype of, 93, 95; stories picked up by other media, 107; story on Han Han, 93–94; success in Africa, 21; vetting of incoming stories, 72; visit by Xi Jinping, 164; work environment, 81, 95, 100; Zim-babwe bureau, 25. *See also* "Annie"; *Globe* magazine; Gui, Eric; Han Song; *Interna-tional Herald Leader*; Li Congjun; Liu Hong; Liu Ying; *Oriental Outlook* maga-zine; *Reference News*; "Tom"; Wang Chao-wen; Xinhua Finance; Yang Qi; Ying Qiang

Xinhua08 business wire, 98

Xinjiang, 126, 158

xuanti (approved topics), 56, 59

Xu Xiao, 34

Xu Xiaonian, 146

Yahoo, 112

Yan Xuetong, 48, 164

Yang Qi, 24

Yang Xiao, 49
Yanukovich, Viktor, 129
Yao Bin, 64–65
Yaoundé, 10
Yasukuni Shrine, 67
Ying Qiang, 38
you chang wu wen (remunerated lack of
   news), 41. *See also* extortion
Young, Doug, 55
Yu Liang, 36
Yuan Bingzhong, 25–26, 63; *I Was a White
   House Correspondent*, 63
yulun daoxiang (guiding public opinion), 28
yulun jiandu (supervision by public opin-
   ion), 28
Yves Saint Laurent art collection, 92

Zambia, 124
Zhang Gang, 103–5
Zhang Weiwei, 48

Zhang Yihe, *The Past Is Not Another
   Country*, 161
Zhang Yiwu, 48
Zhao Jing (Michael Anti), 50
Zhao Juan, 96–98, 99, 131–32
Zhejiang Daily, 33
Zhejiang Media Group, 33
Zhongguo bu ke qi (China Will Not Be
   Bullied), 64
Zhongnan Duihua (China Goes Global),
   170
Zhou Xiaoping, 35, 163
Zhou Yongkang, 117
Zhou Yu, *Democracy in Detail*, 104
Zhu Feng, 90–92, 95
Zhuang Qiaoyi, 49–50
Zigon, Jarrett, 155
Zimbabwe, 25, 148
Zuckerman, Ethan, 84
Zuo Zhixian, 19, 169

Milton Keynes UK
Ingram Content Group UK Ltd.
UKHW041310210924
448482UK00001B/5